CONNOISSEURS OF CHAOS

Connoisseurs of Chaos

IDEAS OF ORDER IN MODERN AMERICAN POETRY

Denis Donoghue

SECOND EDITION

Columbia University Press

New York 1984

Excerpts from "Florida," "The Man-Moth," "The Weed," "Sonnet," "Sandpiper," "The Armadillo," "The Unbeliever," "At the Fishouses," "Over 2000 Illustrations and a Complete Concordance," and "Crusoe in England" from THE COMPLETE POEMS 1927–1979 by Elizabeth Bishop. Copyright © 1938, 1939, 1947, 1948, 1957, 1962, 1971 by Elizabeth Bishop. Copyright renewed © 1974, 1975 by Elizabeth Bishop. Copyright © 1983 by Alice Helen Methfessel. Reprinted by permission of Farrar, Straus and Giroux, Inc.

Columbia University Press, New York

Columbia University Press Morningside Edition 1984

Printed in the United States of America

Clothbound editions of Columbia University Press books are Smyth-sewn and printed on permanent and durable acid-free paper.

Library of Congress Cataloging in Publication Data

Donoghue, Dennis.
   Connoisseurs of chaos.

   Includes bibliographical references and index.
   1. American poetry—19th century—History and criticism. 2. American poetry—20th century—History and criticism. I. Title.
PS316.D65 1983 811'.009 83-20935
ISBN 0-231-05734-2 (alk. paper)
ISBN 0-231-05735-0 (pbk. : alk. paper)

For Frances

ACKNOWLEDGMENTS

The material in this book, in somewhat briefer form, was given as the George Elliston Lectures at the University of Cincinnati in January, 1965. I am grateful to the Faculty and associates of that university for hospitality far beyond conventional requirement. To mention, in particular, Professor and Mrs. William S. Clark is merely to acknowledge two of many sources of kindness in that city.

Some of the preparatory reading for this study was done at the University of Pennsylvania, where I was a Visiting Scholar for the year 1963–64. This happy arrangement was effected by the American Council of Learned Societies, which granted me a Fellowship for the occasion. I am especially grateful to Robert Spiller and Richard Downar for placing their time, goodwill, and energy at my disposal. I have also to thank the Governing Body of University College, Dublin, and particularly President Jeremiah J. Hogan, for releasing me from my teaching duties for that year.

Apart from the specific debts recognized in the footnotes, I owe words of thanks to Reuel Denney, Robert Buttel, Arnold Stein, Alex Blackburn, Milton Hindus, and (as a memorable group) those participants in "English S-160" at the Harvard Summer School who helped me to clarify some of the ideas in the following pages.

Finally, I thank the publishers who have allowed me to quote from the following works:—

Walt Whitman, *Complete Poetry and Selected Prose*, ed. James E. Miller, Jr. (Boston; Houghton Mifflin, 1959).

Frederick Goddard Tuckerman, *Sonnets*, ed. Witter Bynner (New York; Knopf, 1931).

Herman Melville, *Collected Poems*, ed. Howard P. Vincent (Chicago; Packard, 1947).

Emily Dickinson, *Complete Poems*, ed. Thomas H. Johnson (Cambridge; Harvard University Press, 1955. London; Oxford University Press, 1955).

E. A. Robinson, *Collected Poems* (New York; Macmillan, 1961).

Robert Frost, *Complete Poems* (New York; Henry Holt, 1949. London; Jonathan Cape, 1951).

Wallace Stevens, *Collected Poems* (London; Faber and Faber, 1955).

Wallace Stevens, *Opus Posthumous* (New York; Knopf, 1957. London; Faber and Faber, 1959).

William Empson, *Collected Poems* (London; Chatto and Windus, 1955).

J. V. Cunningham, *The Exclusions of a Rhyme* and *To What Strangers? What Welcome?* (Denver; Alan Swallow, 1964).

Acknowledgments

Theodore Roethke, *Words for the Wind* (Bloomington; Indiana University Press, 1961. London; Secker and Warburg, 1957).

Theodore Roethke, *The Far Field* (New York; Doubleday, 1964. London; Faber and Faber, 1965).

Robert Lowell, *Life Studies* (London; Faber and Faber, 1959).

Robert Duncan, *The Opening of the Field* (New York; Grove Press, 1960).

Dublin, *March 19, 1965.*   DENIS DONOGHUE

CONTENTS

CONNOISSEURS OF CHAOS

CONNOISSEURS OF CHAOS was published in 1965. Most of it was written in the United States during a sabbatical year—I was a visiting scholar at the University of Pennsylvania, on a grant from the American Council of Learned Societies—but it was based on reading I had done, over several years, in Dublin. When I was an undergraduate at University College, Dublin, we had no courses in American literature. A few of the major books were mentioned, in passing, as adjuncts to English muses, but American independence was not yet recognised.

Besides, there were very few American books in Dublin libraries. I first read the American poets and novelists by courtesy of the United States Information Service, which opened an office in Dublin and kept it going for several years. American music, too, was available from the same source. I recall presenting, on Radio Éireann, a series of six programmes on modern American music, with recordings—Copland and Barber, to begin with—I had borrowed from the U.S.I.S. A few years later, a Congressman remarked that America was already so deeply understood and loved in Ireland that the office could safely be closed. I still own several books—Faulkner's short stories, Frost's poems, O'Neill's plays, a one-volume collection of Carson McCullers among them—which bear the stamp of the U.S.I.S. The director of the office let me take my pick of them a few days before the library was closed.

By then, I was a committed reader of American poetry and the criticism that accompanied it. When my colleagues in University College were reading F. R. Leavis and *Scrutiny,* I was reading John Crowe Ransom, Cleanth Brooks, Kenneth Burke, R. P. Blackmur, Lionel Trilling, and Robert Penn Warren. When I started teaching at University College, I argued American poetry with my friend Donald Davie, who was teaching at Trinity College. I recall the day on which, in his rooms at Trinity, he recited Yvor Winters's poem "On Teaching the Young," intoning with Yorkshire conviction its final lines—

> The poet's only bliss
> Is in cold certitude—
> Laurel, archaic, rude.

It troubled me then, as it still does, that Winters valued in life only the knowledge of it, and that he didn't even commit himself to knowledge till he felt it as cold certitude. But this is an old dispute with Davie; we have put it aside along with other questions.

It is hard to remember that American literature, during those years, had little footing in Europe, and that those European scholars who taught it and wrote of it had missionary zest to keep them going. The European Association for American Studies brought them together; there was also the Salzburg Seminar. Several years later, we started the Irish Association for American Studies, and arranged little conferences in the usual manner.

There was also, from time to time, an opening for American themes on the B.B.C., especially on its Third Programme, which was willing to receive occasional talks—twenty minutes the limit—on the poets. I gave a few talks, including one called "Three Directions in Modern American Poetry," undertaking to show that one could make sense of the new poets by thinking of them in diverse association with Frost, Stevens, and Williams. I still think the argument sound, but it had this disability, that nearly every poet anyone in Dublin or London could name had issued in some form from Williams's overcoat. Nobody in Europe at the time was reading Ammons or Ashbery or indeed any of the poets who took Stevens as their master. Frost's voice was so distinctively quirky that it was hard to name any other poets who cared to risk sounding like him. In Dublin, we were content to believe that the Beats came from Williams by way of an elaborate detour called Olson.

I don't claim that it was easier to get the American poets right, reading them at a distance of three thousand miles, than by reading them on the American spot. I don't know what degree of certitude would have animated the experience of reading Frank O'Hara in New York or Robert Duncan in California—though it might have been a special pleasure, like seeing *Chinatown* in Los Angeles. Besides, I don't know or can't remember what we were asking the American poets to do: reading them in Dublin during the Sixties, I thought it must be an immense advantage to a poet to have access to the biggest cast and the widest screen. Lowell, Mailer, Ginsberg, Ferlinghetti: all those readings in amphitheatres, the marches, linked hands, literature as street theatre. Now it is hard to be sure. It doesn't take long, these days, for a stirring event to merge into the decor of its time, for derring-do to become the photograph-album over which one spends a becalmed evening.

The title and subtitle of my book came from Stevens. I was in correspondence with Williams, by the happy chance that he liked an essay I published in *The Hudson Review* on poetry and voice. I had also written an essay on his work, the first account of Williams, I believe—or so Hillis Miller told me—to be published in a magazine in Europe. I was also in correspondence with Kenneth Burke, who was closer kin to Williams than to Stevens. Frost came to Dublin to give a reading, at the end of some State Department tour. I heard him, but not clearly enough to be deeply moved by what I heard. His voice alluded to ways of being alive I didn't much warm to. So I probably missed what makes his poetry count. My misgivings about the chapter on Frost have been sharpened by reading Richard Poirier's book on him: it makes a case for rating Frost with Yeats and Eliot, and I would find the case decisive if it didn't go along with some depreciation of the other two. But it was Stevens's music I most wanted to hear.

I now feel that I heard it too much in one tone. I was reading a good deal of aesthetics at the time, and relished the poems in which Stevens, with hints from Valéry, Santayana, Vaihinger, and Charles Mauron, mused the obscure. But I think I exaggerated the philosophic ambition in Stevens; his meditations now seem more Epicurean, less systematic, than my account of them suggests; he was in poetry for pleasure and desire rather than for epistemological coherence. There is no contradiction, but a change of emphasis would be helpful.

The title of the book I still find satisfactory, but the subtitle is a minor embarrassment. Not the order, but the ideas of it; partly because my sense of ideas and their bearing upon poetry has become more doubtful. How ideas get into a poem, and what happens to them when they get there seems a harder question than I allowed for. There may be principles of order, or intimations, which don't aspire to the completeness we think of as making an idea, and they may work just as well in the poem.

I thought of trying to bring the book "up to date"; but it didn't have a firm date to begin with, and it wasn't planned, in any sense, as a history of American Poetry 1850–1950. I have written about other American poets, as in my *The Ordinary Universe*—on Pound, Eliot, Williams, and Marianne Moore, and more on Stevens—and from time to time I have written reviews and essays on Berryman, Ashbery, Ammons, Plath, Josephine Miles, Kenneth Koch, Hollander, Merrill, and other poets. But I don't feel a sense of the poetry of the past ten or fifteen years securely enough to try to describe it. This is not a matter of decades: Lowell's "tranquillized Fifties," someone's demented Sixties, or the anonymous Seventies. It is more a matter of sects. The audience for poetry today may be as large as it ever was, but it is dispersed into groups, enthusiasts here and there, sects who worship one poet—William Bronk, maybe—initiates who come together to recite some poems issued on fine paper by a saint in Des Moines. I am not complaining, or mounting an argument about the Death of Poetry.

I have let the book stand, then. But I have added a chapter

on Elizabeth Bishop. When I was writing the book, only *North and South* (1946) and *A Cold Spring* (1955) were published: there was no sign of *Questions of Travel* (1965). *Geography III* was many years to come. The achievement of *North and South* was remarkable, but it was impossible to predict how the complete work would appear, and the scale of the last two books.

Lowell once told Stanley Kunitz that he thought Bishop's poems made "a sort of bridge between Tate's formalism and Williams's informal art." That is a way of putting it: in any case, it has particular point in relation to Lowell's own development as a poet. Tate's development from "The Mediterranean" to "The Swimmers" makes "formalism" a barely adequate account of his poetry. Nor is "informal art" adequate to Williams, who was just as formal as Stevens but practised a different sense of formality. I haven't taken up these questions in the chapter on Bishop. I've chosen, rather, to read her poetry in the context of the interests and emphases suggested by the book as a whole.

D.D.
Dublin, August 1983

INTRODUCTION

IN CHAPTER X of his *History of the United States During the Second Administration of James Madison* Henry Adams said that sometime around 1815 the American character acquired, for the first time, a form, sufficiently fixed to be considered, discussed, defined. It was not a particularly beautiful form. For one thing, its activities were largely mechanical, routine, "matter for a census rather than for history." They offered no evidence to show that the Americans were at all "conscious of a higher destiny." [1] This was Adams' fated theme: the higher destiny, and the American failure to rise to it. It was also the theme that troubled most of the American writers in the first half of the nineteenth century, but these writers still thought it an open question. The story of nationalism in American literary thought in the nineteenth century is an interesting story as far as it goes, and it has been well told; there is no need to tell it again. But it may be useful to think of Adams' experience, as refracted through the novels, the *History*, the *Education*, *Mont-Saint-Michel and Chartres*, and the *Letters*, and to set beside that experience a few texts to qualify its image.

In September, 1817, the *North American Review* published one of the most famous poems in American literature, Bryant's "Thanatopsis." The poem is still widely esteemed, with little justification. It merely paraphrases early Wordsworth, adding a little graveyard *décor*. Nature is the Great Teacher, a friend to man, and the virtuous man passes mildly away:

> So live, that when thy summons comes to join
> The innumerable caravan, which moves
> To that mysterious realm, where each shall take
> His chamber in the silent halls of death,
> Thou go not, like the quarry-slave at night,
> Scourged to his dungeon, but, sustained and soothed

By an unfaltering trust, approach thy grave,
Like one who wraps the drapery of his couch
About him, and lies down to pleasant dreams.[2]

Most of Bryant's poems are in this tone. Nature is God's witness. "There is a Power whose care/Teaches thy way . . ." Truth is pastoral. Whatever is, is right. This is largely the lesson, simple as it is, that Bryant learned from Wordsworth. It is to be found in such poems as "Summer Wind," "The Rivulet," "The Old Man's Funeral," and "A Hymn of the Sea," in which Bryant looks at the universe and finds it good. But there are several poems in which the lesson is repudiated. In "Rizpah," for instance, there is no attempt to make the events adorn a tale of natural harmony. In the sonnet "Midsummer" "the trout floats dead in the hot stream." What has happened to the harmony of God, nature, and man? Then there is the "Hymn to Death," which turns the pastoral acknowledgments of "Thanatopsis" inside out.

The poem begins by shuffling the conventional counters so that Bryant can take the offense out of death. Death is the executant of a fine poetic justice, at the due moment the scourge of God:

Oh, there is joy when hands that held the scourge
Drop lifeless, and the pitiless heart is cold.

Atheist, extortioner, perjurer, liar are laid low. Death is also a good teacher for those who can still be taught:

Thou dost make
Thy penitent victim utter to the air
The dark conspiracy that strikes at life . . .

And so it continues. But then there is a sudden change:

Alas! I little thought that the stern power,
Whose fearful praise I sang, would try me thus
Before the strain was ended. It must cease—

> For he is in his grave who taught my youth
> The art of verse, and in the bud of life
> Offered me to the Muses.

The victim is one of nature's most devoted pupils, and if it is still appropriate to tell him to "rest in the bosom of God," the words must be deemed to pay more than they owe. The poem ends:

> Now thou art not; and yet the men whose guilt
> Has wearied Heaven for vengeance—he who bears
> False witness—he who takes the orphan's bread,
> And robs the widow—he who spreads abroad
> Polluted hands in mockery of prayer,
> Are left to cumber earth. Shuddering I look
> On what is written, yet I blot not out
> The desultory numbers—let them stand,
> The record of an idle revery.

What is written in many of Bryant's poems is a record of traditional civilities, the obeisance to verities sanctioned by the Wordsworthian strain in English poetry:

> Be it ours to meditate
> In these calm shades thy milder majesty,
> And to the beautiful order of thy works
> Learn to conform the order of our lives.

The shuddering, on the other hand, owes nothing to Wordsworth, Milton, Blair, or Cowper and everything to Bryant's American sensibility, which drains the hymn until it is a revery. To go through Bryant's poems is to see him wavering with some distress between two traditions—an English tradition, strong in its purposes, and an American tradition just barely emerging into form. "The figure the poem makes" in American literature is a question mark.

So we must revise the motto. In Bryant's poems, whatever is, is right sometimes. It is right except when it is, to God's scandal, wrong. Jones Very will imply that whenever

God, nature, and man are out of tune the fault is man's; man's passions are trying to separate God from nature:

> But ever fresh she rises 'neath his rod,
> For she obeys in love her sovereign God.

Bryant is not quite sure. In any event, if the present time is wrong, there is always the future. This is his resolution. Bryant's idea of order is a future condition, toward which he strains as if to free himself from a present tense in which only the easy questions are answered. Whitman exerts maximum force upon the present moment. In Hawthorne the stain of the past is always visible, dead voices always heard. Bryant stretches toward a future of righteousness. His favorite words are "yet" and "shall." We hear his voice in "the peace that yet shall be," "Alone shall Evil die," in every demand that God take up the slack, dispense a justice marvelously poetic. He declares, in "Hymn of the Waldenses":

> Yet, mighty God, yet shall thy frown look forth
> Unveiled, and terribly shall shake the earth.
> Then the foul power of priestly sin and all
> Its long-upheld idolatries shall fall.
> Thou shalt raise up the trampled and oppressed,
> And thy delivered saints shall dwell in rest.

This is one version of something that we find again in Melville's poems and elsewhere in modern American poetry: a craving for rhetorical ease, the full close in a cadence sung by a righteous God. When a nineteenth-century American quarreled with God, his quarrel was here: that God put hard questions into the pilgrim's mouth and never answered them. This is the feeling that, increasingly, sent a poet from "Thanatopsis" to the "Hymn to Death." Later it would sponsor at least one remarkable poem, F. G. Tuckerman's "The Cricket."

Meanwhile Bryant sang as many old songs as he could.

He was an honest man, but he had an extremely limited sensibility. Hence there were many occasions on which the configuration of natural forms gave him the answers he wanted, for the time being. A much more problematic case than Bryant's was presented by Poe, who could never be satisfied with the smiles of nature and would never connive with her to gain a sounding rhetoric. In the first paragraph of *The Fall of the House of Usher* he repudiates the Sublime from Longinus to Burke, "that half-pleasurable, because poetic, sentiment with which the mind usually receives even the sternest natural images of the desolate or terrible." He denies this relation between man and nature because he denies all relations between man and nature. One of Roderick's paintings showed "an immensely long and rectangular vault or tunnel, with low walls, smooth, white, and without interruption or device," far beneath the earth's surface. There was no outlet, no source of light, "yet a flood of intense rays rolled throughout, and bathed the whole in a ghastly and inappropriate splendor." [3]

We think of this light as issuing from Roderick's own mind, a function of his will, the more diseased the more intense. And if Roderick is a man of extreme sensitivity living in a house of ancestral decay, we have only to strain the text a little to think of him as a certain kind of American poet. In that capacity Roderick haunts nineteenth-century American literature: the man for whom the only meaning is a function of his driving will, the only form the improvisation, the guitar impromptu. Even on days of some composure Poe would say, as in the preface to *Eureka,* "What I here propound is true," leaving us to add only "true because you propound it." Hence Poe animates all those aspects of American poetry that we invoke under such phrases as "the disconsolate chimera," the rage of will, isolation ("Thou art not August unless I make thee so"), the breach between man and nature, between man and man, the decay of the world's body ("My house is a decayed house"). He is the chief reason for the common understanding that American poetry tends to be metaphysical without being religious, that it lives fretfully on earth, converting matter into spirit by compulsion, a nervous tic of imagination. There is a sense, then, in which modern American poetry begins with Poe, the first ghost of many in its haunted house. If he leads to Robinson Jeffers and Theodore Roethke, he does so by being an ominous presence in many other poets, great and small. In the present book the only way we can take him is for granted. He repels the summary view. For the moment we can think of him as the poet who filled American literature with question marks.

When we think of answers we think of Emerson. But Emerson wears a coat of many colors: he does not torture himself in the service of coherence. If the issue came to a vote, he voted conservatively:

> Nature, in its ministry to man, is not only the material, but is also the process and the result. All the parts incessantly work into each other's hands for the profit of man. The wind sows the seed; the sun evaporates the sea; the wind blows the vapor to the field; the ice, on the other side of the planet, condenses rain on this; the rain feeds the plant; the plant feeds the animal; and thus the endless circulations of the divine charity nourish man.[4]

Hence in Emersonian theory a man could take his place in the public world, acting with confidence. The life of action was the best life. This was the theory of the matter, and it was a handsome theory. But Emerson knew that it was a daydream. Wherever he looked he saw action confounded; the gap between theory and practice was enormous. Emerson faced this directly on several occasions, but most explicitly while writing of Montaigne in *Representative Lives*. If reason is the law of life, in fifty years we have perhaps half a dozen reasonable hours. "So vast is the disproportion between the sky of law and the pismire of performance under it, that, whether he is a man of worth or a sot is not so great a matter as we say." Young people accuse Providence of "a certain parsimony": "the incompetency of power is the universal grief of young and ardent minds." Seen in this light, man is "this little, conceited, vulnerable popinjay."

There is only one escape. If action is impossible, there is always thought. If you cannot act, you can observe. And if the thought is sufficient, you can even disengage yourself from all those motives in yourself that would confine you to the world of action. In the *Journals* for October 8, 1837, Emerson wrote:

> The constant warfare in each heart is betwixt Reason and Commodity. The victory is won as soon as any Soul has learned always to take sides with Reason against himself; to transfer his Me from his person, his name, his interests, back upon Truth and Justice, so that when he is disgraced and defeated and fretted and disheartened, and wasted by nothings, he bears it well, never one instant relaxing his watchfulness, and, as soon as he can get a respite from the insults or the sadness, records all these phenomena, pierces their beauty as phenomena, and, like a God, oversees himself.[5]

This is one of the classic moments of the genteel tradition in American poetry: the only way to heal the breach between God, nature, and man is by becoming God and rearranging things according to your own "light." The occasion for doing so is provided (if we look ahead beyond Emerson to Wallace Stevens, the greatest poet in the genteel tradition) by the breakdown of supernatural belief and the confusions of epistemology. Hence we say, God and the human imagination are one. The saint is the man of thought. Emerson says (and the voice might well be Stevens') that "when the fact is seen under the light of an idea, the gaudy fable fades and shrivels." But he still speaks as a moralist. The answer to skepticism is "the moral sentiment, which never forfeits its supremacy." The man of thought wins by generalizing, by abstraction, by resisting "the usurpation of particulars." The power that Emerson calls Intellect sees things "cool and disengaged." A truth, separated by the intellect, is no longer "a subject of destiny." "We behold it as a god upraised above care and fear. And so any fact in our life, or any record of our fancies or reflections, disentangled from the web of our unconsciousness, becomes an object impersonal and immortal." [6] A fact, abstracted for our contemplation, ceases to threaten us. Sorrows become, as Emerson says in "Monadnock," "insect miseries." Under pressure we "exist wholly in the mind."

The function of literature, in this setting, is "the conversion of action into thought for the delight of the Intellect," as Emerson wrote in the *Journals* on April 28, 1834. Or as Stevens said, sponsoring his Supreme Fiction, "It Must Be Abstract." Literature is therefore only a formal version of something that "Man Thinking" does every day when he withdraws into his imagination—as Stevens says, "the facts upon which the lovers of truth insist." It is in this sense that literature helps us to live our lives, by offering us instances of the productive imagination at work.

When we think of Emerson and Stevens in this relation we see that Emerson's Over-Soul is as close as we are likely to get to Stevens' Supreme Fiction, and that Stevens' "major man" is the extreme resource of the genteel tradition in American poetry. And this prompts us to see why William Carlos Williams had to carve out a rival tradition in the American grain and could offer little hospitality to either Emerson or Stevens. Both Emerson and Stevens achieved their poetic victories without loss of blood, and Williams found this hard to condone. Their voices are clear but unimpassioned. They don't say yes and they don't say no. While

Stevens was teasing out the problems of epistemology, Williams was hacking through the undergrowth of American history, trying to discover what had happened. This explains why he busied himself with the writers of the American Revolution, with Freneau's essay on verse forms, with John Adams, Jefferson's good taste, Crèvecoeur, and later with Poe and Whitman and Mencken and Gertrude Stein and Stieglitz and Pound; because these people did things (what things?) and with some purpose (what purpose?). All this time Stevens was reading philosophy, corresponding with Yale professors, devising an elaborate terminology of knowledge, structure, being, seeming, and so on. Williams committed himself, rather, to the terms of action, contact, time, history, motive, purpose, direction, end. (But there is a lot more to be said on both sides.)

This has now passed into literary history. It is distinctly possible that Stevens' death brought the genteel tradition to an end. What his poems do they do superbly, disclosing potentialities in the tradition that we had little reason to acknowledge—the *vif* of intelligence, for one thing. But Stevens' poems are so complete in their own terms and so hostile to the encroachment of other terms that the lucidity of their allegiance is likely to work against them in the longer run and to undermine the tradition they define. Or, to put it otherwise, the poems leave out too much. This explains why—to revert to Emerson—so much of late nineteenth-century American poetry seems to have been written by parodying the genteel poets, as if to warn Emerson that his great abstractions—Nature, Compensation, the Over-Soul—mean only whatever their owner can afford to pay them. Indeed, the greatest single obstacle to the genteel tradition was Mark Twain, and the best way to read him, like Swift, Joyce, and Beckett, is to think of what he parodies. The ferocity of "The Mysterious Stranger," for instance, is only partially to be explained in biographical terms. It is basically a parody of Emerson's optimism, ridiculing its coziness. Emerson says, in the essay on Montaigne:

> Although knaves win in every political struggle, although society seems to be delivered over from the hands of one set of criminals into the hands of another set of criminals, as fast as the government is changed, and the march of civilization is a train of felonies, yet general ends are somehow answered. We see, now, events forced on, which seem to retard or retrograde the civility of ages. But the world-spirit is a good swimmer, and storms and waves cannot drown him. He snaps his finger at laws: and so, throughout history, heaven seems to affect low and poor means. Through the years and the centuries, through evil agents, through toys and atoms, a great and beneficent tendency irresistibly streams.

Mark Twain answers in "The Mysterious Stranger":

> Next, Christianity was born. Then ages of Europe passed in review before us, and we saw Christianity and Civilization march hand in hand through those ages, "leaving famine and death and desolation in their wake, and other signs of the progress of the human race," as Satan observed. . . . "And what does it amount to? . . . Nothing at all. You gain nothing; you always come out where you went in. For a million years the race has gone on monotonously propagating itself and monotonously reperforming this dull nonsense—to what end?" [7]

The parody is unmistakable in Satan's ridicule of "The Moral Sense." He keeps bringing up the phrase as if he were tackling in turn all the heavyweight moralists who traded in it—Emerson, Adam Smith, Hutcheson, Shaftesbury, and many others. And closing in upon Emerson again, he makes fun of "intellect" in the Master's terms. In the essay of that name Emerson says that Intellect "separates the fact considered from *you,* from all local and personal reference, and discerns it as if it existed for its own sake." Happiness depends upon the disengaging power of intellect, which "reduces all things into a few principles." But Mark Twain's Satan effects the happiness of Father Peter by driving him mad. As for the disengaging power, it is impertinent, since a human being is nothing in any event but a thought. As Satan tells Theodor at the end of the story:

> "*Nothing* exists; all is a dream. God—man—the world—the sun, the moon, the wilderness of stars—a dream, all a dream; they have no existence. *Nothing exists save empty space—and you!* . . . And you are not you—you have no body, no blood, no bones, you are but a *thought*. I myself have no existence; I am but a dream—your dream, creature of your imagination."

God and the human imagination are what?

We can put the position very briefly. The chief difference between Emerson and Mark Twain is that for Emerson there is always a middle term to mediate between polarities; in Mark Twain there is no middle term. Emerson says, in fact, "Nature is thoroughly mediate. It is made to serve." He means that it is the middle term between God and man, it is made by God to serve man. Mark Twain vetoes this function; nature is not mediate. In the resultant chasm man must do the best he can, which will turn out to be nothing.

The secular equivalent of this can be seen in Henry Adams. If we keep our three terms, God, nature, and man, and if (thinking of Adams) we translate them to read the state, politics, and the citizen, we see why Adams' failure to serve his country in politics had such a devastating effect on his morale; it was the same as being cast off by God. We have to bear in mind that Adams sought "salvation" not only for himself but for the whole American people. What else could justify his talk of the Americans becoming "a higher variety of the human race"? This is his version of getting to heaven. The current orthodoxy was Democracy, in which Adams believed, it almost seems, on the principle that says *credo quia impossibile est*. When this failed, when democracy corrupted itself, the ideal harmony was shattered.

In the novel *Democracy* Madeleine Lee, who has confronted a radical defect in democracy and in herself, longs to "live in the Great Pyramid and look out for ever at the polar star." In effect, she longs to change the whole scene of the drama and confront her "God" directly, with no mediating ministry. In Adams himself there is a corresponding urge to keep changing the scene. He travels to Tahiti, Japan, Sydney, Ceylon, Singapore. But his deepest desire was always to achieve a marvelous harmony, to play a great part in American salvation, a part comparable to Saint Thomas Aquinas' in the medieval church. In Chapter XVI of *Mont-Saint-Michel and Chartres* he says:

> Beginning with the foundation which is God and God's active presence in His Church, Thomas next built God into the walls and towers of His Church, in the Trinity and its creation of mind and matter in time and space; then finally he filled the Church by uniting mind and matter in man, or man's soul, giving to humanity a free will that rose, like the flèche, to heaven.

We need not translate all the terms of this image into their political equivalents; the translation is clear enough as a cry of the alienated heart. And it is but one of many in modern American poetry. We hear it again in Edwin Arlington Robinson, especially in his legendary poems, which flee the scene of alienation in the same spirit, though for different reasons. We hear it more clearly still in the poems of Ezra Pound, another man who longed to define himself by serving an ideal prince. This failing, he did the next best thing, wrote a long poem to coax such a prince into existence —the *Cantos* being, among other less essential things, a mirror for magistrates, a *speculum principis;* but there was no *princeps.* Hence in Pound's case the bitterness, the venom, the hysteria come from a soul's lifelong search for a Master; but there is no Master. As for Adams, we think of him in his most famous image, in Paris in November,

1900, with an old century giving way to a new one. Writing to John Hay he says:

> It is a new century, and what we used to call electricity is its God. I can already see that the scientific theories and laws of our generation will, to the next, appear as antiquated as the Ptolemaic system and that the fellow who gets to 1930 will wish he hadn't. The curious mustiness of decay is already over our youth, and all the period from 1840 to 1870. The period from 1870 to 1900 is closed. I see that much in the machine-gallery of the Champ de Mars. The period from 1900 to 1930 is in full swing, and, gee-whacky! how it is going! It will break its damned neck long before it gets through, if it tries to keep up the speed. You are free to deride my sentimentality if you like, but I assure you that I,—a monk of St. Dominic, absorbed in the Beatitudes of the Virgin Mother—go down to the Champ de Mars and sit by the hour over the great dynamos, watching them run as noiselessly and as smoothly as the planets, and asking them—with infinite courtesy—where in Hell they are going.[8]

It is a famous occasion. Seventy years before, on an occasion only a little less famous and quite as significant, Poe asked in his sonnet "To Science":

> Hast thou not dragged Diana from her car,
>   And driven the Hamadryad from the wood
> To seek a shelter in some happier star?
>   Hast thou not torn the Naiad from her flood,
> The Elfin from the green grass, and from me
> The summer dream beneath the tamarind tree?

Science, Darwin, Spencer, the War between the States, Reconstruction, the democratic dogma, the white whale, Amherst, two great wars—in the following pages we shall have to take these, like Poe, for granted, along with a multitude of private disorders in the poets themselves, which we shall take on the evidence of their poems, for the most part silently. The terms of our discussion are order and chaos.

NOTES

1 Henry Adams, *History of the United States During the Second Administration of James Madison* (New York: Antiquarian Press reprint, 1962), III, 220. See also his *History of the United States During the Second Administration of Thomas Jefferson* (New York: Antiquarian Press reprint, 1962), I, 212.

2 William Cullen Bryant, *Representative Selections,* ed. Tremaine McDowell (New York: American Book Company, 1935), p. 5.

3 Edgar Allan Poe, *Complete Poems and Stories,* ed. A. H. Quinn and E. H. O'Neill (New York: Knopf, 1946), I, 263.

4 Ralph Waldo Emerson, *Works* (Boston: Houghton Mifflin, 1903–1904), I, 13. All quotations, unless otherwise specified, are from this edition.

5 Emerson, *Journals,* ed. Edward Waldo Emerson and Waldo Emerson Forbes (London: Constable, 1910), IV, 315–316.

6 Emerson, *Works,* II, 327.

7 *Selected Shorter Writings of Mark Twain,* ed. Walter Blair (Boston: Houghton Mifflin, 1962), pp. 370, 371.

8 Adams, *Letters,* ed. Worthington Chauncey Ford (Boston: Houghton Mifflin, 1938), II, 301.

CHAPTER 1

WALT WHITMAN

"CONNOISSEUR OF CHAOS" is an elegant dialogue by Wallace Stevens that holds aboriginal experience at the safe distance of contemplation. The first voice says that the law of inherent opposites, of essential unity, is "as pleasant as port." The contrast of life and death is "pretty," presumably because it is suavely contained in the essential unity. "The squirming facts exceed the squamous mind," yes, but nevertheless "relation" appears and expands, and as April comes to summer, it seems good. The second voice speaks with distaste of an order too fixed, too "Plantagenet," and conjures a pensive man, a man of saving grace, the grace of imagination:

> The pensive man . . . He sees that eagle float
> For which the intricate Alps are a single nest.[1]

If the pensive man is the "man-hero" of Stevens' "Notes toward a Supreme Fiction," we are at the center of Stevens' world, his *"fluent mundo."* There is no better place from which to view the athletic *mundo* of Walt Whitman, because Stevens gives us all the terms we need, and his fluency shows us how much sweat and spirit Whitman had to expend before an American poet could deploy those terms with such control, such elegance. I have in mind such terms as chaos, order, the great disorder which is itself an order, "relation," "the pensive man." Whitman wielded all these, or their rugged equivalents, and he had to press them into being before Stevens could put them on show, like Yeats' circus animals. Whitman's version of Stevens' pensive man, for instance, is the "equable man" invoked in the preface to the first edition of *Leaves of Grass* and again in "By Blue Ontario's Shore," and in both cases identified with "the poet," a generic figure, master of the intricate Alps. And if we need Whitman's tone of voice to shape the meaning of the phrase, we have it: "Now there shall be a man cohered out of tumult and chaos." The man thus cohered is not Whitman himself or any particular man, not even Lincoln, but a man still in vision, in prophecy. Whitman sees him whenever he looks into the middle distance or enters a brown study. Once, for Edward Dowden's benefit, he described the "spine or verteber principle" of *Leaves of Grass* as "a model or ideal (for the service of the New World & to be gradually absorbed in it) of a complete healthy, heroic, practical modern Man." [2] Indeed, the best way to read *Leaves of Grass* is to consider it Whitman's notes toward a supreme fiction; the supreme fiction that in Whitman and Stevens is Man.

I have no wish to force upon Whitman and Stevens a congruity foreign to their tempers. Indeed, Whitman's shadow falls more directly upon the poems of Ezra Pound and William Carlos Williams than upon Stevens' philosophical discriminations. So we will not push the association too far. But even the differences between the two poets are vivid. Stevens' poems press toward a moment of stillness in which perception is acute and all the harmonies sing. I think of this as Stevens' answer to that quite different stillness in T. S. Eliot's poems in which the poet, like a celebrant priest, hands over his individuality to the ritual of the sacrifice, and the result is a calm of self, all stillness, all repose. Whitman is not interested in such "moments," either Eliot's or Stevens', nor is he interested in the spectacular moments of Hart Crane or Marius the Epicurean. He demands that the continuities shall flow all the time, not merely at Key West but wherever a man happens to be. The peaks of feeling do not satisfy him; he wants the whole landscape, nothing less.

Hence the defining "figure" of Whitman's mind is the equals sign—equals, not plus or minus. Where the New England Fathers set up a covenant with God, based on severance and inequality, Whitman set up a covenant with nature, governed by the energy that makes all things equal. If he found two things traditionally considered enemies, he would declare their identity, or at least make them friends in a larger community. Ideally, A is A and B is B, and in the flow of energy A equals B.

This explains why Whitman was never troubled by the problem that confronted every major Romantic poet—the nature of the self. He does not hunt and trail and worry the problem, as Coleridge does, or Keats, Byron, Wordsworth, even Emerson. He would never have written a poem like Coleridge's "Frost at Midnight," never have tried to write Wordsworth's *Prelude*, because Wordsworth and Coleridge in those poems are vexed by question marks, plus and minus signs, and Whitman's act of faith has erased these as impertinent. For him life is—in Yeats' phrase—"the fire that makes all simple"; simple because equal. He would speak of "the old knot of contrarieties," but he was always sure he could open it. (At least until the Civil War; later he would tell a different story.)

Hence he begins by saying, Let x equal the self. Then x equals A plus B plus C plus D plus E, and so on, where each letter stands for a new experience contained and possessed, and the self is the sum of its possessions. This is the law of Whitman's lists. If you say that the self—x—is the sum of its possessions, $A, B, C, D,$ and so on, then the more you add to the right-hand side of the equation, the more you enrich the left, and you do this without bothering about the "nature" of the x. You assume, as most Romantic poets did, that the self is not at any moment fixed, complete, or predetermined, and then you are free to develop or enlarge it at any time by adding to its experience. This is one of the differences between Whitman and Joyce, two writers who wanted to "put everything in." Joyce wanted to put everything in so that he could exhibit the power of a mind in control of whatever it contained. Whitman wanted to put everything in so that he could declare the essential unity of a world rampant with multiplicity. He gives the principle, the law of his equation, in "Our Old Feuillage":

O lands! all so dear to me—what you are, (whatever it is,) I
    putting it at random in these songs, become a part of that,
    whatever it is,
Southward there, I screaming, with wings slow flapping, with the
    myriads of gulls wintering along the coasts of Florida . . .

He can put it in at random—or seems to do so—because once in, it will take its proper place. And in this equation it doesn't matter, mathematically, whether you put M before or after N; the equation persists. The great advantage of the equation is that while it is at any moment true and valid, you can add further items to the right-hand side without disrupting it; the x, the self, is "growing" at the same rate.

Whitman was thrilled and sometimes dazzled by the felicities of his equation. He never lost faith in it; and if he questioned it, notably in "As I Ebb'd with the Ocean of Life," the question merely testifies to the power of the sea as a symbol of "merging" and obliteration, one of the perennial temptations of American literature. In one of the recurrent "moments" of American literature the imagination confronts reality in the guise of a poet gazing at the sea. The imperious singer in Stevens' "The Idea of Order at Key West" walks by the sea and partly invents it with her song. But whether she invents it or discovers it, she will master it, because she stands and walks and sings for Wallace Stevens, not another poet. Whitman is more representative of American experience when the sea throws down a challenge to his selfhood that he is not sure he can survive, and in one of his rare and extreme moments he says:

O baffled, balk'd, bent to the very earth,
Oppress'd with myself that I have dared to open my mouth,
Aware now that amid all that blab whose echoes recoil upon me I
   have not once had the least idea who or what I am,
But that before all my arrogant poems the real Me stands yet
   untouch'd, untold, altogether unreach'd . . .

The sea is Stevens' reality, and Whitman's too, and for once in this extreme moment Whitman fears that the sea has obliterated all the dense particulars of reality on which his equation depends—and then there is nothing but the void. In *Sea-Drift* he will be his own man again, but only when he has settled and populated the sea with ships and sea captains and swimmers and a child and her father walking on the beach at night, feeling the "vast similitude" that "interlocks all." The equation is, in the nick of time, verified.

But it is verified. In the essay "Experience" Emerson says that one of the consequences of the Fall of Man is that the Me is utterly separated from the Not-Me. But Whitman disposes of the problem briskly by declaring that the Me is simply the sum of the Not-Me it contains. And he implies, of course, that it is the part of prudence as well as faith to make that sum as large as possible. One should keep adding to the self as Whitman kept adding to *Leaves of Grass,* thereby gaining the best of all possible worlds, being and becoming. Any experience genuinely assimilated adds to what Whitman calls "the Me myself." Hence he will say, "The press of my foot to the earth springs a hundred affections," and again, "Is this then a touch? . . . quivering me to a new identity . . ." The equation would also allow for the incorporation of any and every kind of experience. There would be no problem, for instance, in the rivalry of poet and scientist, one of the issues warily touched in Wordsworth's great *Preface*. Whitman can bring science into the equation simply by calling it, as he does in the preface of 1872, "a new sunrise." He can therefore avoid the slough of self-pity that we call "romantic irony." And he can evade one of the perennial problems, that of appearance and reality, simply by declaring their identity. He would never have said, as Stevens did, "Let be be finale of seem." Whitman wants the whole opera, not just the finale, so he declares that what seems is, here and now, and is good. Freed from metaphysical embarrassments, Whitman could devote himself to his equations, collecting experiences as the dominant culture of his day collected material possessions, and—in a sense—for "similar" reasons: because the verification of the self depended upon an exhibited affluence, perhaps even upon conspicuous waste. T. S. Eliot has spent many years persuading us that our possessions are vulgar, ephemeral. Hence we attend to him as we listen to our consciences, and no more frequently. Whitman spent most of his life sponsoring an affluent society, with this admonition, that our possessions should include sympathies, accords, pleasures, marriages, pains, passions, the sun and the stars as well as gadgets. But judged simply as an esthetic—though how simple is that?—Whitman's creed was uncannily faithful to the dominant metaphors of his place and time. He did not repudiate the metaphors; he thought they were excellent and would serve every occasion, if only you worked them hard enough, put everything in, material and spiritual.

Because his equations were designed to include everything, like and unlike, city and country, they could also include evil. It was William James, I think, who brought into critical currency the notion that Whitman lacked a sense of evil. In a lecture of 1895 he spoke of "our dear old Walt Whitman's works" as the handbook of that "temperamental optimism" that is "incapable of believing that anything seriously evil can exist." [3] What James started Yeats continued, in a famous passage in *A Vision*. But it will not do. No one will ask Whitman to speak like Saint Augustine, Kierkegaard, or that accomplished neo-Augustinian of our own day, Graham Greene. But it is willful to argue that Whitman was blind to evil or that he felt it sluggishly. Some of the most haunting passages in "Song of Myself" are apprehensions of sickness and pain, "the silent old-faced infants and the lifted sick." It is not that Whitman was insensitive to the pain of others, but—I concede only this—that he was a little too ready to assimilate this pain to the genial law of his own equation. In "Song of Myself," after a long passage invoking pain and suffering, he says:

All this I swallow, it tastes good, I like it well, it becomes mine,
I am the man, I suffer'd, I was there.

Even if we read this as a hymn to the sympathetic imagination, or, alternatively, in the Nietzschean sense that life is somehow justified by the courage its endurance requires, still we jib at its fluency. It is one thing to suffer, and it is another thing to sympathize with the suffering of others, and these experiences are not identical, no matter what Whitman's equations say. In an earlier part of "Song of Myself" he says:

The pleasures of heaven are with me and the pains of hell are with me,
The first I graft and increase upon myself, the latter I translate into a new tongue.

It is the ease with which he translates the pain of others that constitutes the failure of response. This is why, reading the poems, we are so relieved and assuaged to come upon the poem "I Sit and Look Out" in the collection *By the Roadside*, where Whitman says, toward the end of a vision of pain:

I observe a famine at sea, I observe the sailors casting lots who shall be kill'd to preserve the lives of the rest,

I observe the slights and degradations cast by arrogant persons
upon laborers, the poor, and upon negroes, and the like;
All these—all the meanness and agony without end I sitting look
out upon,
See, hear, and am silent.[4]

If Whitman's equations can include evil, they should have
no difficulty with death. Sometimes he euphemistically translates death to read "immortality," as in the last lines of "To
Think of Time," which read in the first version:

I swear I think there is nothing but immortality!
That the exquisite scheme is for it, and the nebulous float is for
it, and the cohering is for it,
And all preparation is for it . . . and identity is for it . . . and life
and death are for it.[5]

And generally Whitman assumes that death merely inaugu-
rates a new cycle of life and is therefore not a thing to fear
or bewail. There were moments in which, like many nineteenth-century poets and dramatists, he was more than half
in love with easeful death. Several passages, even in *Sea-
Drift*, sound like program notes to Wagner's *Tristan*, the
motif being "the low and delicious word Death," whispers
of heavenly death. But for the most part death and evil are
contained in the expanding self, the x, and therefore "justified."

Given the primary equation by which the self is identified
with the sum of its contents, Whitman goes on to declare
other equations, especially where the old orthodoxies
luxuriated in antagonism—soul and body, for instance,
which in Whitman's animal faith are distinct but without
difference. He would eliminate the distinction with an equation, thus earning D. H. Lawrence's celebrated praise.
Throughout *Leaves of Grass* this equation persists, and
Whitman returns to assert it several times in *A Backward
Glance*. "Behold, the body includes and is the meaning, the

main concern, and includes and is the soul," he says in "Starting from Paumanok," and again, in effect, in *Children of Adam* and "Song of Myself." A later poet, W. B. Yeats, in at least one of his moods would present the fullness of being as "a perfectly proportioned human body" in splendid animation, and he would point to certain passages in Dante for theory and to "certain beautiful women" for proof. The same hope would send Yeats into the theater and toward certain spectacularly theatrical poems, poems all gesture and nonchalance. Yeats would bring his thought to drama, to crisis. But Whitman was not content with a few fine crises. The electrical body would have to certify the soul at all times, and he would "sing" it to encourage it to do so. Where Dante had behind him the doctrine and incitement of the Incarnation, the word made flesh, Whitman had only the prompting of his own animal faith. But for him it was, of course, enough. This is why, discussing Yeats, we constantly need terms drawn from the theater; but these are useless in reading Whitman. In Whitman—both in our reading and his writing—the relevant terms are those that define the entire range of experience centered on the body. Above all, Whitman needs terms that evade the importunities of an arrogant and jealous consciousness, because he is honorbound to dissolve the old dichotomies of soul and body, mind and matter, consciousness and experience. In short, he needs all those words that are themselves equals signs, terms that denote the intersection of subject and object, the Me and the Not-Me. In a long list the central term is "contact."

From the first page of the first edition of *Leaves of Grass* this word reverberates through the poems and prose. "I am mad for it to be in contact with me," he says of the atmosphere, and in "A Song for Occupations," "I pass so poorly with paper and types . . . I must pass with the contact of bodies and souls." *Children of Adam* is virtually a tone poem on contact. And even when the key terms are more general, they are acceptable to Whitman only if they can prove their origin in bodily experience; many are phrenological terms. He chooses words like *inhale, adhere, respiration, adhesiveness, meeting, inspiration, acceptation, realization, give, receive, press, swallow.* In *The Mechanical Operation of the Spirit* Swift's irony challenges us to deny that our terms for the "higher" exertions are drawn directly from the "lower" bodily and mechanical facts, the "high" being therefore merely a sublimation of the "low." Whitman is not interested in such irony; he has no wish to entrench himself in a fort from which he can deflate our pretensions. He convinces by praise, by celebration, by allowing himself to be fully known. And this is a kinetic, muscular process. In "Resolution and Independence" Wordsworth trusts in his own wise passiveness to register the meaning of the old man's life. He takes it in as he takes in the landscape in which the old man figures; he assumes that such meanings come "naturally" and quietly to the suitably qualified observer. But when Whitman in the third stanza of "I Sing the Body Electric" confronts an old man and enters the meaning of his existence, we can almost foretell that the last grace of the encounter will be a touching, a contact, not just a "seeing":

When he went with his five sons and many grandsons to hunt or fish, you would pick him out as the most beautiful and vigorous of the gang,
You would wish long and long to be with him . . . you would wish to sit by him in the boat, that you and he might touch each other.

Emerson would worry because objects can touch each other only at one point. Whitman did not worry. One point was enough; you had only to ensure that there would be, always, one. In reading Samuel Beckett, if you derive any comfort from the impingement of subject and object, you will be advised that the incorrigible mobility of the subject makes the entire experience a humiliation. In Whitman the general rule is that subject and object are verifiable, trustworthy, sufficiently stable to merit local habitations and names and to justify the pleasure we take in their contact. And because this contact is to be felt now and will persist indefinitely as the sweet law of our lives, Whitman's favorite tense is the continuous present.

A life of such continuous intimacy, a life of contact, is Whitman's ideal human image. It will blur the distinction between man and God, thus setting up yet another equation, the largest in intention. Whitman effects this equation in "A Song of Joys" and celebrates it in "Song at Sunset":

To be this incredible God I am!
To have gone forth among other Gods, these men and women
   I love!

This divinity flows and sanctifies, by contact, everything it sees, hears, touches, tastes, or smells; it is Whitman's version of the laying on of hands. Stevens will say, "God and the human imagination are one," and he will offer as proof the extreme reaches of his own perception. But this is not Whitman's faith. Stevens is convinced that man is God to the degree of his vision, his perception, his visual imagination. Whitman is convinced that man is God to the latitude of his contact. In Whitman's heaven we communicate by touch. In "Song of the Redwood-Tree" the new earth and the new heaven are one, an earthly paradise of contact, silent because it is itself the ultimate poem that renders all lesser poems redundant. Kenneth Burke says that man craves images of "perfection," is "rotten with perfection." Whitman claimed, in the world of experience, everything, simply —like mountaineers possessing themselves of Everest—because it was there. If it existed, Whitman had to touch it; if it was possible, it was for that very reason a necessity, a compulsion. And because the limits of the possible and the actual must coincide, and this requires extreme pressure of invocation, he must command the High Style, almost the Sublime.

The sources of this compulsion—much more than a "vision" of life—are not at all clear. Whitman found a few of the signposts he needed in Emerson, and he pursued them far beyond the point at which Emerson elected to rest. He picked up a certain spirit of the age from the German idealists by way of Coleridge and the transcendentalists. A few echoes of Oriental lore reached him from Thoreau. From Hegel he took the consolation of historical approval. His debts to Carlyle and the American poets he favored are another story, and hardly an exciting one. But in fact his own native temper, I think, dictated most of his lines. What we loosely call his optimism, what we loosely call his romanticism, were matters of temper rather than theory or conviction. But it is worth while to relate optimism and romanticism quite specifically in Whitman, bearing in mind that A. O. Lovejoy has connected these motives in one of his famous *Essays in the History of Ideas*. It is all the more necessary to rehearse this motif, now that optimism has become almost an insulting term in criticism and we are admonished to dedicate ourselves to the proposition that good poems—especially good American poems—are written only on the dark side of the moon.

In linking romanticism and optimism Lovejoy argues that what distinguishes romanticism is a renewed delight in the plenitude, the mystery, the variety, of the created universe. And he traces this feeling back to the old notion that God allows evil to exist and flourish rather than have a missing link in the marvelously diverse chain of being. Anything rather than a lack. This joy in the plenitude of the universe is the difference between Reynolds and Blake. And in "Song of Myself" it sets Whitman praising "manifold objects, no two alike, and every one good," praising "my own diversity." This joy resounds through *Leaves of Grass,* and it persists even in the rueful prose of *Democratic Vistas.* Indeed, even if Whitman had loved "these States" for no other reason, it would have been enough that they exhibited "always the free range and diversity."

Hence one of his fundamental equations is the identification of value with being, not with progress or perfectibility, though he praised Darwin. "Song of the Open Road" is not a myth of perfectibility. Value resides, the poem implies, in the spirit of the journey, not in promissory notes redeemable at the end of the road. In "To Think of Time" he says:

It is not to diffuse you that you were born of your mother and
  father, it is to identify you,
It is not that you should be undecided, but that you should be
  decided,
Something long preparing and formless is arriv'd and form'd in
  you,
You are henceforth secure, whatever comes or goes.

He means secure in being, in identity. In *Democratic Vistas* he says: "The quality of BEING, in the object's self, according to its own central idea and purpose, and of growing therefrom and thereto—not criticism by other standards, and adjustments thereto—is the lesson of Nature." This virtually summarizes the aggressive remarks that Blake wrote in the margin of Reynolds' *Discourses,* though the inflection is unmistakably Whitman's. Indeed, it is also the point of contact between Whitman and Hopkins. When Hopkins wrote "The Leaden Echo and the Golden Echo" and registered kinship between his own mind and Whitman's, what he recognized was joy in the multiplicity of created being, joy that his friend Bridges could not feel in such measure. In the essay "Compensation" Emerson spoke of Being as "the vast affirmative, excluding negation, self-balanced, and swallowing up all relations, parts and times, within itself." This is close enough to Whitman for most purposes. But the best text, for our present purpose, to set beside *Leaves of Grass,* is that passage in *Specimen Days* in which Whitman speaks again of the tie between the Me and the Not-Me. Offering this as "the most profound theme that can occupy the mind of man," Whitman rehearses the several positions of Kant and Schelling and votes resoundingly for Hegel. The whole earth, with all its differences and contrarieties, he says, embodies "the endless process of Creative thought, which, amid numberless apparent failures and contradictions, is held together by central and never-broken unity— not contradictions or failures at all, but radiations of one consistent and eternal purpose." [6] In fact, the great purpose is the greatest of all equations.

Whitman will doubt this in certain rare and extreme moments, notably in the beautiful poem in *Calamus* called "Of the Terrible Doubt of Appearances," where the only answer to the doubt of being and identity is the present satisfaction of companionship, love. But for the most part Whitman's poems move upon a very simple epistemology, a realist faith. The "base of all metaphysics," he finds in the poem of that name, is:

The dear love of man for his comrade, the attraction of friend
    to friend,
Of the well-married husband and wife, of children and parents,
Of city for city and land for land.

So philosophic idealism and its doubts will touch him, but will never really endanger the security of being and identity. In *Democratic Vistas* he says: "There is, in sanest hours, a consciousness, a thought that rises, independent, lifted out from all else, calm, like the stars, shining eternal. This is the thought of identity—yours for you, whoever you are, as mine for me. Miracle of miracles, beyond statement, most spiritual and vaguest of earth's dreams, yet hardest basic fact, and only entrance to all facts." This is the spirit of Whitman's poetry, the temper of his greatest things. We seldom think of him as a poet of plot, act, and event. We think of him as a loud voice, a prophet, and often wish in weariness that he would cultivate the piano. But in fact his greatest poems are written in devotion to being, identity, time, event, and action. He is the guardian of being, and he is content to let essence take care of itself, or, better still, to let it reside silently and confidently in being. When Stevens says "the imperfect is our paradise," he is Whitman's pupil, his ephebe, as again when he says "the gods of China are always Chinese." Stevens would often try to disengage essence from being, to have spirit in some "essential" purity, but his greatest poems lay aside this metaphysical chemistry. And so too with Whitman. When he pours all his trust and joy into "contact," the actual, the finite, the verifiably human, the harmonies rise with wonderful grace and tact. I have in mind, among many, the twenty-eight men bathing, the beautifully tender "Out of the Rolling Ocean the Crowd," "We Two, How Long We Were Fool'd," the marriage of the trapper and the red girl—this has often been impugned, but it can stand any amount of critical strain— the runaway slave, the "old-time sea-fight," the wounded whale in "A Song of Joys." These represent the strongest elements in Whitman and are not at all dependent upon his lungs, his *fortissimo*. They are contact poems written by a poet in easy possession of his powers, touching an object, a human action, and touching it not at all to destroy it but to acknowledge it; there is no bravado.

These things were possible because Whitman acknowledged a reality good enough—rich enough, vivid enough— to celebrate. To develop or explode into being is to verify a primal energy; and to celebrate that energy is to share in it, to possess it. This is again the romantic joy in plenitude, in being. The Romantic poet solves the problem of the self by celebrating energy as a value in itself, a primal, non-ethical value, a principle of being, upon which a genuine ethic depends—as in Whitman. Because the religious motive —to take this example for the moment—is clearly an energy, poets were loath to reject it. And even when they refused religious belief and turned away from the theologies, they translated the motive into secular terms. This is the secularization of spirituality whose guardian angel is Hegel.[7] Those who condescend to Whitman as an apostle of the good heart have not attended to the sturdiness of his images. In *A Backward Glance* he says: "The profoundest service that poems or any other writings can do for their reader is . . . to fill him with vigorous and clean manliness, religiousness, and give him good heart as a radical possession and habit." It is easy to sneer at these terms if we take them individually and with a certain glib sophistication. But when we take them all together, each one supporting the others, we can still sneer, but our vulgarity is clear, even to ourselves. Again, in *Specimen Days* Whitman says, in the same spirit, that the really human purpose is "to bring people back from their persistent strayings and sickly abstractions, to the costless average, divine, original concrete." And the necessary principle of energy is to be found—where else?—in nature.

Indeed, one of the notable things in Whitman is his attempt to draw a little of the old meaning of the word "nature" into the new romantic ethos of plenitude. Sometimes he speaks of nature, admittedly, when he has in mind only daffodils and the great outdoors, but more often—as in "Song of Myself"—nature means "the perfect fitness and equanimity of things," and it will certainly include what he calls, in the original preface, "the eternal tendencies of all toward happiness." Nature is the principle of energy allowing that a thing shall be itself. After this the thing can be implicated in hundreds of relationships; and these in turn will depend for their vitality upon the original blessing of identity. Nature is, to use Yeats' terms on another occasion, "self-creating, self-delighting," and as Whitman says in "Myself and Mine":

Let others finish specimens, I never finish specimens,
I start them by exhaustless laws as Nature does, fresh and modern
   continually.

In short, nature is the principle that exhibits itself in being, delights in plenitude, and reconciles difference. It is the new decorum.

Hence the proper attitude, the secular equivalent of religious piety, is Emerson's "nonchalance." When the principle of energy is diffused through all things and courses through an individual man, the proof is ease, grace, tact. In "One Hour to Madness and Joy" Whitman invokes it: "To find a new unthought-of nonchalance with the best of Nature." This nonchalance will, of course—like Stevens' Supreme Fiction—give pleasure; and it is part of Whitman's morality to disengage the pleasure principle from an antecedent scruple. In his world the principle of pleasure is verified by the energy that animates it, and it is therefore, in the easiest of his translations, "good." When Yeats thought of nonchalance and praised it—as he often did—he took the word from Castiglione's *sprezzatura* and borrowed its air of high breeding, aristocratic hauteur, a handsome spread of civility and splendor. But just as Whitman celebrates the average and calls it divine, so also he commandeers a traditional aristocratic term and hands it over to his new democratic man. And one of the promises he makes on these ceremonial occasions is that the democratic man of nonchalance will be released from the current obsession with time and transience. It is the part of faith and prudence to accept the flow of time, to set aside the "quest for permanence." If Saturday is succeeded by Sunday, this is the natural course and order of things and not at all an instance of what Samuel Beckett, glossing Proust, will call "the poisonous ingenuity of Time in the science of affliction." Stevens is again the poet who has most vividly acknowledged the natural course of things, and he has done something to liberate us from our bondage to Grecian urns and the idiom of bangs and whimpers. In this he stands with Whitman, and, if anything, more firmly, because the Whitman of the later poems sometimes slipped back into the feeling that, alas, death's the end of all. But both poets find, even in the shadow of time and death, that unities are still possible. Each poet goes his own way, singing unities of self in quite different terms. But they share the basic feeling. Whitman's nonchalant hero will not always satisfy Stevens, even when the hero walks among his peers with superb presence in "Song of the Answerer," and finds gratifying harmonies in "Song of the Rolling Earth." It isn't characteristic of Stevens to celebrate the glamorous resources of ordinary people—their nonchalance—as he did, for once, in the poem "Ordinary Women."

We are concerned with the nature of Whitman's poetry in its most characteristic phases, in the years before the war. After the war, as students of Whitman agree, there is a notable change. Whitman's "bumps" would persist, his cast of mind would remain substantially what it had always been, he would make the same demands upon himself and others. But most of the demands would be frustrate and the great equations would not, finally, work out. It was too late to change, and there were no kindly spirits to bring him, as they would bring Yeats, new metaphors, new analogies. Postwar America disappointed Whitman precisely because it failed to live up to the demands of the old metaphors—demands of tact and grace. He would still try to "human-ize" the new world with the old familial metaphors; he would try to hold the new fact close to the old value. And he would resist as long as possible the feeling that the new world of "things" was hostile to the freedom of man. A naturalistic philosophy was already audible that would seal man's faith, his obliteration beneath the mountains of alien things. But Whitman would resist. He would insist and then hope and finally pray that products are not hostile to their producers, nature is not hostile to man's purposes. But it was to be a rear-guard action, as "Song of the Exposition" makes clear, and more and more the rueful note would win out, the old equations now subverted by the new mathematics. And when fact split apart from value, when relation was impossible, then of course the grammar of contact was impossible too. It was the only grammar Whitman knew, the only grammar certified by the human body. Once this failed, a genuine culture was impossible, a culture, that is, based on the "daily toils" of all the people, the nature of human sympathies, the axioms of the body. If man is cut adrift from nature, the next step is the separation of man from man—no contact. Some poets can bear this; a few thrive on it; and some, like Emily Dickinson, have their own resources of metaphor that allow them to proceed. But the destitution of Whitman's later poetry arises from the gap between the old metaphors and the new facts; and Whitman could fill the gap only with petulance, the tone of the broken sage.

(But in a sense, when this happened, his crucial work was already done. So we can go back.)

To get the beauty of Whitman's poetry hot, one should quote it in long, rolling stretches. No poet was ever less revealed in the single word, the crystallizing phrase, the reverberating epithet. The unit in Whitman's verse is indeed the phrase, a loose-limbed structure of four or five words easily held together and moving along because the cadence is the limit of the speaker's breath. This is part of what William Carlos Williams learned from Whitman—the natural cadence, the flow of breath as a structure good enough for most purposes and better for humanity than the counting of syllables. For both poets the ideal is what Williams called "a redeeming language," a language to bridge the gap between subject and object, thereby certifying both and praising bridges. And, again, in both poets the function of language is to verify an intricate network of relationships, contacts, between person and person, person and place, person and thing. Williams once praised a poem by Marianne Moore as an anthology of transit, presumably because the words wasted no time sitting down to admire themselves but got on with the job of transmission. The same applies to many of his own poems and to most of Whitman's. No wonder Whitman loved bridges, ferries, and wrote some of his finest poetry in "Crossing Brooklyn Ferry"—a passage like this, for instance:

I too many and many a time cross'd the river of old,
Watched the Twelfth-month sea-gulls, saw them high in the air
    floating with motionless wings, oscillating their bodies,
Saw how the glistening yellow lit up parts of their bodies and
    left the rest in strong shadow,
Saw the slow-wheeling circles and the gradual edging toward
    the south,
Saw the reflection of the summer sky in the water,
Had my eyes dazzled by the shimmering track of beams,
Look'd at the fine centrifugal spokes of light round the shape of
    my head in the sunlit water,
Look'd on the haze on the hills southward and south-westward,
Look'd on the vapor as it flew in fleeces tinged with violet . . .

If we take this as poetry of description or invocation, it is obviously flat. We have only to compare Whitman's sea gulls with Hopkins' windhover to see that Whitman doesn't even begin to compete in that line. Where Hopkins loads every vein with ore, Whitman waits for another day. But this is superficial, and the real difference escapes. Hopkins, from the whole range of being and multiplicity, seizes upon one moment, one action, and forces it to disclose all the meaning there is. His methods are pressure, force, concentration; he is a specialist in applied pressure. But Whitman is a general practitioner; for him each existent is a zone of consanguinity, a place where people gather for "natural" worship. Hence in his esthetic it is more important that the poet annex his objects by terms of contact than that he should bear down hard upon any one of them. In "Crossing Brooklyn Ferry" Whitman is not describing the scene with the aid of sea gulls, vapors, ships, and summer skies. He addresses a future man and claims fellowship with him by showing that he too—Walt Whitman—was an eligible participant in the same scene. And his proof is the network of sympathetic relationships that he establishes between all his objects. What he calls, in "I Sing the Body Electric," "the flush of the known universe" is nearly as much his theme as it is Hopkins'. But Hopkins drills for it at a few likely spots and writes his poems when the juice spurts out and sometimes, in desolation and bitterness, when it doesn't. Whitman does not drill. He is an electrician and he believes that electricity is everywhere and can be carried along in wires and lines. Every human recognition, every contact, adds to the great network. And because this is an eminently human activity, he will speak of it in human and natural terms. He will say "many and many a time" instead of "often," because the first is traditional to the storyteller before printed books and the isolated reader. He will make each line a breath length, because this is the natural division of speech. He will begin each line, especially in the definitive version, with the word of contact—*watch'd, saw, look'd*—until all the relationships are ensured, winding out the wires. This is the great electrical circuit, not the chain, of being.

Hence the energy released in Whitman's poetry is invariably directed to extend the lines of contact. And once contact is effected he tends to leave his objects alone. He has no interest in fidgeting with metaphors to amplify the objects; each is what it is. We often think of him as an incorrigibly adjectival poet, forgetting that he wrote hundreds of lines that are as lean as words can be when we want them to be lean. A line like "The flags of all nations, the falling of them at sunset" does not claim, by itself, to be "interesting." It refuses the attention of the anthologist and directs him to move along to more spectacular places. It does not even parade its modesty. It is one part of the network, no more, no less. "The falling of them at sunset" is a little more idiosyncratic than "their falling," which would be the bare notation, but even this is a modest claim. What we attend to in this line is the grace, the civility, of the two phrases, laid side by side to record an event that is significant because the whole network, the vast similitude, is significant, and not otherwise. This is why, reading Whitman, we have to attend to his Grand Style, yes, his Sublime; but we have also to attend to that marvelously pure middle style and the civility that enabled him to write a poem like "There Was a Child Went Forth." The qualities of the middle style are too often taken for granted, as if we could all possess them if only we could manage a free weekend. But we have to attend to them all over again if we are to give Whitman his due. Indeed, one of Whitman's greatest contributions to modern poetry—and therefore to modern life—is the grace that enabled him to write this:

There was a child went forth every day,
And the first object he looked upon and received with wonder
    or pity or love or dread, that object he became . . .

I might push the argument a little further. If Whitman did not exist, American poets in search of the Grand Style would not need to invent him; they could find what they want in Whittier and Bryant. But without Whitman's verse and Emerson's prose, I cannot see how Williams would have written "To Daphne and Virginia" or Frost "An Old Man's Winter Night," each with his high grace in the middle style.

In fact, the question to ask about Whitman is not, How did he manage it? Rather, Why, since he has so much, does he not have everything? Why are so many of his poems tainted with the meretricious, the provincial? Why does he trail away and in later years peter out in muscle-bound verse and prose, in gawkiness and excess? Why does he lose what Williams called "measure"? Why, to be specific, are the first three editions of *Leaves of Grass* so much more controlled, more finely adjudged, than the others? Why are so many of his poems, as he said of Dr. Schliemann's letters, "interesting but fishy"?

I have already suggested part of the answer: the failure of the old metaphors to cope with the new facts. And there is also, of course, the risk entailed in his devotion to his own equations, the risk of facility. We are unhappy with Emerson when he soars too easily above the facts of the case, and we praise Thoreau for a scruple foreign to his master. The difficulty in Whitman's equations is that once the equals sign is inserted, the transaction is finished, and can only be succeeded by another in the same form. Yeats said, in a celebrated formulation, that from the quarrel with others we make only rhetoric, from the quarrel with ourselves, poetry. Perhaps the trouble is that Whitman's equations virtually eliminated the quarrel with himself. To write poetry at all, Whitman had to trust himself; doubts, hesitations, scruples would have killed the poems even before they were properly born. And to write his own particular kind of poem, Whitman needed to trust himself in all weathers—totally. This meant not only that he was temperamentally disinclined to quarrel with himself but that his imagination was deployed at large, along a broad range, rather than in minute adjustments and measures. He would never have written poems like Yeats' "Dialogue of Self and Soul" or "Vacillation," because the first is all conflict and the second is all hovering, and to vacillate or to hover is to break the electrical circuit, in Whitman's world an act of gross disloyalty. He is one of the great praisers, and this is one of his most admirable qualities, but it made it practically impossible for him to test his own insights. Once he had them, they became his very own, and like a father he loved all his children equally.

A few sentences from André Gide will show another kind of temper, radically different from Whitman's, will show what it means to be born with a critical scruple, like a birthmark. In his *Journal* for January 3, 1892, Gide wrote: "And every moment, at every word I write, at each gesture I make, I am terrified at the thought that this is one more ineradicable feature of my physiognomy becoming fixed: a hesitant, impersonal physiognomy, an amorphous physiognomy, since I have not been capable of choosing and tracing its contours confidently." [8] This would never have distressed Whitman. Both Whitman and Gide thought of each experience as an addition to the self, but while this delighted Whitman, it terrified Gide. Whitman was content to live and work with the given; he did not demand the privilege of creating himself, literally, out of nothing. In these matters he who hesitates is not lost, he is a special kind of writer, and very often his scruple will save him and he will be stronger as a result. Whitman never hesitated: his animal faith in himself was an everlasting yes. The world was all before him, and he walked through it, a new Adam.

But when we read Whitman with our own scruples—such as they are—we often feel that a more scrupulous poet would have made more of what was there. For one thing, he is the poet of the new day, the present tense and a declared future, but he scants the verifiable past, and the loss to his own poetry is grievous, because the past is one of the great critics of our actions. There is a poem by Stevens called "The Prejudice against the Past" implying that to children every object is what it is, now, this moment, seen as if on a clear day with no memories, whereas the "aquiline pedants" treat each object as if it were the relic of the heart or the mind. This is a strong image, and we do well to attend to it. It reminds us that there is a childlike element in Whitman's vision, as if all his poems were written on a clear day with no memories. But the loss is grievous. I often wish that Whitman had written a book called *In the American Grain,* because it would then have come at the right time, and later poets could have used it without waiting for William Carlos Williams to write it. It would have come appropriately in its time, from Whitman, a fine garnering of acts and sufferances and values in the United States—the available past. Because Whitman did not write it, we have the impression that America in 1855 had only a brief and insignificant past; and this is an error to which Henry James gave classic status. Fenimore Cooper knew that America had a past, and he helped to define it in his sturdier social novels. But he was not satisfied, and he longed to give America a mythology, a heroic anthropology, as well. Indeed, Hawthorne was the only major American writer who attended to an American past on the understanding that it was palpably there and that it could be invoked for present lucidity. And, later, Edith Wharton would write *The Custom of the Country* on much the same understanding.

Whitman, in "Starting from Paumanok," claimed that he "conn'd old times," and he protested his respect for the ancients, but he sent them away, though with blessings on their heads. Even in *Democratic Vistas,* courtesy to the past was as much as he could manage. If we would believe De Tocqueville, this is implicit in democracy itself. "Democracy," he says, "shuts the past against the poet, opens the future before him." It may be so, but this is not our concern. When Whitman says, in "Pioneers! O Pioneers!," "All the past we leave behind," the gesture is framed by his own temper, for which we do not need to posit national compulsions. The significant acts performed in America in the centuries before 1850 were matters of little moment to Whitman because he could not demonstrate his possession of them. He could demonstrate his possession of the present, by celebration, by praising its plenitude, and he could assert his fellowship with the future. But it is frustrating to see him, in "Song of the Exposition," roaming with weary elegance through the history and mythology of England, France, Germany, and Egypt at a time when the verifiable meaning of his own country was still waiting to be inspected. He did about as much—or as little—homework on his fated subject as a later poet, Hart Crane, a man of similarly grand intention.

But it would be quite wrong to imply that because Whitman wrote his equations from an American present and an equally American future he is merely an American "problem," a case study in something-or-other. Whitman is at the center of American literature—at least as relevant as Poe and Mark Twain, more relevant than Emerson—but his significance extends far beyond the United States, because it is moral significance. If it is not that, it is nothing. I am not speaking of his overt influence on European writers, though that influence has been great and is likely to be greater. I have in mind a certain moral bearing, an attitude to life that is defined in Whitman with strange resonance. One can find it elsewhere; its range is broad. I am thinking of his work as an endorsement of certain parts of life that are now, alas, in some disrepute among the elite, what he called the commonplace, the average, that great middle range of experience that is now so maliciously despised. Modern literature has disdained this experience on the grounds that it is a middle-class property and therefore contemptible. The loss to the literature is very great. This is the point at which Whitman impinges upon a failure of response that is no more American than European or Asiatic. We should invite his poems to offer the kind of critique that Thomas Mann's Tonio sent to Lisabeta in that great letter in which he said: "As I write, the sea whispers to me and I close my eyes. I am looking into a world unborn and formless, that needs to be ordered and shaped; I see into a whirl of shadows of human figures who beckon to me to weave spells to redeem them: tragic and laughable figures and some that are both together— and to these I am drawn. But my deepest and secretest love belongs to the blond and blue-eyed, the fair and living, the happy, lovely and commonplace." [8a] I think the achievement of Whitman's greatest poems resides here: that they restore the dignity of the commonplace.

There is very little evidence that contemporary poets are taking Whitman's poems in this way—though it is the only way, I should argue, in which the poems will bear any severe strain. In contemporary American poetry *Leaves of Grass* is put to work for many masters, but often it is the wrong work. Some poets, like Louis Simpson, bring the book into their poems partly out of reverence and partly in the hope that it will lift some of their own burdens. But it won't. Allen Ginsberg brings Whitman into his poems for a dozen modish reasons, and he seems to think that by drop-ping Whitman's name often enough he will make everything clear. In "A Supermarket in California" Ginsberg has done everything that is required of a poet except the one essential thing—to write his poem. And then there are the poets who use Whitman to imply that all you need to be a great poet is homosexual experience and a copy of *I and Thou*.

Indeed, very few poets seem to me to use *Leaves of Grass* for a genuine purpose. Robert Duncan is exceptional. *The*

Opening of the Field sets itself the high object of completing the work that *Leaves of Grass* started. At one point Duncan says:

> It is across great scars of wrong
> I reach toward the song of kindred men
> and strike again the naked string
> old Whitman sang from.[9]

Duncan's "optimism" ("Flickers of unlikely heat/at the edge of our belief bud forth"), his joy in plenitude ("A bush puts forth roses upon roses/to illustrate the afternoon /abundancies of white, scarlet, yellow—/the beautiful profusion takes me"), his image of man as moral agent ("salmon not in the well where the/hazelnut falls/but at the falls battling, inarticulate,/blindly making it"), even his neo-Elizabethan songs, and especially his idiom of Contact ("There is no touch that is not each/to each/reciprocal" and "Transient beauty of youth/that into immortality goes direct,/forsaking us? Aye, but bedded in touch,/ever-remembered Lord of Sensualities"): these modes of feeling are certified by Whitman. Part of Duncan's care is to take possession of them without injuring them or, worse still, domesticating them, and to proceed from that possession.

So I return to Whitman's equations. The scale of their achievement (which is not to be confused with the length of a shopping-list) is inseparable from the energy and goodwill with which he insisted that all was not yet lost. There were still values to be found in place and time. The proper study of mankind was still man, the world, relationships, places, things, in their temporal being. Reading him again today we are struck by the fact that the equations had to be declared: they came when he called them, but only then and with some reluctance. And we are apt to feel that much of Whitman's sound was invoked to calm his own fury. But we should not push this too far. He committed himself to his equations and to the validity of human life. This was his vote, his voice, to "redeem the time."

NOTES

1 *Collected Poems of Wallace Stevens* (London: Faber and Faber, 1955), p. 215.

2 Walt Whitman, *Correspondence: Vol. II 1868–1875*, ed. Edwin Haviland Miller (New York: New York Univ. Press, 1961), p. 154. Letter of Jan. 18, 1872.

3 William James, *The Will To Believe* (New York: Dover Publications, n.d.), pp. 32ff.

4 Whitman, *Complete Poetry and Selected Prose*, ed. James E. Miller, Jr. (Boston: Houghton Mifflin, 1959), p. 197. All verse quotations, unless otherwise specified, are from this edition.

5 See the first edition, reprinted with an introduction by Malcolm Cowley (New York: Viking Press, 1959), p. 104. Later Whitman changed "death" to "materials." See *Complete Poetry and Selected Prose*, p. 308.

6 Whitman, *Prose Works, 1892: Vol. I: Specimen Days*, ed. Floyd Stovall (New York: New York Univ. Press, 1963), p. 259.

7 See Lionel Trilling, "On the Modern Element in Modern Literature"; in Stanley Burnshaw (ed.), *Varieties of Literary Experience* (London: Peter Owen, 1963), pp. 407–433.

8 *The Journals of André Gide*, trans. Justin O'Brien (New York: Knopf, 1955), I, 18.

8a *Death in Venice; Tristan; Tonio Kröger*, translated by H. T. Lowe-Porter (London: Penguin Books and Secker & Warburg, 1955), pp. 189–190.

9 Robert Duncan, *The Opening of the Field* (New York: Grove Press, 1960), p. 64.

CHAPTER 2

FREDERICK GODDARD TUCKERMAN

WHITMAN'S FAVORITE TENSE is the present, his favorite mood the indicative, with this qualification, that his indicatives tend to acquire the force of imperatives by pressure of tone. He is rarely content to state a fact and leave it; his "is" sounds like "ought" or "must," his facts are instruments for the transportation of value. His particular significance in American poetry is that he "made it new" by forcing issues that had never before claimed a voice. The issues wandered about the American landscape, timid and fretful, until Whitman brought them to the pitch of definition. But Whitman did not capture the entire imagination of American poetry. Even after *Leaves of Grass* it was still possible to write in one of the old ways, or even in a new way that owed nothing to Whitman's novelty. For instance, in the years immediately after *Leaves of Grass* one of the best poets in America was Frederick Tuckerman. But to read Tuckerman after Whitman is like moving into a private realm of worry and silence. The silence is heavy with questions, the only discernible movement is the movement of thought, the attendant figure is "Man Watching" rather than "Man Thinking," and the voice (when it comes) is an American voice only because it has to be. Whitman's world, more than ever in this context, is noisy, clamorous, aggressive, a world of concentration and insistence.

But at certain points the two worlds coalesce. Whitman and Tuckerman are typical American poets in assuming that for the work in hand they must rely upon their own resources. Each is, to himself, Robinson Crusoe. Tuckerman is a private man, an amateur, a scholar, astronomer, botanist, recluse; Whitman thinks of his role in much more public terms. But each poet assumes that no relevant assistance is available from other men, that none of the work can be entrusted to others. Much of the pressure in Whitman is the force, beyond any average poetic requirement, that he must generate in the absence of relevant companions. He would praise other poets, but only on the understanding that their poetry made no essential difference to him. Bryant might be an admirable poet in his way, but his work left Whitman's still to be done in its own way. There was no question of a "common pursuit"; every job was a one-man job. Tuckerman was much less grand in his ambition—he never hoped to change the world by his sonnets. But he always assumed that value, form, and meaning were personal achievements, to be won by private resolution. Sustenance would come from those intangible powers certified by his own imagination, notably God and nature. But the relation between self, nature, and God was a closed system; no experience outside the system was relevant.

A poem by Tuckerman, therefore, tends to place an observer at a chosen point inside this "triangle," and to have him survey the scene, often a landscape, a house, a mountain, sometimes the landscape of the past, as it seems to bless or threaten him. In "Margites," for instance, the poet leans from his window in autumn and finds evidence in the landscape that his life is "well-lost," that "all things seem the same." [1] The poet is invariably alone, and whether he finds intimations of ease or pain in the landscape, he is never tempted to blur the line of demarcation between himself and nature, the Me and the Not-Me, subject and object. A typical poem reads:

> And so the day drops by; the horizon draws
> The fading sun, and we stand struck in grief,
> Failing to find our haven of relief,—
> Wide of the way, nor sure to turn or pause,

And weep to view how fast the splendour wanes
And scarcely heed that yet some share remains
Of the red after-light, some time to mark,
Some space between the sundown and the dark.
But not for him those golden calms succeed
Who while the day is high and glory reigns
Sees it go by,—as the dim pampas plain,
Hoary with salt and gray with bitter weed,
Sees the vault blacken, feels the dark wind strain,
Hears the dry thunder roll, and knows no rain.

This is typical because the suffering observer is in the poem
when it begins and is still there when it ends; nothing that
happens in the poem releases him from the fate of merely
watching and suffering. It is like *Waiting for Godot.* Tuckerman points this up by pressing down hard on the verbs in
the last couplet: the one who sees the vault blacken, feels
the dark wind strain, hears the dry thunder roll, and knows
no rain is the one who can do nothing, take no action; he
can't even move away. This is to exemplify, with a vengeance,
the "point of view." Tuckerman's hero is transfixed, nailed
to one spot, condemned to see, feel, hear, and—hardest of
all—know.

This is why so many of Tuckerman's poems are melancholy visions—as if the Greenfield astronomer, happy enough
with his telescope when it was time for stargazing, wanted
in his poems the rival satisfactions of action, mobility, par-
ticipation. Indeed, there are a few poems in which Tuckerman asks, literally, for something far more outgoing than
his normal poetic experience. "Let me give something!" he
cries at one moment, and only then do we realize how much
constriction he suffered inside that triangle. The extreme
point is reached when "all things seem the same," and, as
Stevens says, "in such seeming all things are." If the terms
of a poet's life commit him to vision and knowledge, he is
well advised to still his "active" ambition and hope that the

matter to be seen and known will be dense and rich enough
to satisfy him. This is the only tolerable kind of silence.

Tuckerman was a recluse by choice and, for a hundred
reasons, a man of vision and knowledge. We identify him
with his "point of view" because this is his chief term of
reference. On dog days there is for such a poet not enough
to see, and one thing seems insufficiently distinct from another in the ways that count. As for taste, touch, and smell,
the experience of the poems rarely comes in this fashion;
he is not Keats. And as for hearing, I have said that Tuckerman's was a silent world. His "natural" mode of knowledge
was by sight, vision, the interpretation of what was visibly
there. This is the norm of his poems. Hence it is entirely
in keeping that the great release comes, when it does at all,
in sound, noise, voice. When nature "contradicts" herself
and gives far more than she has promised, when she goes
far beyond her contract in plenitude, the bonus comes in
sound; the terrible silence is relieved and the air is full:

> For Nature daily through her grand design
> Breathes contradiction where she seems most clear:
> For I have held of her the gift to hear
> And felt, indeed, endowed of sense divine
> When I have found, by guarded insight fine,
> Cold April flowers in the green end of June,
> And thought myself possessed of Nature's ear
> When by the lonely mill-brook, unto mine,
> Seated on slab or trunk asunder sawn,
> The night-hawk blew his horn at sunny noon;
> And in the rainy midnight I have heard
> The ground-sparrow's long twitter from the pine
> And the cat-bird's silver song, the wakeful bird
> That to the lighted window sings for dawn.

This is how relief invariably comes in Tuckerman's world.
When the importunities of order and chaos and knowledge
are in abeyance and the poet's spirit is drenched with ease,

the ease is sound. In one poem he says, "And even the present seems with voices kind/To soothe our sorrow; and the past endears. . . ." When he invokes his dead wife, as he does in several poems, he enters a world of voice, in which the questions are assuaged in answers constantly audible ("Her voice is in mine ears, her answer yet"). Indeed, when it is a case of direct response, whether the message is hard or easy, it comes as voice. The childhood memories are oral. When sorrow pours upon the poet's soul and it is too late to repair the defenses, the facts are given as sounds: the bird "seemed to cry out his warning at my ear," the night wind divides itself into two voices to express the poet's grief, and the clock that is rarely heard is heard now—"The morning bell/Into the gulfs of night dropped *one*."

But this merely emphasizes the fact that when Tuckerman stands before a world that he hopes to see and know (or that he sees and despairs of ever knowing), it is at best a world of silent, visual relations. One of his later poems begins with an invocation to the wood fern, sand grass, and pitch pine of his landscape, "and over these the incorruptible blue." Then he says:

> Here let me gently lie and softly view
> All world asperities, lightly touched and smoothed
> As by his gracious hand, the great Bestower.

It is not his finest poetic moment, but it is characteristic of Tuckerman in this respect, that he is "assuaged and soothed" when he sees evidence in landscape of the great Bestower. He was not a botanist, an astronomer, and a naturalist for nothing; these are silent worlds. After his wife died the silence seems to have become total. In the later poetry she is a haunting absence; absent herself, she spreads absence all around. (In Tuckerman's poems one is only named to be marked absent, like the two lovely sisters, Gertrude and

Gulielma: "Gertrude! with red flowerlip, and silk black hair!/Yet Gulielma was by far more fair!")

I am arguing that Tuckerman's loneliness was intensified by his commitment to the "point of view," the lexicon of vision, the interpretation of experience as silent relations, lines of influence—his position inside the triangle of self, nature, and God. We can sum up very bluntly: even if nature is, in one of Tuckerman's poems, "the old Mother," she keeps her own counsel, goes about her business without explanation or apology. And if her "invention and authority" are God's, He is not speaking. At best, God leaves silent messages, in clouds, rivers, and trees—hieroglyphs, not words, and the "scholar of one candle," to use Stevens' phrase, deciphers as best he can. This is Tuckerman's predicament in one of his greatest poems:

> But man finds means, grant him but place and room,
> To gauge the depths and views a wonder dawn,
> Sees all the worlds in utmost space withdrawn
> In shape and structure like a honeycomb,
> Locates his sun and grasps the universe
> Or to their bearings bids the orbs disperse;
> Now seems to stand like that great angel girt
> With moon and stars; now, sick for shelter even,
> Craves but a roof to turn the thunder-rain—
> Or finds his vaunted reach and wisdom vain,
> Lost in the myriad meaning of a word,
> Or starts at its bare import, panic-stirred:
> For earth is earth or hearth or dearth or dirt,
> The sky heaved over our faint heads is heaven.

The motto for this is given in the preceding poem:

> Where they prefigure change, all signals must yet
> Fail in the dry when they forebode the wet . . .
> I know not.

The beau linguist, bent on interpreting the marks, demands that the words stay still; Tuckerman often feared that they wouldn't. T. S. Eliot in *Burnt Norton* says:

> Words strain,
> Crack and sometimes break, under the burden,
> Under the tension, slip, slide, perish,
> Decay with imprecision, will not stay in place,
> Will not stay still.

Tuckerman's sonnet begins as if by quoting Marlowe it could get over the problem of deceptive signals: "But man finds means . . . Sees all the worlds in utmost space withdrawn." Then it calls to Milton for reinforcements: "Now seems to stand like that great angel girt/With moon and stars." But the slip from "sees" to "seems" throws Tuckerman off his rhetorical guard, and almost before he knows it he is in a starker tradition, *King Lear*-land: ". . . now, sick for shelter even,/Craves but a roof to turn the thunder-rain—," and the relation between word and matter, parodied by Goneril, is known to be askew. William Empson, ephebe of ambiguity and complex words, says in "Manchouli":

> I find it normal, passing these great frontiers,
> That you scan the crowds in rags eagerly each side
> With awe; that the nations seem real; that their ambitions
> Having such achieved variety within one type, seem sane;
> I find it normal;
> So too to extract false comfort from that word.

But the interpreter who stands and stares at the scene, hoping to read the signs, always extracts false comfort from the words. The Fool in *Lear* says, "He's mad, that trusts in the tameness of a wolf, a horse's health, a boy's love, or a whore's oath." But if all our evidence is on earth, and if "earth is earth or hearth or dearth or dirt," what then? What then, to the visualist who must either read the signs or die? "I know not." Knowledge amounts to this: "The sky heaved over our faint heads is heaven."

Tuckerman was not always so keen. But he always knew that reading the signals is a complex affair. In several of the early poems he grieves because the "import" of natural forms is alien to him. And there is always "that dark doubt." Sometimes he tries to tease himself out of doubt by dreaming and asserting the validity of the dream, clearly to escape the despotism of the eye. Sometimes he recites a transcendentalist lesson: "If evil sneereth, yet abides the good." But he is never convincing in this note. More often when he invokes transcendentalist terms ("And ills seem but as food for spirits sage"), he goes on to say that for him they simply don't work: "But vain, oh vain, this turning for the light!" When the past drops away, the signs are few, there is not enough to read:

> As when down some broad river dropping, we
> Day after day behold the assuming shores
> Sink and grow dim, as the great water-course
> Pushes his banks apart and seeks the sea,
> Benches of pines, high shelf and balcony
> To flats of willow and low sycamores
> Subsiding, till where'er the wave we see
> Himself is his horizon utterly—
> So fades the portion of our early world.
> Still on the ambit hangs the purple air;
> Yet while we lean to read the secret there,
> The stream that by green shore-sides splashed and purled
> Expands, the mountains melt to vapours rare,
> And life alone circles out flat and bare.

To a writer like Tuckerman who is deeply committed to the reading of signals, leaning to read the secrets, it is natural to draw comfort from the imaginative or "faith-ful" techniques of interpretation, especially from the procedures exemplified by such terms as *analogy, metaphor,* and *cor-*

respondence. If nature is a text, the words should mean and mean abundantly, else the reader is frustrated. But Tuckerman was very scrupulous on this point. He read the text, but he would not go beyond it or "amplify" it for a sounding rhetoric. Indeed, in one of his finest poems (which is also one of the best short poems in the language) he examines with great severity the entire myth of "correspondence":

> Yet wear we on, the deep light disallowed
> That lit our youth. In years no longer young
> We wander silently and brood among
> Dead graves and tease the sun-break and the cloud
> For import. Were it not better yet to fly,
> To follow those who go before the throng,
> Reasoning from stone to star, and easily
> Exampling this existence? Or shall I—
> Who yield slow reverence where I cannot see
> And gather gleams where'er by chance or choice
> My footsteps draw, though brokenly dispensed—
> Come into light at last?—or suddenly,
> Struck to the knees like Saul, one arm against
> The overbearing brightness, hear a voice?

Tuckerman walks broodingly; others "fly," relieved of his scholarly scruple. Those who go before the throng are, presumably, the popular preachers who achieve great awakenings by the suppression of evidence and common sense. But "reasoning from stone to star" seems particularly directed against Swedenborg and the Swedenborgians. In the *De Caelo* Swedenborg distinguishes things of the earth as three kinds, called kingdoms, one of which is the mineral kingdom. "The things in the mineral kingdom are correspondences in the third degree because they neither live nor grow"; that is, they are of the "lowest" degree. To reason from stone to star is therefore an extreme leap of reason in faith. When he comes to effect his translations, Swedenborg says that "Stone . . . signifies the truth of faith"; else-

where he equates it with "the Divine Truth." But the leap
is made a good deal "safer" when Swedenborg discusses the
stars. "Glittering stars, which are at the same time wandering," he says, "signify what is false; but glittering and fixed
stars signify what is true." Again, "Stars in the Word signify
the knowledge of good and truth, consequently truths." [2]
Reasoning from stone to star is therefore an easy matter,
if you start by taking the validity of correspondence for
granted, on faith or trust. Emerson, now predictable, praised
Swedenborg for the spirit of this trust, and drew the line
only when Swedenborg insisted on translating the "things
of the earth" into purely theological terms. Emerson wanted
the things translated into moral terms, and was grieved by
Swedenborg's theological pedantry.[3] But Tuckerman was not
impressed one way or the other; we have to give full weight
to his saying that he yielded slow reverence "where I cannot
see." In the second half of the sonnet the idea of finding the
truth as seeing the light is linked to the two "ways" of conversion. In "The Wreck of the Deutschland" Hopkins invokes this idea, citing as its exemplars Saint Paul and Saint
Augustine:

> Whether at once, as once at a crash Paul,
> Or as Austin, a lingering-out sweet skill.

Tuckerman takes the ways more slowly but just as effec-
tively. The best he can hope for is the Augustinian way, by
gathering broken lights to "come into light at last." And the
tentative nature of the hope is given in the syntax, the separation of the subject from its verb by three lines and a
multitude of slow footsteps. The second possibility, Saul's
conversion into Paul, is given as an emblem, the victim
struck by the blow of the sublime truth. And because this
would be the greatest consolation of all, it is given as sound
—"hear a voice." In another poem, when Tuckerman finds
in heaven "no sign," "the lights are strange and bitter voices

by." And in a third he says of the stars, so cozily touched by Swedenborg:

> Nor reck those lights, so distant over us,
> Sublime but helpless to the spirit's need
> As the night-stars in heaven's vault.

It is clear from the poems that Tuckerman yielded up the consolations of "correspondence" very reluctantly but with a scruple that he could not put by. Indeed, this was deeply involved in his melancholy, and it went along with a particular part of it, the feeling that he was cut off from the public analogies of his time. We don't know what he thought of Darwin and the Evolutionists, for instance, but there is a poem in which he laments that evolutionary metaphors are alien to him:

> What profits it to me, though here allowed
> Life, sunlight, leisure, if they fail to urge
> Me to due motion or myself to merge
> With the onward stream, too humble, or too proud?—
> That find myself not with the popular surge
> Washed off and on, or up to higher reefs
> Flung with the foremost when the rolling crowd
> Hoists like a wave . . .

And there are other poems in which he grieves that by failing these metaphors he has lost the faculty of action altogether ("No onward purpose in my life seems plain"). Even when his conscience spurs him on by telling him that "Truth is not found by feeling in the pocket,/Nor wisdom sucked from out the fingers' end!" the best he can manage for consolation is the hope that he may still make something of his sorrow. And he keeps returning to his fear:

> Where will the ladder land? Who knows?—who knows?
> He who would seize the planet zone by zone
> As on a battle-march, for use alone,
> Nor stops for visionary wants and woes

But like the Bruce's, on, his heart he throws
And leaves behind the dreamer and the drone?
Great is his work indeed, his service great,
Who seeks for Nature but to subjugate,
Break and bereave, build upward and create
And, hampering her, to carry, heave and drag
Points to results,—towns, cables, cars and ships.
Whilst I in dim green meadows lean and lag,
He counts his course in truth by vigorous steps,
By steps of stairs; but I add crag to crag.

The easy way out is to turn back to early Wordsworthian recollections of childhood and mastery:

> . . . when glorying
> I stood a boy amid the mullein-stalks
> And dreamed myself like him the Lion-King.

Tuckerman has two or three poems in this spirit. But normally the past was no escape. For one thing, Tuckerman's sense of the past was a feeling for the human acts and sufferances that it disclosed. Looking at a house with lights and curtains and vases, he recalls that "but a lifetime back," "Here in the forest-heart, hung blackening/The wolf-bait on the bush beside the spring." And in the next poem he thinks back to "The Shay's-man, with the green branch in his hat,/Or silent sagamore, Shaug or Wassahoale." Indeed, if it is a question of reading the signals of nature, Tuckerman is much more inclined to trust his "quick savage sense," as if he were an Indian trapper, than to sentimentalize with the analogists. And knowing a hawk from a handsaw, he knows that a loss is a loss, untranslatable:

> Under the mountain, as when first I knew
> Its low black roof and chimney creeper-twined,
> The red house stands; and yet my footsteps find,
> Vague in the walks, waste balm and feverfew.
> But they are gone: no soft-eyed sisters trip

Across the porch or lintels; where, behind,
The mother sat,—sat knitting with pursed lip.
The house stands vacant in its green recess,
Absent of beauty as a broken heart.
The wild rain enters; and the sunset wind
Sighs in the chambers of their loveliness
Or shakes the pane—and in the silent noons
The glass falls from the window, part by part,
And ringeth faintly in the grassy stones.

Tuckerman was committed, then, to the hieroglyphs of
nature. There were moments in which he felt that he was
dealing with a corrupt text, but generally he thought it fairly
reliable, if read with a stubborn concern for scholarship. It
was possible to say that nature brings a "consenting color"
to "heal" a place blasted by storm, provided you saw with
equal accuracy that the place was in fact blasted. You could
say, "Look, where the gray is white!" provided you retained
a clear distinction between the two colors. "We see what is
not shown/By that which we behold"; yes, but "Nature's
secrecies" are still intact. Tuckerman speaks of "the natural
heart" and on one extreme occasion refers to nature as "an
embracing Friend," but he is not committed to these assur-
ances. Wordsworth speaks in the "Prospectus" of 1800 of the
"great consummation" by which "the discerning intellect of
Man" is "wedded to this goodly universe in love and holy
passion." Tuckerman thought the universe goodly enough,
but he was never tempted to spousal metaphors. At best, the
relation between himself and nature was a cool affair, a
matter of knowledge, signals, ciphers; there were no further
intimacies. And when the situation was extreme, especially
after his wife's death, there was no sign of the embracing
friend:

Each common object too—the house, the grove,
The street, the face, the ware in the window—seems

Alien and sad, the wreck of perished dreams;
Painfully present, yet remote in love.
The day goes down in rain, the winds blow wide.
I leave the town. I climb the mountain-side,
Striving from stumps and stones to wring relief,
And in the senseless anger of my grief,
I rave and weep. I roar to the unmoved skies;
But the wild tempest carries away my cries.
Then back I turn to hide my face in sleep,
Again with dawn the same dull round to sweep,
And buy and sell and prate and laugh and chide,
As if she had not lived, or had not died.

Impersonal nature is exemplified by the sea, which comes
and goes "as though the wet were dry and joy were grief."
So Tuckerman is never tempted to identify himself with
nature beyond the limit of discretion. Whitman's equations
are Whitman's business. Tuckerman always felt that even
if you went to the outer limit of nature's observances, you
would still leave many of your strivings unfulfilled. Wordsworth might talk of "the individual Mind" and "the external
World" as being exquisitely "fitted" to one another, but
Tuckerman played this theme very softly. For one thing,
he thought that man's religious motive was a separate thing,
not at all to be assuaged by a "religion of Nature." This follows, of course, from his distrust of "correspondences":

Still craves the spirit: never Nature solves
That yearning which with her first breath began
And in its blinder instinct still devolves
On god or pagod, Manada or man
Or, lower yet, brute-service, apes and wolves.
By Borneo's surf, the bare barbarian
Still to the sands beneath him bows to pray.

The new problem is, What happens now, when man can
worship only himself?

And what remains to me who count no odds
Between such Lord and him I saw today,
The farmer mounted on his market-load,
Bundles of wool and locks of upland hay—
The son of toil that his own works bestrode,
And him, Ophion, earliest of the gods?

Mostly, Tuckerman implies, we "falsely claim and blindly say,/'I am the Truth, the Life too and the way.'" But we don't take the full weight of this, and fend it off by present gratifications:

Watching my fancy gleam, now bright, now dark,
As snapping from the brands a single spark
Splits in a spray of sparkles ere it fall,
And the long flurrying flame that shoots to die.

What more can one do? Tuckerman suggests that if nature's text is baffling, there is one consolation: the human mind itself has a certain stock of light. He says this in one of his most beautiful passages:

Nay, for the mind itself a glimpse will rest
Upon the dark; summoning from vacancy
Dim shapes about his intellectual lamp,
Calling these in and causing him to see;
As the night-heron wading in the swamp
Lights up the pools with her phosphoric breast.

However, this is not final. There are several poems in which Tuckerman speaks of God in the old way: "the round natural world" does not hold "the reconcilement," nor does "the deep mind"—only God. And God is to be sought by giving up the meretricious struggle, "leaving straining thought and stammering word":

Across the barren azure pass to God:
Shooting the void in silence, like a bird,—
A bird that shuts his wings for better speed.

Often Tuckerman's answer is, Lie quietly within yourself, contain the vaunting will. It is as if, in a world of necessary silence, he were to make silence his ethic. And he did so. Just as time will bring "oblivion of annoy," so also silence will "bind the blows that words have lent." In the later poems, giving up his claims to action and the name of action, he makes "giving up" his "way," his decorum:

> And peace will come, as evening comes to him,
> No leader now of men, no longer proud
> But poor and private, watching the sun's rim,
> Contented too to fade as yonder cloud
> Dim fades and, as the sun fades, fading likewise dim.

In another poem the soul defends itself, like an embattled city, by retiring "even to her inmost keep and citadel." And in a third the soul is warned to keep within its tower, thoughtful, meditative, quiet:

> But shun the reveries of voluptuous thought,
> Day-musings, the floralia of the heart
> And vain imaginations.

This is one of the major tensions in Tuckerman: the pull between the official commitment to rest, quiet, limitation, and the unofficial, wild desire to pursue things "to the end of the line." Briefly, he wanted a wider scene, a larger circle of reference. His official commitment to thought and meditation disclosed other possibilities, and if these seemed "vain imaginations" on cool days, there were other days in which they were exciting precisely because of the wider circumference they ensured. There is a sonnet in which Tuckerman faces this:

> Nor strange it is, to us who walk in bonds
> Of flesh and time, if virtue's self awhile
> Gleam dull like sunless ice; whilst graceful guile—
> Blood-flecked like hematite or diamonds

With a red inward spark—to reconcile
Beauty and evil seems and corresponds
So well with good that the mind joys to have
Full wider jet and scope nor swings and sleeps
Forever in one cradle wearily:
Like those vast weeds that off d'Acunha's isle
Wash with the surf and flap their mighty fronds
Mournfully to the dipping of the wave,
Yet cannot be disrupted from their deeps
By the whole heave and settle of the sea.

It is one of Tuckerman's most daring poems. He does not deny to the human mind its mighty fronds and deeps or its implacable vote for virtue, but he confronts the possibility that meditative quiet may be nothing more than inertia, a static, graceless condition. This is the observer, in moments of greatest pressure, detaching himself from his "point of view" and making it his local object for challenge and scrutiny. If the poem is also one of Tuckerman's most "modern" pieces, it is for this reason, that it achieves immunity to irony by taking up, itself, a rival stance. Tuckerman rarely does this. He makes his commitments as each occasion offers, but he rarely hedges his bet. He votes and takes the consequence. The poorer poems are propaganda for "the deep soul that knoweth heaven and hell." To swing and sleep forever in one cradle is like lying in Abraham's bosom all the time, with this difference: that Tuckerman for once finds the experience a weary matter, hardly human at all, "like those vast weeds . . ." What he is rejecting, if only for the time of fourteen lines, is not only his own commitment to the esthetic-ethic of "content" and limitation but the entire tradition of which Milton's Platonist scholar in the lonely tower is a central manifestation. Tuckerman is not merely giving Byronism its due, he is challenging himself by pointing beyond the sleek ensolacings in which he has often indulged himself. And if some of the blame falls upon Wordsworth, let it fall. In the "Esthétique du Mal" Stevens speaks of syllables that would form themselves, in time, "and communicate/The intelligence of his despair, express/What meditation never quite achieved." This is what Tuckerman's poem does, expressing what his official meditation fended off. Indeed, the "Esthétique" is a useful parallel text. The moon, Stevens says,

> . . . evaded his mind.
> It was part of a supremacy always
> Above him. The moon was always free from him,
> As night was free from him.

Hence the despair. But Tuckerman's despair is his feeling that the vaunted relation between man and nature, Wordsworth's exquisite fitting of mind and world, amounts to a very inert relation. When nature, like the sea, is impersonal, aboriginal, subhuman, the mind reacts by acquiring immunity, narrowing its vision, closing itself into itself, to its own loss. The poem is therefore much closer to Coleridge's "Dejection" ode than to anything in Wordsworth; except that Coleridge blames himself for his "sullenness," while Tuckerman blames the tradition of which he is a part.

Tuckerman's masterpiece is "The Cricket." The best introduction to the poem is a sonnet in which Tuckerman meditates upon the cricket's cry and the sea break:

> Yet even mid merry boyhood's tricks and scapes,
> Early my heart a deeper lesson learnt,—
> Wandering alone by many a mile of burnt
> Black woodside, that but the snow-flake decks and drapes.
> And I have stood, beneath Canadian sky,
> In utter solitudes where the cricket's cry
> Appalls the heart and fear takes visible shapes,
> And on Long Island's void and isolate capes
> Heard the sea break like iron bars. And still

In all I seemed to hear the same deep dirge
Borne in the wind, the insect's tiny trill,
And crash and jangle of the shaking surge,
And knew not what they meant.—Prophetic woe?
Dim bodings? Wherefore? Now, indeed, I know.

What he knows is the burden of "The Cricket," an ode in five long stanzas.

The poem begins by setting up a courtly relation between the poet and the cricket. As the bee purrs over his flower, so the poet attends the cricket, serving him with a promise of reward. In the second stanza the relation is animated by placing it in a dense setting, a collusion of the senses. What is common to the participants is the burden of their different natures. The "burdened brook" flows by, muttering and moaning; the horizon is "swooning-blue"; "Let the dead fragrance round our temples beat,/Stunning the sense to slumber"; the day "declines," and the noise of the crickets, louder still, is like the rising and falling of the sea. The third stanza is Tuckerman's greatest achievement and one of the finest passages in modern poetry. I quote it in full:

Dear to the child who hears thy rustling voice
Cease at his footstep, though he hears thee still,
Cease and resume, with vibrance crisp and shrill,
Thou sittest in the sunshine to rejoice!
Night-lover too; bringer of all things dark,
And rest and silence; yet thou bringest to me
Always that burthen of the unresting sea
The moaning cliffs, the low rocks blackly stark;
These upland inland fields no more I view,
But the long flat seaside beach, the wild seamew,
⁣   And the overturning wave!
Thou bringest too, lost accents from the grave
To him who walketh when the day is dim,
Dreaming of those who dream no more of him—
With edg'd remembrances of joy and pain:

And heyday looks and laughter come again;
Forms that in happy sunshine lie and leap,
With faces where but now a gap must be
Renunciations, and partitions deep,
And final tears, and crowning vacancy!
And to thy poet at the twilight's hush
No chirping touch of lips with laugh and blush,
But wringing arms, hearts wild with love and woe,
Closed eyes, and kisses that would not let go.[4]

Paraphrased, the fourth stanza reads thus: So also were you loved in ancient Greece, when the setting was different— gods, heroes, great ships; there too you brought pain as well as the skill of its expression. In the fifth stanza Tuckerman associates himself with "the Enchanter old," who sought among the poisonous plants for magical powers:

> And touched the leaf that opened both his ears
> So that articulate voices now he hears
> In cry of beast or bird or insect's hum—

This is Tuckerman's prayer: "Might I but find thy knowledge in thy song." The cricket's knowledge would be "ancient as light," aboriginal, a foreign tongue, all the more precious for that reason. I paraphrase again (because the next lines are difficult): If the poet could acquire this alien knowledge, he would dare to sing it to the human world, driving through "denser stillness" and even deeper darkness than the cricket penetrated to come here. The world might then listen. It might even applaud the poet, modestly of course; these are high matters, minority communications, and a larger applause would only prove that the truth itself, the communication, was diminished in the handling:

> For larger would be less indeed, and like
> The ceaseless simmer in the summer grass
> To him who toileth in the windy field
> Or where the sunbeams strike

Naught in innumerable numerousness.
So might I much possess
So much must yield.

This may be otherwise put: Because there are so many sounds, we do not attend to any; because there are so many illuminations, sunbeams, we do not attend to any. The poet loses everything between the little actual and the possible. Nonetheless the cricket is still dear, even if its secrets remain alien to man:

Then cricket, sing thy song! or answer mine!
Thine whispers blame, but mine has naught but praises.
It matters not.—Behold! the autumn goes,
     The Shadow grows,
The moments take hold of eternity;
Even while we stop to wrangle or repine
     Our lives are gone
     Like thinnest mist,
Like yon escaping color in the tree:—
Rejoice! rejoice! whilst yet the hours exist
Rejoice or mourn, and let the world swing on
Unmoved by Cricket-song of thee or me.

And the poem ends. It began with a courtly relation, at one stroke meant to establish a relation between the poet and everything represented by the cricket: his antique "otherness," the primitive, prehuman element, the element that resists the sentimental harmonies imposed by man on nature.

The relation once established, Tuckerman thinks of it as the truth of things, especially the truth of pain and time and death. He must bring this truth to the world, like Shelley proposing a similar purpose to the west wind in a more hectic aspiration. But this public purpose is null, Tuckerman reflects; the same misunderstandings would persist. So he turns back. But now he identifies himself not with the human world that he proposed to inform, but with the cricket—each a fretful, noisy being, speaking to deaf ears. One can only persist, rejoicing or mourning—Tuckerman's *materia poetica.* In a poem of the same title Emily Dickinson thinks of the crickets celebrating their rituals under the grass, utterly foreign to man, "enlarging loneliness." But in this case the ritualists, like the ancient Druids, are thought to "enhance" nature. If the crickets have secret lore, antique disciplines, Emily Dickinson is content that this should be so and that the secrets remain intact, the discipline contained. If she claims such privacy for herself, why deny it to the crickets? Tuckerman, so fully committed to reading the text of nature, cannot bear the thought that there are parts of the text that are indecipherable. It is as if a scholar, studying the received texts, came upon certain fragments of a great sacred book, prophetic in tone, and gave the rest of his life to their company. The cricket's noise, like the sound of the sea, is unknowable; hence its fascination as an image of that chaos of which we must become the connoisseurs. In "A Grave" Marianne Moore says:

Man looking into the sea,
taking the view from those who have as much right to it as
           you have to it yourself,
it is human nature to stand in the middle of a thing,
but you cannot stand in the middle of this;
the sea has nothing to give but a well excavated grave.

And the next lines annotate the grave with footnotes on the sea's rapacious look. Then the poem ends:

and the ocean, under the pulsation of lighthouses and noise of
                bell-buoys,
advances as usual, looking as if it were not that ocean in
    which dropped things are bound to sink—
in which if they turn and twist, it is neither with volition nor
    consciousness.[5]

This is our parable. Wallace Stevens' voice in "Sunday Morning" says that "we live in an old chaos of the sun." Tuckerman looks into the sea as into an old chaos of the sun, but he does not hope to take its measure, to stand in the middle of it. He is as decorous in his way as Marianne Moore in her different way. But to both poets the sea is the place where volition and consciousness die, even if bones deposited in that grave continue to twitch and roll as if they were human. The sea, as Williams said in *Paterson Five,* is not our element. American poets are brought up to know this. "The river is within us, the sea is all about us," as one of the voices says in "The Dry Salvages."

"The Cricket" is therefore an exemplary American poem and one of the greatest poems in its tradition. Tuckerman is the isolated figure caught between two worlds: behind him is the human world, deaf, obtuse, vulgar; in front and all around is a world that owes no obeisance to man. This second world is an impenetrable text, "sublime but helpless to the spirit's need"; it contains all of life that we have never known or, knowing, have forgotten. The human world has given itself over to its gross Now. So if the equities are frustrate and it comes to a choice, Tuckerman chooses to be a scholar of one candle, even if most of the text is impenetrable. And he leaves the human world "unmoved."

NOTES

1 *The Sonnets of Frederick Goddard Tuckerman,* ed. Witter Bynner (New York: Knopf, 1931), p. 13. All quotations, unless otherwise specified, are from this edition. The *Complete Poems,* ed. N. Scott Monaday (New York: Oxford University Press, 1965), arrived too late to be of use to me.

2 Emanuel Swedenborg, *De Caelo et eius Mirabilibus, et de Inferno ex Auditis et Visis,* translated as *Heaven and Its Wonders and Hell* by J. C. Ager (London: Swedenborg Society, 1958), p. 50. See *Earths in Our Solar System* (London: Swedenborg Society, 1940), pp. 91, 303, 24.

3 Cf. Elizabeth Sewell, *The Orphic Voice* (London: Routledge and Kegan Paul, 1960), pp. 186–190.

4 Tuckerman, *The Cricket* (Cummington Press, 1950), n.p. The poem was printed from Tuckerman's notebooks. Since its 1950 printing a later version has been found. I have incorporated one change in the third stanza, "with

laugh and blush" instead of "and tittering blush" in the Cummington text. In several places the Cummington text seems highly doubtful: the word "dorcynium," for instance, should be "dorycnium." My attention was drawn to the poem by Yvor Winters, whose review of it is in the *Hudson Review*, III, (Autumn, 1950), 453–458.

⁵ Marianne Moore, *Collected Poems* (New York: Macmillan, 1952), pp. 56–57.

CHAPTER 3

HERMAN MELVILLE

IT IS THE COMMON UNDERSTANDING that Melville was a great poet only in his prose. I have no wish to disturb that view, except perhaps to remark that it states a problem and does not solve it. We might make the same evaluation of D. H. Lawrence, for instance, and live happily enough with it until the differences declared themselves. They would do so almost at once. For the first impression we take from Lawrence's poems is that they do everything he wanted them to do. They are always in command of themselves, minding their own business, going their declared ways. If they are slight things, this is because Lawrence wrote them with a modest object in view, as a kind of courtesy book, a small showing of vivid relationships offered to us lest we miss the point and fail the challenge of the novels. They are a grammar school of courtesies. When we have learned the grammar we are better people, more qualified readers, more graceful in our behavior. Or if we are not, we know the code we infringe. The poems are akin to Lawrence's literary essays, parables, fables, featuring animals, plants, and fish for the lucidity of the demonstration, the accuracy of the grammar. They rarely go wrong, partly because they do not propose to go far. They are Lawrence's ABC of living, and he puts the rest of the alphabet—or as many letters as he commands—directly into the fiction. In that sense the poems exist for the sake of the fiction, as footnotes to the great text.

So the comparison of Melville and Lawrence in this respect is not useful. For most of Melville's poems give us precisely the opposite impression. They lack the fine, modest adequacy of Lawrence's poems; they are sometimes more and more often less than their occasions. Many of the war poems, for instance, were written up from the files of *The Rebellion Record* and often written up too high, too large. And many of the travel poems sound as if they should have been something else—sermons, perhaps, or pamphlets, lectures, mottoes, speeches. And then there is the special problem of *Clarel*, which clearly would have been a novel of ideas, like *The Magic Mountain,* if Melville had found such a genre to sustain him and a public of some good will to read him.

If we think of another novelist who traded in poems, Thomas Hardy, again the differences obtrude. For Hardy was a poet from the beginning, a verse man, and he took to fiction to gain a hearing and went back to his first love when the hearing became too furious to bear. But he was a poet all his life. True, when he found an engrossing theme—the breakdown of the English agricultural communities and the destruction of certain values for which the communities provided a home—he knew that the theme required the wide, loose range of fiction and he was willing to take it up. But his general vision of life was always well served by verse, and the verse-fable was, I think, his favorite instrument. He would not have tackled *The Dynasts* if he had not considered that his verse-fables could stretch themselves to take in the new task. And if we think, on the whole, that his confidence was excessive, this is only another way of saying that drama is inhospitable to strangers; it recognizes its own brethren and warns foreigners to move along. Hardy was not a dramatist, he was a poet. And he was fortunate to find the habits of prose fiction sufficiently varied to accommodate him when the occasion arose. When a later occasion sent him back to verse, it was like going home, he spoke like a native.

Not so Melville. Melville's theme—the exacerbations of a private vision for which the public world provides no form, no haven, no relief—clearly required one of the several modes of prose fiction, and he drove it relentlessly in such works as *Pierre, Moby-Dick,* "Benito Cereno," and "Bartleby." When *The Confidence Man* was published in 1857, Melville's theme was merely held at bay; in no sense was it resolved. And thereafter he gave up fiction, with the single exception of *Billy Budd,* his last act. For more than thirty years he laid aside his great art and took to verse, writing hundreds of short pieces and one enormous poem, the albatross called *Clarel.*

Several explanations have been offered for this strange fact: poor health, the neglect of his recent fiction, a steady job that enabled him to become his own man and do what he wanted to do. Yes, but the question is, Why did he want to do—among all the possible things—*this?*

My own feeling is that after 1857, when he had driven himself to distraction with private visions, elemental forms, and strange obliquities, he craved the comfort of simplicity. He wanted the relief of strong, easy attitudes, massive commitments, solid images. He wanted, in short, to live like other men. So he turned away and tried to live with conventional forms, the rhyming couplets of a life at last normal. This was his program, his dearest, tired wish. I would also suggest—as one part of his problem—that even in the dead days beyond recall he was never really the democrat he thought himself; he was an aristocrat, and he needed the privacy of the poems to give free rein to those alien feelings. Some of his best and some of his worst poems were written to soothe those feelings. One of the worst of them, "The Age of the Antonines," offers the first chapter of Gibbon's *Decline and Fall of the Roman Empire* as a comment upon the America of 1877:

> Orders and ranks they kept degree,
> Few felt how the parvenu pines,
> No law-maker took the lawless one's fee
> In the Age of the Antonines!

Under law made will the world reposed
And the ruler's right confessed,
For the Heavens elected the Emperor then,
The foremost of men the best.
    Ah, might we read in America's signs
    The Age restored of the Antonines.[1]

I should argue that Melville turned to conventional verse forms because the author of *Moby-Dick* craved a condition in which law would be made will, for that very reason—as a way out, for relief. And in those years he wrote hundreds of poor poems and about fifteen poems of the first order that give him a place in American poetry beside Whitman and Emily Dickinson.

A poet in search of a way out will often try to break down his problem into manageable parts. All the better, then, if he can tackle each part separately. This was Yeats' strategy, for instance, in setting up tangible polarities. If you divide your world into soul and self, or matter and spirit, at least you know where you stand; you can define your problem and perhaps side with one part against the other. You can win battles even if the war is in constant danger of being lost. Anything is better than the vague cloud of unknowing that is indivisible and incorrigible. Think how much indecision, complexity, frustration is resolved, one way or another, when we have recorded a vote, yes or no. It is my argument that Melville, during those thirty years of poetry, tried to still his beating brain by dividing his world into yes and no. The alternative was to live with those "heartless voids and immensities of the universe" that Ishmael thought he saw in the malignant whiteness of the whale.

I think this accounts for those poems in his first volume, *Battle-Pieces*, that celebrate the heroism of war, poems like "The March into Virginia," "Lyon," "Ball's Bluff," "On the Photograph of a Corps Commander," "The Cumberland," "The Battle for the Mississippi," and "The Fall of Richmond." It is characteristic of their simplifying vision that in these and similar poems Melville associates Cushing with Adonis, Worden with Hercules, Lincoln with Christ, a particular person—whoever he is—with a counterpart in myth and legend. Conventional memorial poems work in this way, and in all "sincerity" Melville wants to speak and feel like other men. Hence he speaks like them so that he can feel like them. And if it works, the new feelings will be easier to live with than the old. In the last stanza of "The Fall of Richmond" Melville says:

> Well that the faith we firmly kept
> And never our aim forswore
> For the Terrors that trooped from each recess
> When fainting we fought in the Wilderness,
> And Hell made loud hurrah;
> But God is in Heaven, and Grant in the Town,
> And Right through might is Law—
> *God's way adore.*

It is not enough to say that this is bad poetry or a parody of Browning. True, the relation between God in heaven and Grant in Richmond is much too close for good taste or comfort. But we are unlikely in any event to lose ourselves to the rhetoric. Melville wrote those lines not because he felt in that way but because he desperately wanted to feel in that way. And he would have been happy to write any number of bad poems if he could have brought it off, if in taking up an easy, manly rhetoric he could have lived an easy, manly life. As the *Collected Poems* show, he tried—hundreds of times.

Perhaps we can put this another way, linking it with Melville's own fiction. In "Benito Cereno" the character of that name is a man of will, who pushes his vision to extremes, driven by his demon. He is like Kurtz in *Heart of Darkness*. And in the same story there is Captain Delano, who is rather like Conrad's Captain MacWhirr, a steady, good man, a man of limits, devoted to rule and order, a man who lives by not seeing too much. Melville the poet fears that he is, by nature and temper, Benito Cereno, and he thinks that the only way out is to become Captain Delano. He wants, if he can have nothing else in safety, an order most fixed, most Plantagenet. And the events of the story itself are there to imply, for his comfort, that sometimes indeed the innocent are saved, the meek inherit the earth.

This will go some distance to explain why Melville during those thirty years seized every occasion on which a strong, simple, public emotion was possible. When the War between the States ended, for instance, he wrote "A Canticle: Significant of the National Exaltation of Enthusiasm at the Close of the War." The first stanzas are a loud hosanna, "Hosanna to the Lord of hosts,/The hosts of human kind . . . ," and the rhetoric sets up a confusion of noise that ends in the drums of the last stanzas:

> The Generations pouring
>   From times of endless date,
> In their going, in their flowing,
> Ever form the steadfast State;
>   And Humanity is growing
>   Toward the fullness of her fate.
>
> Thou Lord of hosts victorious,
>   Fulfill the end designed;
> By a wondrous way and glorious
>   A passage Thou dost find—
>   A passage Thou dost find:
> Hosanna to the Lord of hosts,
>   The hosts of human kind.

Clearly this is wishful thinking, wishful noise. But it is difficult to conceive that the Melville of the novels, or the Melville who repudiated the cozy meliorism of Derwent in *Clarel,* was taken in by the progressivist myth of a humanity growing toward the fullness of her fate. We think of another poem written on a similar occasion, on the signing of the armistice in November, 1918. Hardy's poem is called "And There Was a Great Calm," and halfway through he says:

> So, when old hopes that earth was bettering slowly
> Were dead and damned, there sounded "War is done!"
> One morrow. Said the bereft, and meek, and lowly,
> "Will men some day be given to grace? yea, wholly,
> And in good sooth, as our dreams used to run?"

It is only a question at this stage, and the poem is only half-way through. There are three more stanzas to mark the calm for what it was, merely a more or less temporary parenthesis in a violent text; and the last stanza comes:

> Calm fell. From Heaven distilled a clemency;
> There was peace on earth, and silence in the sky;
> Some could, some could not, shake off misery:
> The Sinister Spirit sneered: "It had to be!"
> And again the Spirit of Pity whispered, "Why?"

The sinister spirit is the spirit of irony, who is never taken in by anything. We are meant to feel that he has the better part of the argument and most of the chapters of history on his side. But we also feel that it is not a time for argument, and even if the spirit of pity is to lose out, his last word, "Why?" is the one that fills the air. But of course there is no resolution; the poem is a fine question mark. The fact to dwell upon, when we hold these two poems together, is that the spirit of irony who figures in Hardy's poem is barred from Melville's. This is not because Melville does not know him—for he roams at large through the fiction—but because Melville desperately wants to banish him on this occasion. He cannot run the risk of having him.

Admittedly, fifty years of European history made a difference. The hopes of 1865 could hardly raise their heads in 1918; they already felt dead and damned. But if we bridge the gap with war poems like Stephen Crane's, which were written in the last days of the old century and long before Sarajevo and Versailles, we see that Melville wrote his poems as a deliberate act of will, against the grain of his temper. In the book so ruefully called *War is Kind* Crane spoke of the "Little souls who thirst for fight," and those souls were hardly distinguishable from the young men who marched into Virginia, in Melville's poem, "chatting left and laughing right." If Melville sounds like Southey, and the spirit of irony flies into Hardy and Crane, this does not mean that Melville is Southey; it means that he put those sounds together to keep himself from falling apart.

But he could not keep it up. He kept it up long enough or often enough to serve his basic purposes, and if self-preservation is the first law of life, these poems are beyond dispute. If poems do so much for their author, what they do for us is of secondary importance; they have served. But reading through the *Collected Poems* we come upon a poem once in every fifteen or twenty pages in which Melville could not quite keep up the rough, manly tone and then he falls back into his own natural temper and says no in rain if not in thunder. These are the best poems, and without them we should hardly have read the big book at all.

I have in mind, as such a poem, "The House-Top," which deals with certain riots in New York in July, 1863, after the publication of a list of those named for military service:

> No sleep. The sultriness pervades the air
> And binds the brain—a dense oppression, such
> As tawny tigers feel in matted shades,
> Vexing their blood and making apt for ravage.
> Beneath the stars the roofy desert spreads
> Vacant as Libya. All is hushed near by.
> Yet fitfully from far breaks a mixed surf
> Of muffled sound, the Atheist roar of riot.
> Yonder, where parching Sirius set in drought,

Balefully glares red Arson—there—and there.
The town is taken by its rats—ship-rats
And rats of the wharves. All civil charms
And priestly spells which late held hearts in awe—
Fear-bound, subjected to a better sway
Than sway of self; these like a dream dissolve,
And man rebounds whole aeons back in nature.
Hail to the low dull rumble, dull and dead,
And ponderous drag that jars the wall.
Wise Draco comes, deep in the midnight roll
Of black artillery; he comes, though late;
In code corroborating Calvin's creed
And cynic tyrannies of honest kings;
He comes, nor parlies; and the Town, redeemed,
Gives thanks devout; nor, being thankful, heeds
The grimy slur on the Republic's faith implied,
Which holds that Man is naturally good,
And—more—is Nature's Roman, never to be scourged.

We don't think of Southey, we think of Dryden invoking
Virgil, or of some of Johnson's great *Prologues*. Melville
is not merely writing "I agree" in the margin of Hobbes'
Leviathan; the vision is his own as he turns his back upon
the sentimental idealism that is the spirit of the age and
the motto of his own worst poems. The difference between
this poem and "The Age of the Antonines" is the difference
between an inescapable vision and a campaign speech. But
the vision is declared in a context of values fully understood
and acknowledged. It is not exacerbated until it becomes a
purely private anguish, a demon. The values of intelligence
and civility that sustain the poem give the feeling a status
in the public world that the purely private anguish always
needs and never has. This is why Melville can bring to his
occasion the massive resources of a moral tradition that he
inherits and acknowledges; and among these resources a
place is reserved for his own moral sense, which comes into
the poem as a special tone:

> In code corroborating Calvin's creed
> And cynic tyrannies of honest kings.

This tone is unusual in nineteenth-century American poetry. Indeed, if we do not take it in Melville we shall look in vain for it elsewhere. And, as we have seen, it is not always available even in Melville. We find something like it in the prose of "The Lightning-Rod Man" and in "Poor Man's Pudding and Rich Man's Crumbs" in reply to Blandmour's benevolism, and in a handful of poems. But it is rare enough. It is not even in *Pierre*, which is a little romantic in its irony.

Another poem that exhibits the same classical strength, the same refusal of easy victories, is "The College Colonel," a poem in praise of the young Harvard man, William Francis Bartlett, who distinguished himself in the 20th Massachusetts. The poem begins with a few lines of description—the young wounded colonel, his war-worn regiment, the homecoming, the welcome, the shouts and the flags. The hero has come home, and lo! he is still a boy. There could be no easier occasion for the loud, crude emotion, and there are several poems by Melville himself to prove it. But "The College Colonel" is different. After describing the young man's appearance—pale, rigid, with an Indian aloofness—Melville presents in him the rift between consciousness and experience. In most of the war poems the rift is obliterated by the clamor of glory and renown; such rifts are visible only in silence. To the young colonel the gods have revealed, as their last gift, the essential truth of things, and even in the noise of his own experience he will possess it—his eagle—in silence. And Melville, giving all this and more, says:

> It is not that a leg is lost,
>   It is not that an arm is maimed,
> It is not that the fever has racked—
>   Self he has long disclaimed.
> But all through the Seven Days' Fight,
>   And deep in the Wilderness grim,

> And in the field-hospital tent,
>   And Petersburg crater, and dim
>   Lean brooding in Libby, there came—
>   Ah heaven!—what *truth* to him.

Far out in *Pierre* Melville said: "For the more and the more that he wrote, and the deeper and the deeper that he dived, Pierre saw the everlasting elusiveness of Truth; the universal lurking insincerity of even the greatest and purest written thoughts." [2] Perhaps so. Perhaps truth comes, if it does, only in silence, and goes away again in speech. Certainly it goes away in noise, especially on the great public occasions. Melville would often forget this, or he would try to bury the fact under more noise. But in certain poems he would confront the possibility that truth, the enemy of sound and fury, discloses itself in action—if only the action be great enough, selfless enough, silent enough.

This brings us to another version of his predicament. During those thirty years Melville wanted value to reside in the great public occasions, and he would give those occasions the benefit of all conceivable doubts and some doubts hardly conceivable at all. He wanted to come in out of the storm —the personal storm—into the shelter of other men. But he knew—at least when he was true to himself—that truth has a bad time in the market place. More often than not it lives in isolation and feeds on silence. Hence, partly in fury and anger, Melville joined Hawthorne in saying no. In a famous letter in April, 1851, Melville tried to couch this option in decorous terms:

> There is the grand truth about Nathaniel Hawthorne. He says No! in thunder; but the Devil himself cannot make him say *yes*. For all men who say *yes*, lie; and all men who say *no*,— why, they are in the happy condition of judicious, unencumbered travellers in Europe; they cross the frontiers into Eternity with nothing but a carpet-bag,—that is to say, the Ego. Whereas those *yes*-gentry, they travel with heaps of bag-

gage, and, damn them! they will never get through the Custom House.[3]

This letter is one of the great occasions in the history of American experience. It is well known and has been widely discussed, but I am not sure that we take it quite in the spirit of its deliverance. It is commonly taken to mean that one should swim against the public streams, the law of the imagination being, as Kenneth Burke said on another occasion, "When in Rome do as the Greeks." But I think Melville goes one step further. If you say "When in Rome do as the Greeks," you opt out of one allegiance by taking up another. And this is only to say yes in another way, down another street. I think Melville wanted to disengage himself from all allegiances, partly for self-preservation, partly in devotion to the privacy of truth. In his worst poems, as we have seen, he said a simple, hearty, crude yes; in far better poems he said no; but in his best poems we find him struggling toward a position above both yes and no. This is so in the best of the poems and, before that, in *The Confidence Man*.

I must offer a good deal of evidence for this view. To make a start, there is the frequency with which Melville disavows both the optimistic and the pessimistic positions. Even without assimilating him to Thomas Hardy, one would have expected him to side with the pessimists, if it were to come to a vote. And this is so as long as it is a question of voting. But his favorite position is the one he expressed in a letter to James Billson in January, 1885, when the talk came round to Thomson and his *City of Dreadful Night*. "As to his pessimism," Melville says, "altho' neither pessimist nor optimist myself, nevertheless I relish it in the verse if for nothing else than as a counterpoise to the exorbitant hopefulness, juvenile and shallow, that makes such a bluster in these days—at least, in some quarters." [4] And think how often he implies, as between rival philosophies, "a plague on both your houses." This is how he offers the commitment to events, especially in *Pierre:* "For Faith and philosophy are air," he says, "but events are brass." I assume he means that events are silent truths, they are what they are—for better or worse. Faith and philosophy are words, speech, talk, and therefore subject to the "everlasting elusiveness" already invoked in the same novel. The only answer lies in another perspective, somehow above the wars and rivalries, beyond the no and the yes. Perhaps the nearest thing we have to it is the perspective of comedy, which somehow lives above irony and pity, optimism and pessimism, skepticism and trust. *The Confidence Man* is Melville's most systematic attempt to achieve that perspective, to control his demon by subjecting it to an alien comic spirit.

We are arguing that Melville needed this stance for his own deliverance. And it is significant that when he thought of this, he often found the pattern for it in two analogies that stared him in the face: the idea of God and the idea of nature.

In one of Melville's finest poems, "The Conflict of Convictions," the human conflicts leading into the war are encircled by the derision of Satan on the one hand, and "Heaven's ominous silence" on the other. The ominous silence is that of truth, ominous because alien, indifferent to man. God turns the wheel of necessity:

> The people spread like a weedy grass,
>   The thing they will they bring to pass,
> And prosper to the apoplex.

And so it goes:

> Age after age shall be
> As age after age has been . . .

Life is, we assume, positive, and death, as the poem has it, is a silent negative. But the poem ends:

> Yea and Nay—
> Each hath his say;
> But God He keeps the middle way.
> None was by
> When He spread the sky;
> Wisdom is vain, and Prophesy.

The middle way has nothing to do with Aristotle or the stance of the traditional reasonable man of Western literature; it is the way of indifference. None was by when God spread the sky, so He is responsible to none, indifferent to the blood and mire. And if that is God's way, might it not, should it not, also be Melville's? If Melville takes a leaf from the divine book, who can blame him?

It is the spirit of nature too. In "Poor Man's Pudding and Rich Man's Crumbs" Blandmour sings hymns to "the blessed almoner, Nature," but the story confronts him with the facts and sets him down. In "The Stone Fleet" the old sailor recounts his life, the ships lost, scuttled, sunk. And in the last stanza he says:

> And all for naught. The Waters pass—
> Currents will have their way;
> Nature is nobody's ally; 'tis well;
> The harbor is bettered—will stay.
> A failure, and complete,
> Was your Old Stone Fleet.

Nature is nobody's ally. Natural process is not a friend to man, and if man extracts the notion that he is nature's favorite son from the fact that winter is followed by spring, that is his funeral, he has been warned. In *The Confidence Man* the herb doctor says to the Missouri bachelor: "Is it not to Nature that you are indebted for that robustness of mind which you so unhandsomely use to her scandal? Pray, is it not to Nature that you owe the very eyes by which you criticize her?" And the Missourian answers: "No! for the privilege of vision I am indebted to an oculist, who in my tenth year operated upon me in Philadelphia. Nature made me blind and would have kept me so." [5] We have come a long way from Blake, Wordsworth, and Coleridge. Whitman would sing of a natural principle diffused through the plenitude of multiplicity, and he would assume that nature favors multiplicity as a father favors his children. Melville feels the multiplicity and acknowledges nature, but he assumes that it is indifferent to man and interested only in going its own way. The only comparable vision in Wordsworth arises when Lucy's death is the signal of a break in the benevolent relation between nature and man. Melville says, "The Waters pass—Currents will have their way"; Wordsworth says,

> No motion has she now, no force;
> She neither hears nor sees;
> Rolled round in earth's diurnal course,
> With rocks, and stones, and trees.

And in both cases now the natural processes are indifferent.

Indeed, we can see where Melville got the idea of a comic perspective, and how deeply he needed it, in a poem like "Malvern Hill," which starts off as if it were by Akenside but goes on to bleaker things:

> Ye elms that wave on Malvern Hill
> In prime of morn and May,
> Recall ye how McClellan's men
> Here stood at bay?

We are moving between Akenside and Southey thus far, but there is still no sign of the spirit of irony, who is introduced only in the second stanza when Melville has described the battle and the dead, and says, "Does the elm wood/Recall the haggard beards of blood?" But even yet there is no sign of the spirit of comedy. And the third stanza ends with an echo of the second: "Does Malvern Wood/Bethink itself, and muse and brood?" Or—another way of putting it—has nature any sympathy, any feeling, a conscience, perhaps? But in the epilogue to the poem Malvern Wood speaks for itself: the spirit of nature can answer all questions by answering them indifferently. The merely human are embarrassed by ignorance, rival claims, the responsibilities that begin in dreams; Nature has all the freedom of irresponsibility:

> We elms of Malvern Hill
>   Remember every thing;
> But sap the twig will fill:
>   Wag the world how it will,
> Leaves must be green in Spring.

So nature and God, if distinguishable at all, share the same attitude—the safety of indifference, the comic perspective, the middle course above yea and nay, a plague on all your houses—not anarchy, comedy. So that, strictly speaking, the more "natural" we are in our behavior, and the more seriously we take the idea that we are made "in the image of God," the more energetically we seek the comic position. This becomes the "right" thing to do. Prudence and devotion are identical.

To mark the extent to which Melville runs against the wind of nineteenth-century American literature in this respect we have only to recall a few simple texts. Emerson, for instance, in the essay "Nature," which he published in 1836, says: "The lover of Nature is he whose inward and outward senses are still truly adjusted to each other; who has retained the spirit of infancy even into the era of manhood. His intercourse with heaven and earth becomes part of his daily food. In the presence of nature a wild delight runs through the man, in spite of real sorrows. Nature says,—he is my creature, and maugre all his impertinent griefs, he shall be glad with me." Later in the same essay we read: "The moral law lies at the centre of nature and radiates to the circumference"; and finally: "Nature is made to conspire with spirit to emancipate us." This benign conspiracy, translated into familial terms, is the motif of Longfellow's sonnet "Nature," which first appeared in 1875:

As a fond mother, when the day is o'er,
  Leads by the hand her little child to bed,
  Half willing, half reluctant to be led,
  And leave his broken playthings on the floor,
Still gazing at them through the open door,
  Nor wholly reassured and comforted
  By promises of others in their stead,
  Which, though more splendid, may not please him more;
So Nature deals with us, and takes away
  Our playthings one by one, and by the hand
  Leads us to rest so gently, that we go
Scarce knowing if we wish to go or stay,
  Being too full of sleep to understand
  How far the unknown transcends the what we know.

By comparison with these and other chorales, Melville's hour is the eleventh; he points toward Freud, Conrad, Kafka, Grimm's fairy tales. And in the same hour, if we look around in American poetry for a similar spirit, we find it again in Stephen Crane, in a poem like this one from *The Black Riders* (1895):

Walking in the sky,
A man in strange black garb
Encountered a radiant form.
Then his steps were eager;
Bowed he devoutly.
"My Lord," said he.
But the Spirit knew him not.

We take this as we find it—probably, in the first instance, as a parody of a famous devotional poem by George Herbert. And, after that, as the spirit of irony darkening the American landscape after Longfellow, Emerson, and the Civil War. When the man in strange black garb lifts his head and finds that his God is a stranger with no hospitable intention, he walks bitterly into the modern world determined to offer his devotion elsewhere—or nowhere.

So Melville's famous "quarrel with God" is at once a quarrel and an imitation. The quarrel is clear, and one of its results is that Melville imitates God primarily in His comic indifference. Instead of suffering from alienation, he will make alienation the very idiom of his life, and the initiative, this time, will be his own. In that sense, anything God can do, man can do better, better and more thoroughly, because man has more to suffer, more to lose.

Melville has a short story that seems to me to support the argument. In "The Fiddler" a disaffected poet meets an old friend called Standard and a new acquaintance called Hautboy. They go to a circus, and the poet is greatly taken with Hautboy's enjoyment, his healthy mixture of good sense and good humor. And he notes that Hautboy "seemed intuitively to hit the exact line between enthusiasm and apathy. It was plain that while Hautboy saw the world pretty much as it was, yet he did not theoretically espouse its bright side nor its dark side. Rejecting all solutions, he but acknowledged facts. What was sad in the world he did not superficially gainsay; what was glad in it he did not cynically slur; and all which was to him personally enjoyable, he gratefully took to his heart." [6] The sentence we need,—and it is verified in the events of the story—is: "Rejecting all solutions, he but acknowledged facts." We have met something like it before, and will again, for it is Melville's ideal human image. We find it in the character of Rolfe, Melville's spokesman in *Clarel*, whose mind, Clarel tells us in Part IV of the poem, is "poised at self-center and mature." [7] This is essentially the comic poise, the stability that rejects all solutions and acknowledges facts. In this spirit we have no promises to keep and therefore none to break. We can't say "The best is yet to be," but we are preparing ourselves for the worst.

Melville's best poems are written in this spirit. In no particular order I would choose "The House-Top," "The College Colonel," "The Conflict of Convictions," "The Maldive Shark," "The Apparition" in *Battle-Pieces;* "Billy in the Darbies," "Lone Founts," "The Bench of Boors," "Art," "In a Bye-Canal," "The Ravaged Villa," "Greek Architecture," "Misgivings," "The Haglets," and "After the Pleasure Party." These are, I think, the best things in the *Collected Poems.* In *Clarel* there is nothing as fine as the description of corrupt Jerusalem; the rest of it is a gift for the man who already has everything.

"Lone Founts" is another version of the disengagement theme. Instead of immersing ourselves in the destructive element, we are to imagine how this element will appear to posterity, or how it has already appeared to the ancients, and live accordingly:

> Though fast youth's glorious fable flies,
> View not the world with worldling's eyes;
> Nor turn with weather of the time.
> Foreclose the coming of surprise:
> Stand where Posterity shall stand;
> Stand where the Ancients stood before,
> And, dipping in lone founts thy hand,
> Drink of the never-varying lore:
> Wise once, and wise thence evermore.

This sounds a little like the spirit of irony, but it is in fact the spirit of pity driven beyond distraction to seek the comedian's peace. It is certainly the spirit of pity who acknowledges that youth's fables are glorious, and there is no sneer in the admonition to foreclose surprise—surprise being, I assume, the unpredictable and probably fatal, the occasions we can't afford to take on trust. Indeed, what distinguishes this poem from the hundreds of dogmatic trifles with which it could be confused is that in the very act of disengagement the things from which Melville disengages himself are granted their vitality, their juice and sweetness. And there is no bravado, no romantic irony, in those lone founts; they are the sources of Rolfe's "self-center," wisdom hacked from the wilderness.

I take this phrase, with some liberty, from a modern poem in praise of Herman Melville. The poem begins by invoking Melville's "dreadful heart that won Socratic peace." The winning is clear enough, but I am not sure that the peace was Socratic. If we take *Billy Budd* as our sole evidence, we can say, with another modern poet, that Melville "sailed into an extraordinary mildness" with the discovery that "Goodness existed." [8] Both poems suggest that in his last years Melville achieved a marvelous harmony of wilderness and wisdom, perhaps the kind of stillness Wallace Stevens had in mind when the violence without is met by a corresponding violence within. It is every poet's dream. Our modern poet says in his praise of Melville:

> Wisdom and wilderness are here at poise,
> Ocean and forest are the mind's device
> But still I feel the presence of thy will.[9]

In one of his poems Melville speaks of art as a wrestling with the angel, a grappling of opposites, and Jacob is an appropriate figure in high standing with artists. In several poems Melville wrestles with chaos and seems to lose, except that the chaos is, after all, brought to the heel of the mind that apprehends it. A memorable match is the poem "The Ravaged Villa":

> In shards the sylvan vases lie,
>   Their links of dance undone,
> And brambles wither by thy brim,
>   Choked fountain of the sun!
> The Spider in the laurel spins,

> The weed exiles the flower:
> And, flung to kiln, Apollo's bust
> Makes lime for Mammon's tower.

It is easy to underestimate a poem of this kind by scanting the values that sustain it. But we have only to compare it with a poem of similar occasion, Shelley's "Ozymandias," to see that Melville's has an Augustan strength entirely free from the whine of self-pity that pervades Shelley's. Melville's resilience is the power to confront one instance of chaos with a commensurate order from his own resources—from his intelligence and his will. In *Billy Budd* the persuasions of a nature, for once, benign are offset by the impositions of duty and impersonal law, and the book seems to ask in bewilderment, Which is chaos; which is order? That goodness exists is not quite the "new knowledge" the modern poet ascribes to the mature Melville, but we need not quarrel, for the discovery solves nothing. Poor Captain Vere commits himself to law and duty. "With mankind," he says, "forms, measured forms are everything; and that is the import couched in the story of Orpheus with his lyre spellbinding the wild denizens of the wood." [10] But the story, *Billy Budd,* raises the question, If chaos and order are confounded, so that we don't know which is which, what then? Captain Vere opts to identify order with law, and he knows that this order, in the circumstances, is implacable, exorbitant, therefore unjust, but life must persist. Billy is associated with Christ, and both, by long tradition, with Orpheus—scapegoat civilizers, each. But there is nothing in the story to refute the reflection that to God these actors and actions are of no account. In the early poem called "Misgivings" the storm is Melville's text for chaos, social, political—and above all, human:

Nature's dark side is heeded now—
    (Ah! optimist-cheer disheartened flown)—

A child may read the moody brow
   Of yon black mountain lone.
With shouts the torrents down the gorges go,
And storms are formed behind the storm we feel:
The hemlock shakes in the rafter, the oak in the driving keel.

And if we ask who is behind the storms forming behind the storms we feel, the answer is Melville's Great Comedian, adept of neutrality. At the end of *Billy Budd* the ballad that gives the facts of the case contents itself with the facts and offers nothing in relief. Billy's last words are, "I am sleepy, and the cozy weeds about me twist." This is not Socratic peace; it is the patience that abides the question.

Indeed, before we add Melville to the list of poets who chant the dynamic harmony of imagination and reality, we should attend to the poem called "The Berg," in which a ship, impetuous and infatuate—like man—rushes against the stolid iceberg. The iceberg will die, along with the ship it has destroyed. And Melville says:

Hard Berg (methought), so cold, so vast,
With mortal damps self-overcast;
Exhaling still thy dankish breath—
Adrift dissolving, bound for death;
Though lumpish thou, a lumbering one—
A lumbering lubbard loitering slow,
Impingers rue thee and go down,
Sounding thy precipice below,
Nor stir the slimy slug that sprawls
Along thy dead indifference of walls.

In "The Bench of Boors" the poet envies the indolent who see little or nothing. In "The Enthusiast" he admonishes us to "Walk through the cloud to meet the pall." In "Buddha" he begs for absorption and annulment. But an even more characteristic note is sounded in "Fragments of a Lost Gnostic Poem of the 12th Century," when Melville denies the great romantic principle of energy itself because the game is rigged; a malicious sprite, a comedian, has been working to confuse:

> Indolence is heaven's ally here,
> And energy the child of hell:
> The Good Man pouring from his pitcher clear,
> But brims the poisoned well.

Clearly, if the well is poisoned, the culprit is a God horribly indifferent to man. And this, in Melville, is only a special instance of the incorrigible breach between man and nature. Melville's noisy poems are his attempt to drown the voices that remind him of this breach, to shout them down. He wants to set up rousing, public occasions on which private thoughts are impossible. When he fails, he tries to reach a safe position above the yes and no, Godlike, inscrutable. *Clarel* is an attempt to underwrite Melville's own strategy by showing that "the tradition" amounts to nothing more than a heap of pathetically cherished illusions; Western belief is bunk from which we are trying to awake. The author of *Four Quartets* would insist that a pilgrimage undertaken in this spirit is bound to be fruitless, since the pilgrims have demonstrated the impurity of their motives by choosing an object in accordance with their mere "fancies," their self-engendered delusions. The humility that is endless is beyond or beneath such pilgrims because they are concerned less with the Logos than with their own image. But *Clarel* is obscured by its epilogue. The fourth part comes to an end, reasonably enough, when it has nothing further to say:

> Dusked Olivet he leaves behind,
> And, taking now a slender wynd,
> Vanishes in the obscurer town.

He vanishes, that is, when the *via crucis* comes to a dead end. This is bleaker than Adam and Eve taking their solitary way out of Eden, because Milton's "graver subject" belongs at once to him and to the whole human race, while the lack of such a subject is precisely Clarel's discovery. The epilogue is not a rhyming couplet of faith, but it holds out possibilities that the poem itself has specifically disavowed. There is no point in having faith inscribe the sign of the cross on the broken urns when the cross itself has already been carried in the poem without yielding Clarel his "message." One part of the epilogue is true to Melville's essential vision. Above the war of despair and faith "the ancient Sphinx still keeps the porch of shade." Meanwhile there is life, and if we cannot find "a message from beneath the stone," we may at least— as comedians—abide. What else?

NOTES

1 Herman Melville, *Collected Poems,* ed. Howard P. Vincent (Chicago: Packard, 1947), p. 235.

2 Melville, *Pierre* (New York: Grove Press ed., 1957), p. 472.

3 Melville, *Letters,* ed. Merrell R. Davis and William H. Gilman (New Haven: Yale Univ. Press, 1960), p. 125.

4 *Ibid.,* p. 277.

5 Melville, *The Confidence Man,* ed. Elizabeth S. Foster (New York: Hendricks House, 1954), p. 123.

6 Melville, *Selected Writings* (Modern Library ed., 1952), p. 236.

7 Melville, *Clarel,* ed. Walter E. Bezanson (New York: Hendricks House, 1960), p. 418.

8 *The Collected Poems of W. H. Auden* (New York: Random House, 1945), pp. 146–147.

9 Yvor Winters, *Collected Poems* (London: Routledge and Kegan Paul, 1962), p. 121.

10 *Selected Writings,* p. 898.

CHAPTER 4

EMILY DICKINSON

To BRING US QUICKLY into the poems of Emily Dickinson I would offer a motto from René Char, a note in his war journal. "We are stretched on the rack," he says, "between the craving to know and the despair of having known. The goad will not give up its sting, nor we our hope." [1]

The craving to know was part of Emily Dickinson's sense of life, another part was her self-confidence, and the two parts run together. She often reminds us of Keats and his touching faith in his own powers. In one poem she speaks of "that fine Prosperity/Whose Sources are interior," [2] and the prosperity in her own case was clearly a profound belief in her own imagination. The brain, she says, is "wider than the Sky," [632] for it will contain the sky "with ease"; and if any further proof is required, the brain is "deeper than the sea." When she speaks of the "Growth of Man" she gives it as "the solitary prowess/Of a Silent Life," [750] the human imagination minding its proper business. Sometimes she invokes the imagination directly, sometimes she calls it the brain, and once she calls it, quite simply, "revery." By any of its names it is creative. It can make a prairie out of a clover and one bee, and if necessary, out of even less. If this reminds us of Wallace Stevens and his perhaps exorbitant faith in the human imagination, we are not thereby deceived; the poets are in this and other respects cousin. Both poets believe, at least on fine days, that we can "fit our Vision to the Dark" [419] and meet the road erect, or nearly so. The imagination is the "Sinew from within" [616]; it is the source of that "madness" that is "divinest Sense." [435] And there is one poem of some scandal in which Emily

Dickinson attributes all power to the poet and all reality to his poem:

> I reckon—when I count at all—
> First—Poets—Then the Sun—
> Then Summer—Then the Heaven of God—
> And then—the List is done—
>
> But, looking back—the First so seems
> To Comprehend the Whole—
> The Others look a needless Show—
> So I write—Poets—All—   [569]

Hence, when we bring together Emily Dickinson's self-confidence, her belief in the imagination, and her craving to know, we see why meaning exists for her only to the extent that it can be drawn into the poem. She will say, "Each Life Converges to some Centre" [680] when in fact she means that all life, all reality, converges to her poem. We often say that Emily Dickinson withdrew into her room and rejected the busy world, but this is wrong. She withdrew into her room and attracted into it whatever of life her unwritten poem needed. Life is drawn into her room and sometimes entertained there and often trapped there. This is what she means by that "Possession" that is "an Estate perpetual/Or a reduceless Mine." [855] (We are meant to take the pun quite seriously.) Emily Dickinson does not turn the poem outward upon a world now, as a result of the poem, more lucid. The world must look to itself. The only assurance she gives is that she will not hurt it or—to use D. H. Lawrence's phrase—"do dirt" upon it. What is final is the poem. There all roads end. In one of her most impassioned poems she claims, as if by divine right, joys and privileges denied her in historical fact. "Mine," she says, "Mine—here —in Vision—and in Veto!" [528] Within her room she is empress, she has every power, vision and veto; whatever tribute her imagination brings from the outer provinces is hers forever. Indeed, she is very like that "concentred self" which Stevens invokes in "Credences of Summer":

> Three times the concentred self takes hold, three times
> The thrice concentred self, having possessed

> The object, grips it in savage scrutiny,
> Once to make captive, once to subjugate
> Or yield to subjugation, once to proclaim
> The meaning of the capture, this hard prize,
> Fully made, fully apparent, fully found.[3]

This does not mean that Emily Dickinson thought her own order strong enough to control all the chaos of the world, to bring it to the heel of lucidity. "Many Things— are fruitless—/'Tis a Baffling Earth—," [614] she says, and there are several poems in which she makes fun of the childish presumption of power—"pretty estimates/Of Prickly Things." [637] In one of her greatest poems she says, "I felt a Cleaving in my Mind—/As if my Brain had split—," [937] and she doesn't claim the knack of putting the pieces together again. There are circumstances in which even the imagination retires, defeated. "Except the smaller size," she says, "No lives are round—." [1067] And there are many poems in which the attempt to make or keep a life "round" is baffled by the indisputable facts of suffering and death. [1100] But just as she held fast to life when the legal evidence in its favor was slight, so she continued to believe in her imagination, perhaps on the principle that, however poor a thing, it was her own. Indeed, there are three or four poems in which she almost boasts of her prowess. "I can wade Grief—," she says, "Whole Pools of it—," as if tempting a vindictive Providence to strike again. And on at least two occasions she was prepared to make a general rule of her capacities:

> Give Balm—to Giants—
> And they'll wilt, like Man—

        Give Himmaleh—
        They'll Carry—Him!   [252, 310]

Indeed, if we follow this one stage further, we find Emily
Dickinson taking a certain masochistic pleasure in the vision
of horror: " 'Tis so appalling—it exhilarates—," [281] she
says, and goes on to prove it. A starving man is rebuked for
attaching undue significance to distant food; he ought to
know that it was the distance, not the food, that was savory.
[439] In any event, why should we have the capacity to
suffer, if we do not suffer?

    There is strength in proving that it can be borne
    Although it tear—
    What are the sinews of such cordage for
    Except to bear . . .   [1113]

And there are moments in which Emily Dickinson dreams
of impossibility for the refined thrill of defeat:

            I would not paint—a picture—
            I'd rather be the One
            Its bright impossibility
            To dwell—delicious—on—
            And wonder how the fingers feel
            Whose rare—celestial—stir
            Evokes so sweet a Torment—
            Such sumptuous—Despair—   [505]

This is to go far beyond Wallace Stevens in searching out
exotic gratifications. The sweets of defeat were not to his
taste even among the variegated pleasures of *Harmonium*.
And even in Emily Dickinson it is an extreme occasion,
though it has companions. So we should not make too much
of it. A poet who has nothing but her own imagination will
set it off in strange directions, foraging.

    And if she has chosen to live within her room, she will
choose to live there dangerously. "My little Circuit," as she
calls it, [313] will have to be an eventful place. She will

crave to know, and then she will face the despair of having known. Only then, if ever, will she be content. The floor will be a battlefield; her motto will be: "Finite—to fail, but infinite to Venture—." [847] "I dwell in Possibility," she says [657] a little blithely, but more often she will urge her imagination into the valley of death:

> The gleam of an heroic Act
> Such strange illumination
> The Possible's slow fuse is lit
> By the Imagination.   [1687]

The fuse is lit in a hundred poems. "Exultation is the going/Of an inland soul to sea,/Past the houses—past the headlands—/Into deep Eternity—." [76] "Our lives are Swiss," she complains at one point, waiting for the great day of danger to come. [80] And if the danger is slow to come, she will hasten it or invent it. In one poem sunshine on the hills makes her dream of the clash of arms and mighty wars, and she "charges" from her chimney corner—"But Nobody was there!" [152] So dreams of liberty become tremendous escape stories, with chains cut, guns in pursuit, and the like. [277] If a clock stops, it becomes an act of metaphysical defiance, and we hear Satan in the wings. [287] And conjecture itself becomes a scene in science fiction:

> The possibility—to pass
> Without a Moment's Bell—
> Into Conjecture's presence—
> Is like a Face of Steel—
> That suddenly looks into ours
> With a metallic grin—
> The Cordiality of Death—
> Who drills his Welcome in—   [286]

If this use of the imagination needs a supporting theory, perhaps the best one is given when Emily Dickinson says, "I made my soul familiar—with her extremity—/That at the last, it should not be a novel Agony—." [412] Taking a more objective view of it, we could think of it as a life in the middle style craving a taste of the sublime. This would explain a curious feature of Emily Dickinson's poetry: she tends to use traditionally "dangerous" terms as terms of praise—the word "desire," for instance. In Emily Dickinson generally this word refers to a capacity, differing in different people, for imaginative leaps, feats of emotional daring, leaps into the sublime. Those who lack it, or possess it meagerly, are, quite simply, dead. In a poem about heaven she says:

> Heaven is so far of the mind
> That were the Mind dissolved—
> The Site—of it—by Architect
> Could not again be proved—
>
> 'Tis vast—as our Capacity—
> As fair—as our Idea—
> To him of adequate desire
> No further 'tis, than Here—   [370]

Accordingly, in Emily Dickinson's poems everything is here, in her narrow circuit, or it is nowhere. Hence the grammatical figure that is of the greatest comfort to her—more consoling even than metaphor—is synecdoche, which allows the part to stand for the whole, the little thing for the big thing, here for everywhere. (Robert Frost said on one occasion: "I believe in what the Greeks called 'synecdoche'; touching the hem of the Goddess. All that a poet needs is samples.") If you crave to know, and if you live in one room, you will derive great comfort from synecdoche, and you will work your imagination to the bone. And as long as it works, here will be everywhere, small will be all. [284]

But sometimes, in Emily Dickinson, the trick doesn't work. In the love poems especially, when the lovers are separated, here is not everywhere, here and there are rigid, neither will budge. So grammatical principles are no good. One of Emily Dickinson's greatest poems, one of the greatest love poems in the language, begins:

> I cannot live with You—
> It would be Life—
> And Life is over there—
> Behind the Shelf
> The Sexton keeps the Key to—

It ends:

> So We must meet apart—
> You there—I—here—
> With just the Door ajar
> That Oceans are—and Prayer—
> And that White Sustenance—
> Despair—   [640]

This is the despair of having known. Emily Dickinson often speaks of it as vision, vetoed; the light of the sun, put out by night [768]; or (in a remarkable image) the eye of a statue, "That knows it cannot see." [305] In several poems she distinguishes it from common analogues that it might be thought to resemble—death, frost, fire, midnight, and the like—and she opts for chaos as the only approximation, the chaos of a drowning man, in one instance:

> But, most, like Chaos—Stopless—cool—
> Without a Chance, or Spar—
> Or even a Report of Land—
> To justify—Despair.   [510]

And to emphasize that on these occasions here is not everywhere, she says in another poem, "No Man can compass a Despair—." [230] Despair is "Pain's Successor," [396] in the love poems the dreadful boundary between his consciousness and hers, [644] the "fictitious Shores" a drowning man sees, [739] or the "imperial affliction" sent from the air on winter afternoons. [258] It is light that "oppresses," knowledge that kills.

When Stevens speaks of these occasions he touches them much more daintily, and he tries to bend them to his saving figure, the imagination and reality, equal and opposite, a violence within holding an equal violence without. Despair, in Stevens' poems, tends to accompany a blankness of perception, and we rarely feel that the sinews are about to break. Emily Dickinson does not resort to Stevens' image. But she has her own favorite stratagem, good as long as it works: she tries to translate loss, somehow, into gain. And human events are so complicated that this is sometimes possible. Often she will capitalize upon the separation of soul from body, which enables her to say, "Captivity is Consciousness—," but on the other hand, "So's Liberty." [484] Things that are equal to the same thing are equal to each other, as rudimentary mathematics will allow. More often still she will take comfort from the thought that to appreciate joy one must have tasted pain. [73, 684, 771, 1754] A very common motto in her poems is, "Water is taught by thirst," [135, 207, 213, 459, 571, 572, 675] " 'Tis Parching—Vitalizes Wine—," [313] or the last word in bleak translations, "Dying—annuls the power to kill." [358] More consolingly, she speaks of "that Ethereal Gain/One earns by measuring the Grave—," [574] and in another poem [660] she offers the doubtful boon of reflecting that there is only a difference of degree between one woe and another. Danger at the edge of pleasure is good, apparently [807]; and while possibility is "flavorless," impossibility, "like Wine/Exhilarates the Man/Who tastes it . . ." [838] And there is always the consolation, for those who are prepared to pay a stiff price, that agony may get them a seat in the sublime circle that she calls "Tremendousness." [963] Another kind of translation, equally desperate, enabled Emily Dickinson to reflect that "The Missing All—prevented Me/From missing

minor Things." [985] And from here on there is no limit to
the whirling ingenuity of the translator:

> A *Wounded* Deer—leaps highest—
> I've heard the Hunter tell—
> 'Tis but the Ecstasy of *death*—
> And then the Brake is still!   [165]

And there is even another possibility:

> It might be lonelier
> Without the Loneliness—
> I'm so accustomed to my Fate—
> Perhaps the Other—Peace—
>
> Would interrupt the Dark—
> And crowd the little Room—
> Too scant—by Cubits—to contain
> The Sacrament—of Him—
>
> I am not used to Hope—
> It might intrude upon—
> Its sweet parade—blaspheme the place—
> Ordained to Suffering—
>
> It might be easier
> To fail—with Land in Sight—
> Than gain—My Blue Peninsula—
> To perish—of Delight   [405]

Beyond this there is only one consolation, the thought that,
at a certain stage of pain, one can elect to give up the ghost:

> Looking at Death, is Dying—
> Just let go the Breath—
> And not the pillow at your Cheek
> So Slumbereth—
>
> Others, Can Wrestle—
> Yours, is done—
> And so of Woe, bleak dreaded—come,
> It sets the Fright at liberty—

And Terror's free—
Gay, Ghastly, Holiday!   [281]

The craving to know, the despair of having known—anyone who has served his apprenticeship in these trades will be hard to impress. And this is one of Emily Dickinson's distinguishing marks: she stands before the bitterest contingencies of chance, unabashed. She is not imperturbable or fearless. In her poems pain sometimes comes as "One—Imperial—Thunderbolt," [315] and after a while "a formal feeling comes." [341] Or life may be "a brief Campaign of sting and sweet." [159] Or we may have to learn joy by pain "as Blind Men learn the sun!" [167] But there is always the thought that a thing, at the worst, can only be itself; "Defeat means nothing *but* Defeat." [172] Heaven, Emily Dickinson says, "is what I cannot reach." [239] It may not even be true. [121] But agony is true, and convulsion, and despair, and death. [241] Or, bringing many pains together, there may be the despair of having known heaven. [243, 256] Or, again, the soul, having known the heaven that is freedom, may be recaptured and led off like a felon. [512] And there is always the special pain of secret wounds. [1737] But even if none of these facts can be altered, even if reality laughs in the imagination's face, it is still possible to effect a dignified retreat:

I reason, Earth is short—
And Anguish—absolute—
And many hurt,
But, what of that?

I reason, we could die—
The best Vitality
Cannot excel Decay,
But, what of that?

I reason, that in Heaven—
Somehow, it will be even—

Some new Equation, given—
But, what of that?   [301]

Can we not ask here, as Stevens asked on another occasion,
"Are not the imagination and reality equal and inseparable?" [4] Emily Dickinson's poem is a triumph of tone, which
is the same thing as a triumph of imagination. The refrain
is different in each stanza, although the words are the same
—"But, what of that?"—because the words take color or take
fright from the reflections that precede them, and the reflections differ as one part of the mind's life differs from another. In the first stanza the refrain answers and rebukes the
note of complaint, because it is beside the point. In the
second stanza it answers and rebukes the cry of gloom, because it is beside the point. In the third, it answers and rebukes the voice of hope, because it too is beside the point.
Each cry is valid enough and worth attending to, except
for this, that all cries are irrelevant, archaic. (Emily Dickinson is an adept of exclusions. She can clear a space around
her pain in the time most poets take to get from one stanza
to the next.)

The triumph of that poem consists—this is one way of
putting it—in the dignity with which the ground is held, and
held by virtue of Emily Dickinson's own strength. This is one
of the remarkable qualities of her poetry: her images present
themselves on their own authority, which is the authority
she gives them. When she speaks of "the mob within the
heart/Police cannot suppress," [1745] when she says that "the
Outer—from the inner/Derives its Magnitude," [451] she
sets these words down on her own authority, without offering
either evidence or apology. She simply says, in effect, "It
was so." One of her greatest poems goes:

The first Day's Night had come—
And grateful that a thing
So terrible—had been endured—
I told my Soul to sing—

She said her Strings were snapt—
Her bow—to Atoms blown—
And so to mend her—gave me work
Until another morn—

And then—a Day as huge
As yesterdays in pairs,
Unrolled its horror in my face—
Until it blocked my eyes—

My Brain—begun to laugh—
I mumbled—like a fool—
And tho' 'tis Years ago—that Day—
My Brain keeps giggling—still

And Something's odd—within—
That person that I was—
And this One—do not feel the same—
Could it be Madness—this?   [410]

The thing so terrible is not defined, except that having endured it, one is grateful rather than proud, and this is definition enough. The soul as the Aeolian lyre is common
enough, especially in romantic poetry, but the lines about
mending it are entirely characteristic of Emily Dickinson, a
refusal of unearned sublimity. The day as huge as yesterdays
in pairs is some dreadful messenger of doom, vetoing her
vision; and instead of the romantic sighing of the lyre there
is the horrible laugh, the imagination collapsing in hysteria.
The question with which the poem ends is not "Was I mad?"
but "Am I mad?" "Could it be Madness—this?" A contemporary poet will interrupt his dangerous narrative to
say, "My mind's not right," [5] and a few lines later he will call
on Milton's Satan to define his fear. The call seems self-
indulgent now by comparison with the starkness of Emily
Dickinson's poem: "that person that I was—/And this One
—do not feel the same—."

This points up one of the most remarkable characteristics
of Emily Dickinson's poetry: she owes less to authority than

any other American poet of her time. She took very little,
in fact, from the available sources—from other poets, for
instance. Even from her hymnbook she took only the meters.
And she took virtually nothing from the traditional source
of sources, nature. As far as her poems are concerned, natural
forms are vivid, and this is good. But she rarely suggests
that nature should do some of the work for her or should
ease the burden of the doing. She is sometimes coy with birds
and flowers, bees and buttercups, [97, 111, 133, 321, 442, 790]
but even when she entertains nature with sacramental
analogies [130] she does not require that nature bend her
will for the poet's sake. And her acts of celebration are just
that and nothing more. [214, 812, 1068] She will sometimes
use nature as text for a moral lesson on the merits of simplicity, [668] and these are lessons we have conned before.
But normally, far from urging nature to connive with the
poet's emotion, she presents it as more or less indifferent—
not alien or hostile, but simply mindful of its own business.
Indeed, she allows nature the same degree of independence
that she claims for her own imagination. "The Morning
after Woe," she says, nature seems to put on a big parade:

> The Birds declaim their Tunes—
> Pronouncing every word
> Like Hammers—Did they know they fell
> Like Litanies of Lead—
> On here and there—a creature—
> They'd modify the Glee
> To fit some Crucifixal Clef—
> Some Key of Calvary—   [364]

And there is at least one later poem to say, quite specifically,
that "Summer does not care—" [1386] and another to make
fun of pathetic fallacies:

> The Sky is low—the Clouds are mean.
> A Travelling Flake of Snow

Across a Barn or through a Rut
Debates if it will go—

A Narrow Wind complains all Day
How some one treated him
Nature, like us is sometimes caught
Without her Diadem.   [1075]

This is Emily Dickinson's scruple: if she sets up as poet, this is entirely her own affair, and she will not ask nature to sponsor, on her behalf, a Cinderella story.

If we bring together at this stage the characteristics of Emily Dickinson's poetry that we have mentioned—her self-confidence, the craving to know, the despair of having known, her trust in the imagination, the convergence of everything toward the poem, her living dangerously within a narrow room, the principle that small is all, her owing little to others or to nature—we see that these depend upon one assumption, namely, that the poet's soul is the center of the universe. I take this phrase from an essay by Antonio Machado, written in 1917. Machado has been complaining that contemporary artists have lost faith in the value of their own work, and he says: "When the poet doubts that the centre of the universe is in his own soul, his spirit . . . wanders bewildered among the world of objects." [6] We can think of Emily Dickinson as preeminently a poet who valued her own work, who believed that the poet's soul is the center of the universe. She would simply have added, "Why, of course." Without this belief her exaltation of "Circumference" would be meaningless. The belief once granted, we see how she moved with such remarkable grace among the world of objects. She bound herself "cordially" to that world and she treated it with proper tact. She did not smear it with her mystery. Hence there was no bewilderment, no aggression, no broken promise. This explains why she says, in one of her poems:

> Exhilaration—is within—
> There can no Outer Wine
> So royally intoxicate
> As that diviner Brand
> The Soul achieves—Herself—

And although she was little given to theorizing, there is one poem in which she considers her relation to the world of objects:

> Perception of an object costs
> Precise the Object's loss—
> Perception in itself a Gain
> Replying to its Price—
>
> The Object Absolute—is nought—
> Perception sets it fair
> And then upbraids a Perfectness
> That situates so far—

This is to say that an object, perceived, is humanized beyond philosophic redemption and can never again, thank God, be abstract or remote. (This does not invalidate the autonomy of objects or offer warrant for grinding them as grist to our precious mills.)

One of the advantages of this position was that it left Emily Dickinson free to adjudicate between the forces that urged or threatened or cajoled her. Hence the remarkably fruitful tension in her poems between will and law, the inner and the outer compulsions, temperament and tradition, Emily and Amherst. But we should not set these up as violent conflicts. Allen Tate has told us that Emily Dickinson had the great good fortune to write at a time when the New England Puritan doctrines had lost their first power but were still capable of dramatizing the human soul.[7] It may be so, though it is hard to see how such a tremendous burden could be lifted by a subverted or weary faith. In any event I think we make too much of this theme in relation to Emily Dickinson, just as we make too much of the image of the constricted heroine in the white veil. For one thing, Emily Dickinson carried very little theological freight. I do not suggest that she anticipates T. S. Eliot's Cousin Nancy, who in the poem of that name cuts loose in New England and shocks Matthew and Waldo, "the army of unalterable law." But she moved very lightly in matters of religion. It is unlikely that she had what Yeats calls "a talent for conviction." I think we should play the Puritan theme song very quietly when Emily Dickinson is our topic. Perhaps another comparison may make the point. It might be said of John Crowe Ransom that he had the great good fortune to write at a time when the quasi-aristocratic traditions of the American South had lost much of their compelling power but could still present a framework, a "myth," resolute in its remaining character. Ransom was well attuned to that mode of life and thoroughly understood its persuasive terms, but far from being impaled upon those traditions, he moved among them with some freedom and in his later years he found he could live agreeably apart from them. Perhaps it will be argued that he knew more than they, because they were what he knew. Perhaps. In any event there are certain poems by Ransom in which the Southern traditions criticize the individual will, and other poems in which the criticism goes the other way. But it will hardly be urged that he needed the Southern traditions to dramatize the human soul or that the traditions offered him that service. My feeling, in brief, is this: I cannot find enough evidence to show that the Puritan traditions bore more heavily upon Emily Dickinson than the traditions of the South upon Ransom. And as for the alleged constriction, there is really no evidence at all, where it would count, in the poems themselves.

Is it not significant, for instance, that when God comes into Emily Dickinson's poems He is as changeable as the weather, He has no fixed image? Sometimes He is inscrutable, [820] sometimes tender, [78] often capricious, [131, 597, 1751] often indifferent to human purpose, [376, 621] sometimes the Inquisitor, [536] the Good Neighbor, [623] or even the snob. [690] Christ is invariably more reliable, the good teacher, [193] the savior of robins. [153] And there are several moments comparable to this one:

> "Heavenly Father"—take to thee
> The supreme iniquity
> Fashioned by thy candid Hand—
> In a moment contraband—
> Though to trust us—seem to us—
> More respectful—"We are Dust"—
> We apologize to thee
> For thine own Duplicity.   [1461]

There is no constriction here. Emily Dickinson brought to her consideration of divine things precisely the same freedom and flexibility that she directed upon other things. She gave no special dispensation. If it is true for the Puritan writer that "the plain statement of fact vibrates with spiritual overtones," [8] Emily Dickinson was quite capable of reversing the process, testing every spiritual overtone she could find against the edge of human fact.

It is time to examine a few poems in more detail and we shall begin with this one:

> The Soul selects her own Society—
> Then—shuts the Door—
> To her divine Majority—
> Present no more—
>
> Unmoved—she notes the Chariots—pausing—
> At her low Gate—
> Unmoved—an Emperor be kneeling
> Upon her Mat—
>
> I've known her—from an ample nation—
> Choose One—

Then—close the Valves of her attention—
Like Stone— [303]

The grammar is as strange as everyone has remarked. No one knows why Emily Dickinson had such a rooted objection to the third-person-singular form of the verb. The word "present" may be an imperative, as if addressed to a by-standing royal page, and "an Emperor be kneeling" may be a cursory version of the present continuous. (These are desperate suggestions, but they are all I have.) In more fortunate respects the poem is typical of Emily Dickinson's best work. The violence and extremity of the soul's choice are refracted through the formality of the phrases, and the facts are given in such a manner as to balance gracefully between the particular case and a general law. Magisterial generalization is sharpened by the cadence of an individual act ("I've known her . . .") until, like the object perceived, it is indelibly humanized. In "Little Gidding," T. S. Eliot praises "the common word exact without vulgarity/The formal word precise but not pedantic." Emily Dickinson's poem answers. The repetition of "Unmoved" is rather portentous perhaps, but otherwise the style is impeccable.

And it should be said that Emily Dickinson is very rarely portentous, even when she offers moral generalizations. She invariably dramatizes the idea just enough to make us see the meaning in human terms, as a human action—in this poem, for instance:

Did Our Best Moment last—
'Twould supersede the Heaven—
A few—and they by Risk—procure—
So this Sort—are not given—

Except as stimulants—in
Cases of Despair—
Or Stupor—The Reserve—
These Heavenly Moments are—

A Grant of the Divine—
That Certain as it Comes—
Withdraws—and leaves the dazzled Soul
In her unfurnished Rooms   [393]

This is an extremely daring version of a topic, a line of feeling, common enough in poets like Herbert and Vaughan, with this difference: that Herbert especially goes out of his way to make God's case sound reasonable if not generous. Emily Dickinson's God is a shrewd doctor with a certain interest vested in illness. He plays life and illness against one another, adjusting the proportions of each with a view to keeping himself in business, prolonging life only to the extent of ensuring a constant supply of bodies susceptible to illness. And the dazzled soul after each session of stimulation finds herself back in a "deep but dazzling darkness." And her room is bare. Emily Dickinson merely "gives the facts" without any comment except that implied by their choice and disposition. But by placing them halfway between the particular and the general, she makes it impossible for us to shrug them off either as loose generalizations or as exceptions to a divinely benign rule. And sometimes she will begin a poem in very general terms, as if she were reciting a familiar lesson, but before the poem is finished she will have turned it almost into a drama or a novel, full of individual event:

Much Madness is divinest Sense—
To a discerning Eye—
Much Sense—the starkest Madness—
'Tis the Majority
In this, as All, prevail—
Assent—and you are sane—
Demur—you're straightway dangerous—
And handled with a Chain—   [435]

There is no anticipating that chain or the savagery that made it, or that other kind of savagery in Emily Dickinson that placed it there at the end of her poem without apology. Savagery is part of what she knew. She spots it when boys, seeing a mattress flung out from a house where someone has died, wonder "if it died—on that—" [389]; or she sees it in the minister who goes into the house of death:

> The Minister—goes stiffly in—
> As if the House were His—
> And He owned all the Mourners—now—

This is one way of doing it, as if to say, "I did not cause the facts, I merely report them; make what you will of them." This is one of Emily Dickinson's favorite devices. Another version of it is to interpose a neutral force between herself and the difficult facts. Very often between the suffering and the victim she will insert something that has its own life, independent and indifferent. The great example of this is the fly that comes between her and her death:

> I heard a Fly buzz—when I died—
> The Stillness in the Room
> Was like the Stillness in the Air—
> Between the Heaves of Storm—
>
> The Eyes around—had wrung them dry—
> And Breaths were gathering firm
> For that last Onset—when the King—
> Be witnessed—in the Room—
>
> I willed my Keepsakes—Signed away
> What portion of me be
> Assignable—and then it was
> There interposed a Fly—
>
> With Blue—uncertain stumbling Buzz—
> Between the light—and me—
> And then the Windows failed—and then
> I could not see to see—   [465]

This is virtually an anthology of interludes. The stillness is between two storms: the eyes are wrung dry between bouts of tears; the breaths are firm between shocks; and between the failing inner light and the darkening windows there is the fly, with its own stumbles and uncertainties. The windows are said to fail because the light fails, but it would be quite wrong to think that the stumbling uncertain buzz of the fly is an echo, in sympathy, of the uncertain stumbling one who is dying. Quite the reverse. The neutrality of the fly in human affairs is impeccable.

This respect for the facts is part of Emily Dickinson's intelligence and part of her civility. She will keep the lines open, the pavements clean. William Carlos Williams praised Marianne Moore for ensuring that in her poems apples are apples and nothing more, and they are wiped clean so that no symbolic blur adheres to them. Emily Dickinson merits similar praise, with this addition: that while she keeps a clean poetic house she does not, as Marianne Moore occasionally does, fidget with hygiene. She gets on with her chores. In one of the great death poems she begins:

> The last Night that She lived
> It was a Common Night
> Except the Dying—this to Us
> Made Nature different   [1100]

She doesn't say what the difference is—she doesn't need to. Nor is she keeping some monstrous difference up her sleeve to produce at the psychological moment. She has other work to do: she has to convey the resentment, and so on. And, following the resentment, there is the feeling of constriction, attenuation, no room to move. And she gives this:

> We waited while She passed—
> It was a narrow time—
> Too jostled were Our Souls to speak

This is, in the highest degree, civility. "Jostled" is not at all a "brilliant" word; genius apart, it is the obvious word, if one's civility takes the form of a close relation between word and thing, word and act, word and event. And the poem ends:

> And We—We placed the Hair—
> And drew the Head erect—
> And then an awful leisure was
> Belief to regulate—

She means just that—"to regulate." There are many more spectacular possibilities, but Emily Dickinson is too scrupulous to entertain them. Some of the most memorable things in her poems are memorable in this scrupulous way: they stay in one's mind as notable instances of justice, as we remember shopkeepers who never overcharge. The word "surmised" is an instance, in the great poem "Because I could not stop for Death":

> Since then—'tis Centuries—and yet
> Feels shorter than the Day
> I first surmised the Horses' Heads
> Were toward Eternity—   [712]

One would not have balked at a much more dramatic word in the circumstances; the last stanza of a poem like this can be allowed a splendid flourish. But "surmised" is perfect, because we need the note of caution, of shrewdness—of prose, shall we say—to support the flourish of "Horses' Heads" and "Eternity." And there are many other examples of this justice, this civility: from one of the love poems, [418] "Not in this World to see his face—/Sounds long—"; from one of the poems about death, "The Heart asks Pleasure—first—/ And then—Excuse from Pain—" [536]; or again:

> Pain—has an Element of Blank—
> It cannot recollect
> When it begun—or if there were
> A time when it was not—   [650]

This is Emily Dickinson at her greatest: a serious subject, a marvelous propriety of cadence, a scrupulous justice in the measure of word and thing.

Hence her favorite subjects are those that have their own finite value, such as it is. A subject that is indefinite, that refuses limits, is alien to her, and she tends to leave it to others. She much prefers a single clear sound to indefinite reverberations. And therefore a typical poem tends to go like this:

> For Death—or rather
> For the Things 'twould buy—
> This—put away
> Life's Opportunity—
>
> The Things that Death will buy
> Are Room—
> Escape from Circumstances—
> And a Name—
>
> With Gifts of Life
> How Death's Gifts may compare—
> We know not—
> For the Rates—lie Here—   [382]

A name doesn't mean, in Emily Dickinson, fame, repute, a loss felt throughout the nation; it means the fixing of an identity, the definition of a limit. Death gives this, in the sense in which the end of a story fixes the limit of the story. It need not be a great story. Most poets want their stories to have indefinite radiations of indefinite meaning, and they often construe profundity in this flattering sense. Emily Dickinson was content if her stories meant what she wanted them to mean and then stopped.

This may help to explain why she wrote 1,775 short poems and not a single long one. She committed herself, as I have said, to single, definite meanings. "Finite," in her vocabulary, was a term of praise. If one mood supersedes another, well and good; if one fear is replaced by a different fear, they are

all finite occasions of finite poems, and therefore valid. There
is a poem [421] in which she distinguishes between image
and interview, image being the single vision fixed for as
long as attention takes the same form, interview being the
more various scrutiny from several angles over a longer
course. Shall we say that the values of the long poem are
those of interview—adjustment, measure, addition and sub-
traction, the modulation of perspective, the massive deploy-
ment of forces. And image is the short poem, the single
glance. If it requires adjustment, there will be time—we
hope—for another glance, in another poem. Emily Dickinson is one of the greatest masters of image. There is no
reason to think that she had any talent at all for interview.
Indeed, even in some of her shortest poems, the best lines
tend to be the first. Where a poem has two or three stanzas,
the first is invariably the one that does the work, the others
tend to peter out or to dribble away as if the energy leaked.
It almost seems as if her poems began in her mind as
aphorisms, and to make them into poems she had to develop
and amplify those first hints, and often even this degree of
interview was too much for her. There is a poem, for instance, in which she tries to distinguish certain "moments"
in the life of the soul:

> The Soul has Bandaged moments—
> When too appalled to stir—
> She feels some ghastly Fright come up
> And stop to look at her—
>
> Salute her—with long fingers—
> Caress her freezing hair—
> Sip, Goblin, from the very lips
> The Lover—hovered—o'er—
> Unworthy, that a thought so mean
> Accost a Theme—so—fair—

The poem is only halfway through, but already it has spent
its energy; the last two lines are a weary gloss upon the

splendidly bizarre beginning. And now she tries again, picking up the original cadence in the hope of borrowing some energy:

> The soul has moments of Escape—
> When bursting all the doors—
> She dances like a Bomb, abroad,
> And swings upon the Hours,
>
> As do the Bee—delirious borne—
> Long Dungeoned from his Rose—
> Touch Liberty—then know no more,
> But Noon, and Paradise—

This is just barely holding up. And she tries another tack:

> The Soul's retaken moments—
> When, Felon led along,
> With shackles on the plumed feet,
> And staples, in the Song,
>
> The Horror welcomes her, again,
> These, are not brayed of Tongue— [512]

And the poem has collapsed.

What she needed before she could do her finest work was a situation, a figure, that would set out most of the structure for her. She was in trouble whenever some little thing had to be amplified, developed, teased. In the great poems she seizes her theme, normally, not as an idea but as an image or, better still, a relation. And, best of all, the relation has domestic analogies or can be translated directly into domestic or social terms. And then there is a new relation, often a marvelous counterpoint between the intimate relation and the new domestic figure that it has annexed. And the most conclusive example of these felicities is "Because I could not stop for Death":

> Because I could not stop for Death—
> He kindly stopped for me—

The Carriage held but just Ourselves—
And Immortality.

We slowly drove—He knew no haste
And I had put away
My labor and my leisure too,
For His Civility—

We passed the School, where Children strove
At Recess—in the Ring—
We passed the Fields of Gazing Grain—
We passed the Setting Sun—

Or rather—He passed Us—
The Dews drew quivering and chill—
For only Gossamer, my Gown—
My Tippet—only Tulle—

We paused before a House that seemed
A swelling of the Ground—
The Roof was scarcely visible—
The Cornice—in the Ground—

Since then—'tis Centuries—and yet
Feels shorter than the Day
I first surmised the Horses' Heads
Were toward Eternity—   [712]

In this poem all the civilities meet. If we think of it as an achievement of language, we should say at the same time that it has nothing at all to do with a fussy search for the *mot juste*. Once Emily Dickinson had come to the point of imagining the social image—the afternoon visit, the drive into the country—and had perceived its justice, half the battle was won. She would still have to win the rest of it, but she would do that largely by attending to the "facts" as directly as possible. The style is at once dry and noble; but this is a bonus, a grace, given to her because of the fine confidence with which she entrusted the whole affair to the determination of its leading figure. In T. S. Eliot's "Portrait of a Lady" there is also an afternoon visit, but the point of it is that it is sustained by no meaning, personal or social. This is the difference between Emily Dickinson's "And I had put away/My labor and my leisure too,/For his Civility—" and Eliot's lady who says, pressingly, "I have saved this afternoon for you." And just as the modern visit has to be conducted on its own resources—and these are virtually nil—so the pressure upon the language is that much greater. Eliot has to force his language to do the whole job, in the absence of a genuine social pattern, an image, that would have eased his task or made it unnecessary. Both poems are remarkable linguistic achievements, but the linguistic *situations* are quite different. Emily Dickinson can use the language as an instrument, a willing instrument, in the service of realities that are not linguistic at all. The "proportions"—if I may speak of it in this way—are quite different in Eliot's situation. Hence the language, far from being an instrument in the service of something other than itself, is itself—in its purely internal relations—the engrossing object of attention.

The note on which to end is that in a very special sense Emily Dickinson "could not stop" for anything that would restrain her sense of life. This is the impression that emerges from the poems and, almost equally, from her letters. Jonathan Edwards, singing his great praise to the beauty of the world, goes on to say: "Hence the reason why almost all men, and those that seem to be very miserable, love life [is] because they cannot bear to lose sight of such a beautiful and lovely world. The ideas, that every moment whilst we live have a beauty that we take not distinct notice of, brings a pleasure that, when we come to the trial, we had rather live in much pain and misery than lose." [9] But this was not the source of Emily Dickinson's sense of life, and there are very few poems in which the energy comes from that direction. The earth was vivid to her because she lived upon it.

She praises the lark rather than the wren because the lark builds his house upon the ground. [143] In another poem earth is "the Heaven below the Heaven above," [756] and it seems to have the advantage; and if "Exhilaration" is a breeze that lifts us from the ground, [1118] the lift is useful only because it renews us to come down again. There is only one occasion in Emily Dickinson's poems in which she subverts her own earthy faith, when she says in a weary moment that "Earth at the best/Is but a scanty Toy—." But even then she acknowledges the high price we are prepared to pay for it. [1024] Wallace Stevens said that the great poems of heaven and hell have been written, but the great poem of earth not yet. And of course he is right. But Emily Dickinson has written many notes toward that supreme poem, and Stevens added some of his own.

Emily Dickinson is, indeed, a poet of earth, of ground, of time. She always preferred a bird in the hand to two in a promised heaven, and wrote a poem to say so in those terms. [1012] And in case we didn't hear her, she says again, "Forever—is composed of Nows—." [624] And in case we didn't believe her and would make her declare herself even further, she says:

> To be alive—is Power—
> Existence—in itself—
> Without a further function—
> Omnipotence—Enough— [677]

NOTES

1 "Feuillets d'Hypnos," in *Hypnos Waking*, ed. and trans. Jackson Mathews (New York: Random House, 1956), p. 102. ("Nous sommes écartelés entre l'avidité de connaître et le désespoir d'avoir connu. L'aiguillon ne renonce pas à sa cuisson et nous à notre espoir.")

2 *The Poems of Emily Dickinson*, ed. Thomas H. Johnson (Cambridge: Harvard Univ. Press, 1955). The bracketed number after each quotation refers to the number of the poem in this edition.

3 Wallace Stevens, *Collected Poems* (London: Faber and Faber, 1955), p. 376.

4 Stevens, *The Necessary Angel* (New York: Knopf, 1951), p. 24.

5 Robert Lowell, "Skunk Hour," in *Life Studies* (London: Faber and Faber, 1959), p. 62.

6 Antonio Machado, *Obras Completas* (Madrid: 1957), pp. 1219–20.

7 *The Man of Letters in the Modern World* (New York: Meridian Books, 1955), pp. 211–226.

8 Perry Miller, Introduction to Jonathan Edwards, *Images and Shadows of Divine Things* (Yale Univ. Press, 1948), p. 4.

9 *Images and Shadows of Divine Things*, p. 137.

CHAPTER 5

EDWIN ARLINGTON ROBINSON

J. V. CUNNINGHAM

ROBERT LOWELL

In 1933 Edwin Arlington Robinson was the "most famous of living American poets." [1] Today his good gray name is attached to a handful of short poems that are exhibited in the respectable anthologies. But he is no longer an audible voice in poetry except to those sturdy readers who take time to wonder why the long poems are not as good as they should be, or to a few rigorous and lonely poets who find Robinson, for one reason or another, indispensable. But if one poet is indispensable to another, the reason is likely to be interesting. To come upon Robert Lowell reading Crabbe's tales, for instance, is to witness a strange and exhilarating encounter. And if such authority issues from a poet as relentlessly unfashionable as Robinson, we are almost obliged to attend to it. Our text is the *Collected Poems*, a daunting book of almost 1,500 pages.

In offering Robinson as a poet of continuing relevance we shall find it necessary to make some concessions, and it is well to make them sooner rather than later. And it may even be useful to give the largest concession immediately. If we think of T. S. Eliot as perhaps in the highest degree a characteristic poet of this century, then we must concede at once that Robinson either did not know or was indifferent to the movements of feeling that lead to Eliot's revolutionary poems. And we know that such ignorance, such indifference, are hard sins to forgive. We think, for a nearer comparison, of Yeats, almost an exact contemporary, only four years older than Robinson. Genius apart, Yeats clearly ploughs a deeper furrow. We have only to compare Yeats's "Upon a Dying Lady" with Robinson's "For a Dead Lady" to see that Yeats took far greater risks of sensibility and that he seized the advantage of a much deeper personal and social context in which to work. Robinson's lady dies and proves what the poets have always told us, that time is a vicious reaper, going far beyond the duties of his post. Yeats's lady dies not to make a point or to show herself a tragic heroine. A certain kind of death fittingly concludes a certain kind of life, thereby endorsing both; to embody this is her task. Yeats exposed himself to the contingency of other people and knew that the image of his work would have to fit the squirming facts. Robinson at an early age came to know certain things, and he thought that there was nothing else to know. These things became his property, and we have them in the poems in that capacity. Many of the later poems are attempts to protect his property in an age of subversion and falling prices. The things he knew were, for the most part, the old terms, old categories, and he thought that they would serve every occasion. And perhaps in the long run they will. But Robinson underestimated the pressure they would have to bear. A term like "sincerity" is a case in point. Now, after Gide and Mann and D. H. Lawrence, we may still be ignorant of its meaning, but at least we know that the meaning is elusive. Robinson uses the word as if it were his property, impregnable. In "Captain Craig," for instance, he says:

> Take on yourself
> But your sincerity, and you take on
> Good promise for all-climbing.[2]

Again, Robinson pushed his property very hard. He put great stock in the idea of vision and action, and indeed a major theme is the disproportion between the two, the gap between what one can see and what one can realize in action. But it is not endless in its resource. Robinson keeps nudging us to witness his theme and to acknowledge that it is his very own. In "Merlin," for instance, Vivian says:

> Like you, I saw too much; and unlike you
> I made no kingdom out of what I saw—

But if this is Vivian it might equally be any one of twenty speakers in Robinson's poems. People in these poems see too much, or else they see it too late. Either way they are frustrate, and like Seneca Sprague they visit some of their frustration upon the reader, who has heard it all from Robinson before. Too much or too late; we are born at a bad time; vision and action do not synchronize. After a while, in Robinson's poems, this note begins to sound like a list of rules for membership in a gloom club. Robert Frost, irritated by one of George Russell's platitudes in the same key, wrote a splendid poem to say that the times are neither wrong nor right. Robinson never confronted this fantastic possibility, though he could have found it easily by consulting Emily Dickinson. In Book IX of "Tristram" Mark walks the battlements, groaning, "Had I known early/ All that I knew too late . . ." We hear this again in "Amaranth" and in many other poems. In "King Jasper" it isn't even a matter of vision—everything that happens comes, like Zoë, too late. Robinson's trains are scheduled never to arrive on time; we are all men against the sky. To use the terms of "The Wandering Jew," "the figure and the scene/ Were never to be reconciled." Robinson became more and more lugubrious about this in his later poems. Indeed, "Miniver Cheevy" is the only poem in which he treats it lightly, and it is one of his finest poems for that very reason:

> Miniver Cheevy, born too late,
> Scratched his head and kept on thinking:

> Miniver coughed, and called it fate,
> And kept on drinking.

Robinson came to lose this note, and it passed to other hands, notably to John Crowe Ransom in "Captain Carpenter." And in his later years Robinson felt that life consisted entirely of ironies great and little, and he became their devoted chronicler. Indeed, this was true to such an extent that when a phrase from a Robinson poem lodges in the mind or comes up unbidden, it is invariably a gray generalization like "the sunlit labyrinth of pain," "time's malicious mercy," "time's offending benefits," "the patient ardor of the unpursued," or "a dry gasp of affable despair." And the fretful note increased, especially after "The Man against the Sky." Robinson's favorite color was gray, while most readers have now been schooled to prefer, if anything in that line, downright black. Hence we feel that poems like "Cavender's House" have everything that a good poem needs except variety, so that even the well-made sounds become dull, like the "sequestered murmuring" of "Captain Craig." (There is a letter of Hopkins to Baillie in 1864 in which he offers terms for a discrimination of styles, and one of these he calls "Parnassian." This is a kind of style that is all too characteristic of its author. And Hopkins says that when a poet palls on us it is because of his Parnassian: we "seem to have found out his secret." [3] (Robinson has a great deal of Parnassian in those 1,500 pages.)

If we need a phrase to stand for these concessions, Robinson gives one in "The Glory of the Nightingales" when he speaks of "the embellished rhetoric of regret." This is the signature tune of his work, or much of it, apart from its greatest occasions. In "Amaranth" the stranger says:

> I am one Evensong, a resident
> For life in the wrong world, where I made music,
> And make it still. It is not necessary,

> But habit that has outlived revelation
> May pipe on to the end.

And so, alas, it does. But we are almost finished with concession.

It is usual to say that Robinson's good work is to be found in the short narratives, that the long poems are stuffed with sentimental heroes, tragic ironies, melancholy, and moral earnestness. This is a little unfair. None of the long poems is a complete success, but none except "Amaranth" is a mere failure. There are passages and often entire books in the long poems that are remarkable achievements. But I must be specific. Robinson's successful poems seem to me to be these: from *The Man against the Sky,* "Hillcrest," "Eros Turannos," "The Unforgiven," "Veteran Sirens," "Another Dark Lady," "The Poor Relation," and with some reservations, the title poem itself; from *The Children of the Night,* "Aaron Stark," "Luke Havergal," "Cliff Klingenhagen," "Fleming Helphenstine," "Reuben Bright," "The Altar," "George Crabbe." (I would not include the famous "Richard Cory," which seems to me a contrived piece.) From *Captain Craig* I would select "Isaac and Archibald," which is much better than the title poem, and I would add "The Growth of 'Lorraine'." The last book of *Merlin* is particularly good, but there are fine passages also in the third and seventh books. From *The Town Down the River* I would choose "The Master" and "Miniver Cheevy." *Lancelot* is hardly worth its ninety pages, but the conversation between Lancelot and Guinevere in the last book is memorable. In *The Three Taverns* the indispensable poems are "The Mill," "Souvenir," "Avon's Harvest," "Mr. Flood's Party." *Tristram* is also essential, and we will return to it. From *Dionysus in Doubt* I prefer "Haunted House," "The Sheaves," "Karma," "Maya," "Mortmain," and "New England." And at this point, with one-fifth of the *Collected Poems* still in

front of us, we have had the best of it. The last narratives
are all habit, little revelation.

Some of the poems I have named are famous and have
been in the common possession for many years. "Eros
Turannos," for instance, is a masterpiece, and "The Mill" is
equally fine. Several of these poems are maps to a land that
Robinson has made his own and we think of them whenever
we think of lives blocked off before their due date. Robinson is unequaled in the presentation of this land. In Shaw's
play *Heartbreak House* Effie cries out for "life with a blessing!" and Shaw would give it if he could, but the bombs fall
and Effie welcomes them. There are no bombs in Robinson's
poems, no apocalypses, and few blessings. In those poems
blessings are things that have been or never were. In
"Veteran Sirens" Robinson says, "Poor flesh, to fight the
calendar so long!" and this is a common burden in these
poems. "The Unforgiven" is one of the greatest in this line:

> When he, who is the unforgiven,
> Beheld her first, he found her fair:
> No promise ever dreamt in heaven
> Could then have lured him anywhere
> That would have been away from there;
> And all his wits had lightly striven,
> Foiled with her voice, and eyes, and hair.
>
> There's nothing in the saints and sages
> To meet the shafts her glances had,
> Or such as hers have had for ages
> To blind a man till he be glad,
> And humble him till he be mad.
> The story would have many pages,
> And would be neither good nor bad.
>
> And, having followed, you would find him
> Where properly the play begins;
> But look for no red light behind him—
> No fumes of many-colored sins,

Fanned high by screaming violins.
God knows what good it was to blind him,
Or whether man or woman wins.

And by the same eternal token,
Who knows just how it will all end?—
This drama of hard words unspoken,
This fireside farce, without a friend
Or enemy to comprehend
What augurs when two lives are broken,
And fear finds nothing left to mend.

He stares in vain for what awaits him,
And sees in Love a coin to toss;
He smiles, and her cold hush berates him
Beneath his hard half of the cross;
They wonder why it ever was;
And she, the unforgiving, hates him
More for her lack than for her loss.

He feeds with pride his indecision,
And shrinks from what will not occur,
Bequeathing with infirm derision
His ashes to the days that were,
Before she made him prisoner;
And labors to retrieve the vision
That he must once have had of her.

He waits, and there awaits an ending,
And he knows neither what nor when;
But no magicians are attending
To make him see as he saw then,
And he will never find again
The face that once had been the rending
Of all his purpose among men.

He blames her not, nor does he chide her,
And she has nothing new to say;
If he were Bluebeard he could hide her,
But that's not written in the play,

> And there will be no change today;
> Although, to the serene outsider,
> There still would seem to be a way.

We cannot set this aside as one of life's little ironies. It cannot even be disposed of as a domestic tragedy, because there is, literally, no conflict, no drama at all. Indeed, this is how the two lives are defined—by invoking several forms of drama in which these people could not now play a part. They are held as in a faded photograph, a fireside scene without the splendor of fire. They could not be pushed into a classical tragedy, though one might think of them if one were casting a play by Samuel Beckett. Indeed, like Beckett's characters, they are people to whom something once happened; they have had, presumably, "happy days," and now they know with a terrible certainty that the Lord does not hold up "all that fall." This is the point of the last stanza: these people are not only beyond praise or blame, they are beyond speech itself, like Krapp at the end of *Krapp's Last Tape.* Far from being the victims of tragedy, they could not now play a part in a Bluebeard melodrama. And the serene outsiders—you and I—shake our heads and think that perhaps we, like love, could find a way.

Many of Robinson's best poems work along these lines. Like the Wall in *A Midsummer-Night's Dream,* they say, "the truth is so." And the truth is normally set down in a house, a village, a cage, in which people are transfixed. Harry Monchonsey in *The Family Reunion* castigates his aunts and uncles for being people to whom nothing has happened. In many of Robinson's poems they would be featured almost as happy folk. Robinson's characters still cling to the metaphor of action because they have nothing else to do. Their suffering is caused by the fact that, for them, the reality upon which the dramatic metaphor depends is dead. Such words as *decision, choice, do, event,* or

act are their only terms of reference, and these terms are—
for these people—dead.

Another remarkable poem in this way is "The Poor Relation." I give two stanzas, the third and fourth of nine:

> To those who come for what she was—
> The few left who know where to find her—
> She clings, for they are all she has;
> And she may smile when they remind her,
> As heretofore, of what they know
> Of roses that are still to blow
> By ways where not so much as grass
> Remains of what she sees behind her.
>
> They stay awhile, and having done
> What penance or the past requires,
> They go, and leave her there alone
> To count her chimneys and her spires.
> Her lip shakes when they go away,
> And yet she would not have them stay;
> She knows as well as anyone
> That Pity, having played, soon tires.

So pity is a fractious child, if not a naked, new-born babe,
and an afternoon visit to a faded relative is strenuous play
with little in the way of amusement. This is perhaps as sharp
as we like poetic tones to be. What sustains the poem is
that Robinson is scrupulously just to the occasion. He has
no interest in setting the table with well-placed ironies; his
object is—in Yeats' phrase—to hold reality and justice in a
single thought.

Another fine poem in this genre is "Aaron Stark," and
here the search for reality and justice is directed to keep
pity in its place. Indeed, this is common in Robinson's
poems. If his characters break their lives and waste them in
their cages, if life itself is pitiless, at least he will not have
its victims humiliated by your pity or mine. If his people are

isolated, he will leave them their privacy; he will not have it smeared by affluent offers of good will. Nor will he turn his little men into heroes to assuage our guilt:

> Withal a meagre man was Aaron Stark,
> Cursed and unkempt, shrewd, shrivelled, and morose.
> A miser was he, with a miser's nose,
> And eyes like little dollars in the dark.
> His thin, pinched mouth was nothing but a mark;
> And when he spoke there came like sullen blows
> Through scattered fangs a few snarled words and close,
> As if a cur were chary of its bark.
>
> Glad for the murmur of his hard renown,
> Year after year he shambled through the town,
> A loveless exile moving with a staff;
> And oftentimes there crept into his ears
> A sound of alien pity, touched with tears,—
> And then (and only then) did Aaron laugh.

Our response is changed, almost word by word. "Meagre" is neutral so far, and if "unkempt" brings out the beast of sympathy, we are meant to stiffen again with "shrewd" and "morose," and to continue hard with the snarling words and blows. But our sympathy is again enlisted for the figure shambling through the town, and especially for the loveless exile with a stick, who sounds like someone from *Pilgrim's Progress*—so much so that the pity Aaron hears is our pity, the tears are our tears. And only then does Robinson give him the last laugh, although this will serve no purpose except to reassert the claims of a justice poetic if not real.

Life broken against the cage of circumstance, where circumstance is featured as the malice of things and often embodied in another person—a husband, a wife—is Robinson's land of broken images. He doesn't blame God for it as insistently as Thomas Hardy does; his pages are not as relentlessly marked off by those capitalized enemies who, in

Hardy's poems, work for a malignant deity. Robinson took possession of those images, I think, with some ease. The difficulties poured in upon him when he went one stage further, featuring the malice of things within the individual self, the single state of man divided against itself. And of all the forms of division the crucial one in Robinson's poems is that suggested by the juxtaposition of reason and passion. Robinson was engrossed with this problem in some of his best and some of his worst poems. The worst we can tolerate if we think of them now as no more than notebooks in which he made random jottings for his great theme, turning them into verse in a spare hour.

"Demos and Dionysus" is a case in point. It is as bad as a poem can be that is a versified notebook, but it has the interest of a rough draft on a major theme. Demos and Dionysus argue at some length about the forces that we would think of today as totalitarianism and personalism. Demos is the spokesman of reason, the machine age, the elimination of personality. He tells us that in his Kingdom Come the recalcitrant will be "rationed into reason." And of course he is in all this a parody of that reason on which many would pin their hopes. Demos will promise us an administered paradise, a passionless state. Dionysus asks, reasonably enough, "What will be left in your millennium/ When self and soul are gone and all subdued/Insensibly?" And the argument drags its slow length along until Dionysus invokes a higher kind of reason, which we can call (though he does not) imagination. He says to Demos:

> I mean, also,
> An increment of reason not like yours,
> Which is the crucifixion of all reason,
> But one that quickens in the seed of truth,
> And is the flower of truth—not always fair,
> Yet always to be found if you will see it.
> There *is* a Demos, and you know his name

> By force of easy stealing; yet his face
> Would be one of a melancholy stranger
> To you if he saw yours.

It is not an engaging description, I am afraid, and it amounts to little more than the assertion that man in the fullness of time will live by the justice of his imagination rather than by "reason's click clack"—as Stevens calls it. The truth of imagination will set us free and make us whole.

A better parable on the same theme is the poem "Maya":

> Through an ascending emptiness of night,
> Leaving the flesh and the complacent mind
> Together in their sufficiency behind,
> The soul of man went up to a far height;
> And where those others would have had no sight
> Or sense of else than terror for the blind,
> Soul met the Will, and was again consigned
> To the supreme illusion which is right.
>
> "And what goes on up there," the Mind inquired,
> "That I know not already to be true?"—
> "More than enough, but not enough for you,"
> Said the descending Soul: "Here in the dark,
> Where you are least revealed when most admired,
> You may still be the bellows and the spark."

The logic will not stand much pressure, but at least the poem is pushing the problem a little nearer to the terms in which it will be usefully defined—terms of order and chaos, and the minuscule orders that are no answer to chaos at all but merely beg the question. But the very least the poem affirms is that the mind's typical fault is complacency, unless it is prepared to go beyond its own comforts, at which point it becomes imagination, its better self.

The best poem, however, on the theme of passion and reason is "New England," one of Robinson's most controlled achievements:

Here where the wind is always north-north-east
And children learn to walk on frozen toes,
Wonder begets an envy of all those
Who boil elsewhere with such a lyric yeast
Of love that you will hear them at a feast
Where demons would appeal for some repose,
Still clamoring where the chalice overflows
And crying wildest who have drunk the least.

Passion is here a soilure of the wits,
We're told, and Love a cross for them to bear;
Joy shivers in the corner where she knits
And Conscience always has the rocking-chair,
Cheerful as when she tortured into fits
The first cat that was ever killed by Care.

The lines are drawn very sharply here, but not so sharply as to be unjust or merely melodramatic. The images of constriction lead almost immediately into their extreme opposite, images of riot, *la dolce vita*. There is no sense in which the second images offer a serious alternative to the first, nor is Robinson putting them forward in that way. They are as "wrong" as the situation that compelled them, the nearest possibility of the human spirit when all the central imaginative possibilities have been constricted. One of the remarkable qualities of the poem is the control exhibited in the sudden change from the dramatic scene of riot to the mime of New England theory at the beginning of the sestet: "Passion is here a soilure of the wits,/We're told . . ." This prepares the way for the representation of joy and conscience as allegorical emblems, figures in a moral triptych. They are presented without movement, because movement implies an open situation of possibility and these two live in a world of morally constricting finalities long since established. They are the guardians of the law—in T. S. Eliot's phrase—and they reflect their master with daunting exactitude. Indeed, we have to think of them, since Robinson invented them, as the kind of people who inhabit several of his own narratives. Make conscience male and joy female and we have the synopsis of several bleak poems from his own country. In any event, the poem sets up its own values —ease, freedom, nonchalance, possibility—and the kinds of passion, love, joy, and conscience that those values would entertain.

In the long narratives love is often a cross for hero and heroine to bear, but it is sometimes more than that. In the third book of *Tristram* Isolt of Ireland comes to her lover:

> Came nearer still to him and still said nothing,
> Till terror born of passion became passion
> Reborn of terror while his lips and hers
> Put speech out like a flame put out by fire.

Isolt tries to console Tristram, and in one particularly lovely passage she says:

> Something in you was always in my father:
> A darkness always was around my father,
> Since my first eyes remembered him. He saw
> Nothing, but he would see the shadow of it
> Before he saw the color or shape it had,
> Or where the sun was. Tristram, fair things yet
> Will have a shadow black as night before them,
> And soon will have a shadow black as night
> Behind them. And all this may be shadow,
> Sometime, that we may live to see behind us—

And when she speaks of her love, "larger than all time and all places," she contrasts it with the normal, temporal loves in which the violence is subdued to a puny order. She says:

> I do not think there is much love like ours
> Here in this life, or that too much of it
> Would make poor men and women who go alone
> Into their graves without it more content.
> Or more by common sorrow to be envied

Than they are now. This may be true, or not.
Perhaps I am not old enough to know—
Not having lived always, nor having seen
Much else than everything disorderly
Deformed to order into a small court,
Where love was most a lie.

This is Isolt's theme, and it is one version of Robinson's—
the easy, puny formula that replaces the genuine form, the
tiny orders that cut down to size the passions that are the
substance of all orders, and their justification. This is where
the best of Robinson is to be found. He dramatized for
modern American poets one of the problems of a perennial
ethics. Some poets see it as the conflict between reason and
passion, others as that between authority and the self. I want
to think of two poets in this context, and say a little about
them, before coming back to Robinson.

The first poet is J. V. Cunningham, generally considered
a poet of intellectual rigor, who delights in exact statements,
concepts, sentences, resilient surfaces. And this is true. If
there must be a war between reason and passion, or rather,
if one of the perennial wars must be defined in those intoler-
ably simple terms, then he will enlist for reason. Indeed,
many of his poems have seemed to offer readers the comfort of feeling that the firm mind, even yet, can control
disheveled and violent experience. This is not, I think, the
moral of his story, but it is often implied in his poems. In
"The Beacon," for instance, he says:

Men give their hearts away;
Whether for good or ill
   They cannot say
Who shape the object in their will.

The will in pure delight
Conceives itself. I praise
   Far lamps at night,
Cold landmarks for reflection's gaze.

> Distant they still remain,
> Oh, unassailed, apart!
> May time attain
> The promise ere death seals the heart! [4]

This is to say—as Cunningham has said it [5]—that since so many of our desires are functions of our will—objects made by the will in its own likeness—we should try to deceive the will by interposing a safe distance between ourselves and the object, so that its otherness will be secured. We can then contemplate the object intransitively, and if time relents, we may even come to possess it.

Cunningham allows that this is a desperate expedient. Nor will it secure for us a unified life. Far from it. A man must live, Cunningham says, "divided against himself: only the selfishly insane can integrate experience to the heart's desire, and only the emotionally sterile would not wish to." For one thing, there is the fact that one's primary experience is absolute. "What is is, and even this is to say too much." [6] Hence the great achievement would be to integrate the subjectivity of passion with the objectivity of reason, thereby altering both as in a dramatic conflict. For the poet—although Cunningham does not use these terms—this would involve the grappling of opposites; in Coleridge's terms, more than usual emotion with more than usual order. Or in Wallace Stevens' terms, it would be a conflict of two violences, within and without.

When Cunningham speaks of the obstacles to the clear light of reason, he allows for several, including spiritual pride and that area of irrational experience that he symbolizes as the dusk. There is also necessity. And there is passion. In regard to necessity, a man is conditioned by the nature of his awareness. He lives only to accept and to adjust himself to the brutal fulfillment of his insight in the outer world. [7] It follows that "all choice is error," for choice implies "exclusion, rejection, restriction, limitation." This doctrine is closely related to another, the idea of evil as a defect of being. Cunningham interprets this very severely and, I think, goes far beyond the philosophical texts he might offer in his support. He says:

> Any realised particular, anything which is this and not that and that, is by the very fact evil. For to be this is to exclude not only any other alternative but to exclude all else in the universe. Perfection is in possibility, in the idea, but that which is realised, specific, determined, has no possibilities. It is precisely this and nothing else at all. It is lacking in all the being of the universe other than its own particularity. The more realised a thing is the greater its defect of being; hence any particular choice is as such evil though morally it may be the best choice.[8]

I should disagree with this on the grounds that a tulip cannot be said to lack anything in not being an elephant. The quality of being is embodied in particular existents, things that *are*. A thing is defective only if it does not realize its individuating form. A particular woman cannot be said to be defective because there are millions of women not she. Cunningham says that the problem, as he has defined it, is certainly central, "and very likely insoluble":

> For it is not merely philosophy but one's life. If [one] accepts the classic solution in which choice is thought of as the inevitable result in action of reasoned and considered judgment, then choice is completely determined in such fashion that the moral agent may be assured he has inescapably moved toward the best. . . . It is true that in classical ethics the rightness of right reason is considered to be constantly imperilled by passion, against which one must be unremittingly and warily on guard. But the consequence of this position is to enforce an absolute dualism of reason and passion, unmanageable except, perhaps, by religious and ritual means.[8]

The only way out, it would seem, is to go ahead and choose, and then protect oneself against the exorbitance of the choice.

Cunningham has written very few poems that are not involved in this dilemma in some way or other. But two poems seem to me particularly important in its development, a short poem, "August Hail," and a long one, the recent and very remarkable sequence called "To What Strangers? What Welcome?"

The subject of the first, "August Hail," was, he tells us, "the sudden incidence of passion, which comes like an impersonal force and apparently from the outside":

> In late summer the wild geese
> In the white draws are flying.
> The grain beards in the blue peace.
> The weeds are drying.
> The hushed sky breeds hail.
> Who shall revenge unreason?
> Wheat headless in the white flail
> Denies the season.

By giving the situation in meteorological terms, so that unreason comes as hail, Cunningham evades the ethical problem, more or less as Marvell in his "Horatian Ode" evades the problem of judging Cromwell's actions by speaking of them as bursts of lightning, natural events that do not raise an ethical problem, since they are not caused by man. But it is strange to find Cunningham, who is normally severe with the unreason of others, writing in an escape clause here that would make us all innocent. In "To What Strangers? What Welcome?" the issue comes up again in a much more problematic setting.

The new sequence has a very simple plot: a man travels west, falls in love, and comes back. The poems begin with an epigraph from Robinson's long poem, "Merlin," the seventh book, where Merlin leaves Vivian and returns to Camelot. It is worth mentioning, perhaps, that Merlin's speech also evades the ethical issue by positing a neutral

curve of events in which he is implicated. "In Broceliande,"
he tells Dagonet, "Time overtook me as I knew he must."
And a few lines further, in a passage that Cunningham omits,
Merlin says:

> I shall not go back.
> We pay for going back; and all we get
> Is one more needless ounce of weary wisdom
> To bring away with us.

And even if he doesn't go back, Vivian will understand and
say:

> Time called him home,
> And that was as it was; for much is lost
> Between Broceliande and Camelot.

(It is, as Cunningham knows, one of Robinson's most beautiful passages.)

The sequence consists of fifteen very short poems, some
of only four lines, others about twelve or fifteen. It would be
pleasant to go through the poems now, line by line, but I
must jump over many lovely lines and passages to settle upon
those nearest my theme—the tenth poem, for instance, after
the falling in love:

> A half hour for coffee, and at night
> An hour or so of unspoken speech,
> Hemming a summer dress as the tide
> Turns at the right time.
>
> Must it be sin,
> This consummation of who knows what?
> This sharp cry at entrance, once, and twice?
> This unfulfilled fulfilment?
>
> Something
> That happens because it must happen.
> We live in the given. Consequence,

And lack of consequence, both fail us.
Good is what we can do with evil.[9]

When I read this for the first time I thought it exhibited a
weary determinism, almost a version of Manicheanism,
which I found disturbing. Cunningham has argued against
that reading, saying that the statements are "simply human;
more concerned with sorting the experience of a particular
context than with espousing the History of Ideas." [10] So we
must take the statements in the first instance as dramatic
expressions of the moment. If they were to be offered as
anything more—as doctrine, for instance—they would still
seem to me slack, especially the dissolution of an "act" until
it becomes a mere happening. In either event, it seems necessary to interpret "evil" in Cunningham's special sense as
"defect of being," a certain innate paucity of "the given."
And the sequence ends:

Identity, that spectator
Of what he calls himself, that net
And aggregate of energies
In transient combination—some
So marginal are they mine? Or is
There mine? I sit in the last warmth
Of a New England fall, and I?
A premise of identity
Where the lost hurries to be lost,
Both in its own best interests
And in the interests of life.

That is, the narrator, after his experience of passion, is struck
by what Cunningham elsewhere calls "the indeterminable
sources of personal identity," the void region of possibilities
whose principle of being is to be neither this nor that. Love,
"the allegiance of passion to a given external object," betrays
this inner void, forces it to yield up one of those multi-
tudinous possibilities. Hence the effect of the experience

has been to break up the tight order of energies that traded
under the narrator's name. The new order—when it comes—
will be different, because the emergence of that possibility
from the void into the light of historical day changes the
old configuration. At the moment the narrator is only "a
premise of identity," as if he had not yet quite emerged from
the "dusk" of things.

I have, of course, neglected nearly all those qualities in
Cunningham's sequence that make it one of the most beautiful of modern poems—the scrupulous rigor, the finesse of
cadence, the sturdiness and variety of the images. But I have
wanted to make one point: in Cunningham's new poems the
theme of reason and passion—which we isolated in Robinson's work—is extended and dramatized with the greatest
resilience. Far from arranging skirmishes between reason and
passion and fixing the fights in reason's behalf, Cunningham
is offering reason a more stringent challenge than any available in contemporary poetry. In the poem "Socrates" Yvor
Winters speaks of the mind of Athens surpassing the flux,
"when tongue and stone subside, her thought be sure." [11]
We hope it will. And in a recent poem Winters says that
passion running undefined "may ruin what the masters
taught." And we know it will. One part of Cunningham's
achievement is to dramatize the unpredictable run of passion, so that we can the better understand it, even if we
cannot anticipate its next veering. And to stand for all the
poetry I have ignored, I quote without comment the eighth
poem in this new sequence:

> The night is still. The unfailing surf
> In passion and subsidence moves
> As at a distance. The glass walls,
> And redwood, are my utmost being,
> And is there, there in the last shadow,
> There in the final privacies
> Of unaccosted grace,—is there,

Gracing the tedium to death,
An intimation? Something much
Like love, like loneliness adrowse
In states more primitive than peace,
In the warm wonder of winter sun.

The second poet who seems to me distinctly relevant is Robert Lowell. His poems have been offered to us, over the years, in several contexts. For a few years we were advised to consider him a major Catholic poet, and this gave us—depending upon our attitude to Catholicism—either a stick with which to beat the poems or a pilgrim's staff to help us reach them. Either way it was a temporary facility. We have also been told to think of the poems, especially the early ones in *Lord Weary's Castle,* as acts of violence directed against all the forces of constriction wherever the poet feels them—especially those associated with his own New England ancestors, guardians of a deadly law. This has now become critical orthodoxy in regard to Lowell's poems, and we tend to grasp it, on the principle that recommends any port in a storm. But I think we have settled down too easily. It is not very difficult to make a few generalizations about the New England ancestors, accurate or not, but there is very little evidence in the poems to support the sentimental image of a tender poet wounded and darkened by his membership in a great dark family. The occasions that incite those poems are invariably immediate, personal; we don't need to go back to Plymouth Rock.

In fact, I would suggest that the crucial theme in Lowell's poems—authority and the self—is a variant of Robinson's theme, reason and passion, and that the proper context in which to consider it is the context defined by Robinson. Teased out a little it amounts to this: the individual self can rely upon its own resources—such as they are—or it can accept the order provided for it by a compelling, totalitarian force, of whatever kind, or it can spend a lifetime searching for a more benign, more personal order, sufficiently firm to make its edicts persuasive if not legal. If the self refuses all external orders and trusts in its own direction, it runs the risk of exposure, loneliness, a terrible desiccation of spirit, utter chaos. There are several figures of this kind in Lowell's poems, notably the heroine of "Katherine's Dream" and the husband in "To Speak of the Woe that is in Marriage," the husband who "hits the streets to cruise for prostitutes." [12] And the condition itself is generalized in "Christmas Eve under Hooker's Statue" as "our fields are running wild." In "Colloquy in Black Rock" it is given in these lines:

> My heart, you race and stagger and demand
> More blood-gangs for your nigger-brass percussions,
> Till I, the stunned machine of your devotion,
> Clanging upon this cymbal of a hand,
> Am rattled screw and footloose.[13]

If the self takes the first opportunity of coming in out of the storm, it is likely to come upon an authoritarian order, and the price of this shelter is the attenuation of the self until he becomes the no-man favored by all authoritarian states. In Lowell's poems this force is offered in several forms: as "lion-taming Satan" in "The Ferris Wheel"; once as Mammon; sometimes as the narrator's father; once as "my cold-eyed fathers"; once as God; once as Hooker in the poem "Christmas Eve under Hooker's Statue," where he speaks of "the long horn of plenty" breaking like glass in Hooker's gauntlets; and once as Herod in the poem "The Holy Innocents." Indeed, this poem is perhaps the clearest version of the parable: Herod is the totalitarian order, the grip of claw, and the lovely alternative is Christ, whose order is sweet and gracious. But the world in 1945 knows only Herod, so the self, the spirit, suffers:

> Listen, the hay-bells tinkle as the cart
> Wavers on rubber tires along the tar

And cindered ice below the burlap mill
And ale-wife run. The oxen drool and start
In wonder at the fenders of a car,
And blunder hugely up St. Peter's hill.
These are the undefiled by woman—their
Sorrow is not the sorrow of this world:
King Herod shrieking vengeance at the curled
Up knees of Jesus choking in the air,

A king of speechless clods and infants. Still
The world out-Herods Herod; and the year,
The nineteen-hundred forty-fifth of grace,
Lumbers with losses up the clinkered hill
Of our purgation; and the oxen near
The worn foundations of their resting-place,
The holy manger where their bed is corn
And holly torn for Christmas. If they die,
Ah Jesus, in the harness, who will mourn?
Lamb of the Shepherds, Child, how still you lie.

And then, sometimes, there is a benign order. In Robert
Lowell's autobiographical poems this order is often embodied in his grandfather, especially in the poem "Grandparents" in *Life Studies*. In the Christian poems it is figured
in Christian emblems, as for instance the crucifix in the
poem "Concord," set off against "Mammon's unbridled in-
dustry." In many of these poems it is Christ himself, often
the object of prayer. In the poem "Adam and Eve" the narrator says:

> They lied,
> My cold-eyed seedy fathers when they died,
> Or rather threw their lives away, to fix
> Sterile, forbidding nameplates on the bricks
> Above a kettle. Jesus rest their souls!

In "Colloquy in Black Rock" the enabling image is the kingfisher, probably a half-echo from a poem by Hopkins, and
it brings the fire of Christ:

Christ walks on the black water. In Black Mud
Darts the kingfisher. On Corpus Christi, heart,
Over the drum-beat of St. Stephen's choir
I hear him, *Stupor Mundi,* and the mud
Flies from his hunching wings and beak—my heart,
The blue kingfisher dives on you in fire.

Religious belief apart, Christ was a fitting symbol of a new order for this poet, because he contained within himself the knowledge of blood and violence. It would be, in the highest degree, a personal order, not predatory or aggressive. This is why the last stanza of the poem "New Year's Day" is so important:

Under St. Peter's bell the parish sea

Swells with its smelt into the burlap shack
Where Joseph plucks his hand-lines like a harp,
And hears the fearful *Puer natus est*
Of Circumcision, and relives the wrack
And howls of Jesus whom he holds. How sharp
The burden of the Law before the beast:
Time and the grindstone and the knife of God.
The Child is born in blood, O child of blood.

And all of this is implied in the poem "Our Lady of Walsingham." Indeed, the motto that we might use as a way in to those poems in *Lord Weary's Castle* is the line of prophecy—"and the world shall come to Walsingham." Within our terms of reference we could give it a prose translation somewhat like this: The world's order, which shows every proof of out-Heroding Herod and going many steps further in the grip of claw, will one day give up its murderous cruelty and take to the benign order of Walsingham. And Lowell describes Our Lady of Walsingham thus:

Our Lady, too small for her canopy,
Sits near the altar. There's no comeliness
At all or charm in that expressionless

Face with its heavy eyelids. As before,
This face, for centuries a memory,
Non est species, neque decor,
Expressionless, expresses God: it goes
Past castled Sion. She knows what God knows,
Not Calvary's Cross nor crib at Bethlehem
Now, and the world shall come to Walsingham.

If it appears that this new order involves the obliteration of self, some—like T. S. Eliot—would be prepared to accept this, and others would regard the price as exorbitant. But I think we have to read the lines more carefully, and think of them not quite in doctrinal terms. There is a passage in Yeats, in "The Trembling of the Veil," which throws light on this. Yeats has been discussing a certain type of person who must not seek an image of desire but must await that which lies beyond his mind—"unities not of the mind, but unities of Nature, unities of God." Such people, Yeats says, must "hollow their hearts till they are void and without form," must "become the lamp for another's wick and oil." [14] Lowell's version is, "Expressionless, expresses God." And of course if she knows what God knows, she knows the fury and the mire of human veins. So the self is not obliterated; it is transfigured, rather.

If reason and passion—the "antinomies of day and night," as Yeats calls them—are given in this form, then the isolated self is all passion, and reason is the authoritative order, either gentle or rough, Christ or Herod. Where the only available order is authoritarian, totalitarian, the self will squirm and cower, or it will yield. Some of Lowell's most remarkable poems are written to dramatize this situation, where there is no middle term, no gentle order, no Christ, and no hope of finding him, and the self cowers before an angry God. The finest poem in this group is "Mr. Edwards and the Spider," in which Lowell uses the persona of Jonathan Edwards. We are to think of Edwards meditating upon God and man as

the tiger and the spider. The material of the poem is largely
taken from Edwards' boyhood essay on insects and his famous
sermon "Sinners in the Hands of an Angry God." [15] In the
early essay Edwards observed the habits of spiders moving
to their death in the sea. In the sermon he gave a terrifying
picture of God holding us over the pit of Hell as He would
a spider. We are held above the pit, at every moment, only
by God's arbitrary will and pleasure. (I think the difficulties
of the poem are eased somewhat if we take it as a letter written by Edwards to the elder Joseph Hawley. This man,
thrown into despair as a result of Edwards' sermons, cut his
throat and died on June 1, 1735.) The poem reads:

I saw the spiders marching through the air,
Swimming from tree to tree that mildewed day
   In latter August when the hay
   Came creaking to the barn. But where
      The wind is westerly,
   Where gnarled November makes the spiders fly
   Into the apparitions of the sky,
   They purpose nothing but their ease and die
Urgently beating east to sunrise and the sea;

   What are we in the hands of the great God?
   It was in vain you set up thorn and briar
      In battle array against the fire
      And treason crackling in your blood;
        For the wild thorns grow tame
   And will do nothing to oppose the flame;
   Your lacerations tell the losing game
   You play against a sickness past your cure.
How will the hands be strong? How will the heart endure?

A very little thing, a little worm,
Or hourglass-blazoned spider, it is said,
Can kill a tiger. Will the dead
      Hold up his mirror and affirm
        To the four winds the smell

And flash of his authority? It's well
If God who holds you to the pit of hell,
Much as one holds a spider, will destroy,
Baffle and dissipate your soul. As a small boy

On Windsor Marsh, I saw the spider die
When thrown into the bowels of fierce fire:
   There's no long struggle, no desire
    To get up on its feet and fly—
     It stretches out its feet
And dies. This is the sinner's last retreat;
Yes, and no strength exerted on the heat
Then sinews the abolished will, when sick
And full of burning, it will whistle on a brick.

But who can plumb the sinking of that soul?
Josiah Hawley, picture yourself cast
   Into a brick-kiln where the blast
    Fans your quick vitals to a coal—
     If measured by a glass,
How long would it seem burning! Let there pass
A minute, ten, ten trillion; but the blaze
    Is infinite, eternal: this is death,
To die and know it. This is the Black Widow, death.

Edwards is speaking on behalf of an angry God. Hawley
is the recalcitrant self, setting up thorn and briar against the
"fire and treason" in his blood, perhaps still hoping for the
intervention of a benign force with benign images. But
Edwards specifically excludes the possibility; the sickness is
past cure. And he demands that Hawley confront the truth
of the angry God in its authoritarian force, directly, without
mediation. In "Sinners in the Hands of an Angry God" he
says: "You hang by a slender thread, with the flames of divine
wrath flashing about it, and ready every moment to singe it,
and burn it asunder; and you have no interest in any Mediator, and nothing to lay hold of to save yourself, nothing to
keep off the flames of wrath, nothing of your own, nothing

that you ever have done, nothing that you can do, to induce God to spare you one moment." The third stanza of the poem is rather dark. A little thing, a worm, an infection of some kind, shall we say, can kill a tiger. But if the literal tiger can be killed, not so the God-tiger. Will the dead, the poem asks, hold up an image of the tiger and affirm its authority? Perhaps not. But have no doubt about the smell and flash of that other tiger, God, and his authority. If God chooses to destroy you, well and good; thus justice is served. In the sermon Edwards says: "They deserve to be cast into hell; so that divine justice never stands in the way, it makes no objection against God's using his power at any moment to destroy them. Yea, on the contrary, justice calls aloud for an infinite punishment of their sins. Divine justice says of the tree that brings forth such grapes of Sodom, 'Cut it down, why cumbereth it the ground?' "

I am arguing, of course, that this poem dramatizes one of the crucial positions in Lowell's theme, authority and the self. If you set up two terms and hope for the disclosure of a saving third, there must be a stern voice that denies this hope and challenges the self on behalf of a totalitarian God. This voice will have to reckon with others, hence the dialectic of Lowell's poems will canvass all the possibilities. And I am also arguing, of course, that it is better to read the poems in this way than to take them as issuing from his special position as a member of the Lowell family. They are wider in ramification, more general in scope. The search for a mediator between the self and a totalitarian authority is still proceeding in the recent verse plays and the recent poems.

In Robinson's case there was a resolution, of a kind. And it is to be found in the long poems. In *Tristram* after the hero's death Isolt lives with her dreams. *Lancelot* ends with the hero "Not knowing what last havoc pity and love/Had still to wreak on wisdom." Guinevere will not go with him, and he goes away alone, but a voice tells him that "a world has died/For you, that a world may live." And as he rides away he sees what he has always sought, the gleam, the light. The same vision is granted to Archibald in the poem "Isaac and Archibald," "a light behind the stars." *Merlin* ends with darkness over Camelot and Merlin's vision of "two fires that are to light the world." And on the last page of the *Collected Poems* the destruction of King Jasper's kingdom is witnessed by its sole survivor, Zoë:

> She was hearing
> Crashes and rumblings in the house behind her
> That she had left; and over her shoulder now,
> She could see flame within that filled the windows
> With more than fire and light.

Indeed the difference between Robinson's heroic narratives and the shorter poems, length apart, is that the legends offered him a release from the furies of reason and passion; sometimes a new dawn, sometimes an apocalyptic flame, often a gleam, a light. In the short poems, the poems of circumstance, there was often no way out. The Arthurian legends, halfway between time and eternity, gave him a visionary gleam that he could not find on earth and would not posit there. That was why he needed them.

There was another reason. He wanted to give his characters room to move and he thought he could not do so in the modern poetic world. Indeed, he offers little or nothing in the modern ways of poetry; no gargoyles of memorable phrase, no startling juxtapositions. Robinson is a poet as Hardy is a poet, putting most of his capital in people, places, things. But Robinson's best poems are finer than Hardy's, because Hardy's poems are invariably a little innocent, they think they have found the answer when they have barely defined the question. Robinson trusted his answers for truth but not for current application; the modern world would always evade them, making them look archaic. So much the worse. He would persist, composing thousands of words to prove against Yeats that words alone are not "certain good." The "good" resides in human events, people, modes of being, action and suffering: the poet's task is to understand. This is the "tradition" embodied in poems as different in other respects as Robinson's "Eros Turannos" and Wordsworth's "The Old Cumberland Beggar"; masterpieces, both.

NOTES

1 Allen Tate, *The Man of Letters in the Modern World* (New York: Meridian Books, 1955), p. 277.

2 Edwin Arlington Robinson, *Collected Poems* (New York: Macmillan, 1961). The quotations that follow in the present chapter are taken from pp. 151, 280, 709, 456, 348, 1319, 37–39, 46, 911, 917, 900–901, 613, 619, 621–622, 447, 177, 1488.

3 Gerard Manley Hopkins, *Further Letters*, ed. Claude Colleer Abbott (London: Oxford Univ. Press, 1956), pp. 215ff.

4 J. V. Cunningham, *The Exclusions of a Rhyme* (Denver: Alan Swallow, n.d.), p. 23.

5 Cunningham, *Journal of John Cardan*, together with *The Quest of the Opal* and *The Problem of Form* (Denver: Alan Swallow, 1964), pp. 27–28.

6 *Ibid.*, pp. 6, 39.

7 See *Journal*, pp. 27–28.

8 *Journal*, p. 26.

9 Cunningham, *To What Strangers? What Welcome?* (Denver: Alan Swallow, 1964) n.p.

10 Letter of May 10, 1964, from J. V. Cunningham to the author.

11 Yvor Winters, *Collected Poems* (London: Routledge and Kegan Paul, 1962), p. 101.

12 Robert Lowell, *Life Studies* (London: Faber and Faber, 1959), p. 60.

13 Lowell, *Lord Weary's Castle* and *The Mills of the Kavanaughs* (New York: Meridian Books, 1961), p. 15.

14 William Butler Yeats, *Autobiographies* (London: Macmillan, 1956), p. 247.

15 Jonathan Edwards, *Selected Writings*, ed. Clarence H. Faust and Thomas H. Johnson (new ed.; New York: Hill and Wang, 1962), pp. 3–10, 155ff.

ROBERT FROST

ROBERT FROST discovered at an early age that he had an engaging personality. The discovery was unfortunate and might easily have been disastrous. No one, least of all a poet, can afford to admire himself beyond the point of reasonable discrimination. Here is excess:

> Thine emulous fond flowers are dead, too,
> And the daft sun-assaulter, he
> That frighted thee so oft, is fled or dead:
> Save only me
> (Nor is it sad to thee!)
> Save only me
> There is none left to mourn thee in the fields.[1]

The object is supposed to be a butterfly, but the real focus of attention is directed elsewhere, to its handsome observer. The poet is too pleasurably aware that he is an attractive youth and that the flowers of language, those assonances and rhymes, will ask nothing better than to serve his beauty. The butterfly will collaborate, as Grantchester collaborated with Rupert Brooke. But the young poet knows too much, and it is the wrong kind of knowingness, the deadly half-truth that he is worthy to adorn any landscape, fit to give it savor, just by being in it. So the world is his backdrop. He has but to pose in an engaging scene and his distinction will be revealed. It is all done with mirrors. Here is one of many:

> And if by noon I have too much of these,
> I have but to turn on my arm, and lo,
> The sun-burned hillside sets my face aglow,
> My breathing shakes the bluet like a breeze,

I smell the earth, I smell the bruised plant,
I look into the crater of the ant.

We know little or nothing about Frost's escape from the exorbitant self—how it was achieved, what propelled that movement of feeling by which the self was persuaded to give up its privilege. But there it is, in *North of Boston, Mountain Interval, New Hampshire,* and *West Running Brook*—pervadingly, if not always. Frost would never draw a veil over the self, nor would he ever commit himself so deeply to the "otherness" of the object as to put himself into a lower case. He would have nothing to do with objective correlatives or escapes from personality. "Dying to give something life," as Sir Claude Mulhammer puts it in *The Confidential Clerk,* was not in Frost's line. He would always insert a quirk of phrase, a telling rhythm, a knack of attitude, to remind us that we are listening to Robert Frost, not some other fellow. And when he had given modesty its way for several poems, he would regret this laxity and strut about in the robes of a sage. This was his worldly version of that sensitive plant who exhibited himself in *A Boy's Will.* And then he would never lay aside that insidious charm.

But there it is—at its best, a rich personality. Aristotle knew that he who owns such a personality and the ways of revealing it is more than halfway toward communicative success. The critic discussed it in his *Rhetoric* as a method of winning, not by force of reason but by giving the impression of a solid character, true gold. In Frost's case, or that of his persona in the poems, the speaker is rural, though not rustic. He knows sorrow but is reticent about its deeds ("My November Guest"). He can hold his tongue. He has a flair for the behavior of things and for the weird configurations in which, darkly, they can appear ("The Road Not Taken," "Mending Wall"). He knows the code ("Trespass"), just as Faulkner's pious hunters know theirs. He is aware that there

are finalities besides the grave ("The Oft-Repeated Dream").
More, or trying again, he knows that one of his hardest tasks
will be to adjudicate between rival claims and to settle at
last—gently and often inarticulately—for the greatest:

> The woods are lovely, dark and deep.
> But I have promises to keep,
> And miles to go before I sleep,
> And miles to go before I sleep.

So he moves on. He knows that human relationships have
their own rituals and that the good neighbor will allow for
them, thereby celebrating them:

> Baptiste knew how to make a short job long
> For love of it, and yet not waste time either.

He knows that these rituals are often a matter of decent
limits, of letting well enough alone, and he says of John
Smith the explorer:

> It became an explorer of the deep
> Not to explore too deep in others' business.

This man has a stake in the country; he knows its values.
He is gentle as long as he can be, as long as no one trespasses
upon his property. After that, there will be trouble. And in
any event he asks no quarter.

When Frost is secure in his ways, when he does not feel
that he has to throw his weight about, he can often invite the
world into his autobiography without asking it to do his
work. Here is a case in point, one of the love poems:

> As I went down the hill along the wall
> There was a gate I had leaned at for the view
> And had just turned from when I first saw you
> As you came up the hill. We met. But all
> We did that day was mingle great and small
> Footprints in summer dust as if we drew
> The figure of our being less than two

But more than one as yet. Your parasol
Pointed the decimal off with one deep thrust.
And all the time we talked you seemed to see
Something down there to smile at in the dust.
(Oh, it was without prejudice to me!)
Afterward I went past what you had passed
Before we met and you what I had passed.

It might have been a soft poem, self-indulgent with butter-
flies, but Frost tests the feeling as a force behind the words
or under the words. He holds it back or holds it under with
the sturdy geometrical conceit, making it earn its place, making it emerge, if it is good enough, from the rapt attention
to details other than itself. And we err if we think the feeling
is neither out far nor in deep. The fact that this is not a
typical Frost poem merely tells us that our notion of a typical Frost poem may be too narrow. Frost asserts himself only
in the parenthesis "(Oh, it was without prejudice to me!)"
as if he were half afraid of losing his copyright. But he need
not have worried.

We think we have this poet right when we have placed
him beside other poets—beside Emerson, for instance, where
we set him with some assurance because he did it himself.
Or we place him between Clare and Wordsworth—Wordsworth for general affiliation, Clare for his confidence in the
direct word whether it be the *mot juste* or not. And if we
place him, as J. J. Hogan suggests, beside George Herbert,
we are not far astray, though Herbert's country parson has
a more severe role than the speaker in "The Black Cottage"
and—when all is said—a finer intelligence. What Herbert and
Frost share is a sense of "the way things are," though they
adjusted themselves to that sense quite differently. In Herbert that sense was endowed by Christian belief with a
"theoretic form," to which the poet was profoundly loyal
even when his eyes and his fancies played truant. If Frost's
poems have a "theoretic form," it is elusive, though I will

suggest one later and argue for its presence in the poems as an allegiance, whether we approve it or not. One possibility may be set aside. The form cannot be severely of the mind, and is much more likely to be temperamental, even a crotchet of feeling. When we think of the *Cantos* we think of many things in Ezra Pound that we would willingly let die, but the indispensable things include the great hymns to the human intelligence, the emergence of form from chaos, the hymns to light and crystal:

> that the body of light come forth
>> from the body of fire
> And that your eyes come to the surface
>> from the deep wherein they were sunken,
> Reina—for 300 years,
>> and now sunken
> That your eyes come forth from their caves
>> & light then
>>> as the holly-leaf   (*Canto 91*)

This is a note we never hear in Frost—the exaltation, the thrill in the sight of intelligence, mind, lucidity. Frost makes a rather strident gesture in "Sand Dunes," as if someone had challenged him and he wanted to produce his membership card, but it is not convincing. Indeed, reading the *Collected Poems* and the later collection, *In the Clearing*, one is struck by Frost's frugality in the expense of mind, how little he concedes to it. He is happy enough that the mind should be there, but he takes care never to extend it or put it under strain. He will allow it to speculate, to toss up a few possibilities in the air, but always on the understanding that it doesn't really matter, it's only a game. This is one of the things we least admire in Frost, and sometimes we resent it. There are many things in Eliot's poems that we would be happy to lose—his contempt for ordinary people, his reluctance to accept the fact that he is human, his distaste for men like Hardy and Lawrence because they are not Dante—but the one concession we must make is that Eliot has spent a lifetime trying to get things straight and concentrating all his mental powers to that end. With Frost we have the feeling that he used only enough of his mind to fix himself in an attractive pose. And we find this aspect of him tedious. The systematic repudiation of systematic thought cannot help us, at the last, especially if it involves—as it often does in Frost—an undue willingness *not* to understand one's experience. This is nothing like Keats's "negative capability"; it is much nearer to complacency. Often what proclaims itself as detachment or disengagement is merely intellectual slackness:

> I love to toy with the Platonic notion
> That wisdom need not be of Athens Attic,
> But well may be Laconic, even Boeotian.
> At least I will not have it systematic.

He toys too much.

But there it is. Frost communicates through one resource. He has it, and he expects his reader to have it—a sense of "the way things are." He counts on nothing more than humane axioms, self-evident truths incapable of proof:

> The witch that came (the withered hag)
> To wash the steps with pail and rag,
> Was once the beauty Abishag,
>
> The picture pride of Hollywood.
> Too many fall from great and good
> For you to doubt the likelihood.
>
> Die early and avoid the fate.
> Or if predestined to die late,
> Make up your mind to die in state.
>
> Make the whole stock exchange your own!
> If need be occupy a throne,
> Where nobody can call *you* crone.

Some have relied on what they knew;
Others on being simply true.
What worked for them might work for you.

No memory of having starred
Atones for later disregard,
Or keeps the end from being hard.

Better to go down dignified
With boughten friendship at your side
Than none at all. Provide, Provide!

There are poems by Frost that are all manner, all voice, and these are dispensable. And there are poems like "The Most of It" and "An Old Man's Winter Night" that Frost hands over to the facts of the case, committing all the feeling to the facts and giving the famous voice only enough leeway to be audible. These are the great poems, I would argue. And then there are several poems in which the relation between fact and voice is just, however precarious. The present poem, "Provide, Provide," is one of these. What gives the poem its power is its sense of "the way things are." Eliot would give its values short shrift, implying that the difference between the several conditions described is in any event negligible, the difference between boughten friendship and the other kind trivial. In "Little Gidding" the gifts reserved for age are:

First, the cold friction of expiring sense
Without enchantment, offering no promise
But bitter tastelessness of shadow fruit
As body and soul begin to fall asunder.
Second, the conscious impotence of rage
At human folly, and the laceration
Of laughter at what ceases to amuse.
And last, the rending pain of re-enactment
Of all that you have done, and been; the shame
Of motives late revealed, and the awareness

        Of things ill done and done to others' harm
        Which once you took for exercise of virtue.
        Then fools' approval stings, and honor stains.

There is no way of mediating between these voices. Frost
will say that shadow fruit is better than no fruit, fools' approval better than none. Eliot will say that all such distinctions are, in any event, beside the spiritual point. If
judgments are based on the jury system, Frost will win. If
the verdict is given by a rigorous and independent judge
who is strong on ultimate values and the ascetic way to them,
Eliot will be endorsed. But meanwhile we can say this: Frost
is weak on ultimates, but he knows that most of life is lived
in "the element of antagonisms," and this is the source of
the poem's pain. The last dry "Provide, Provide" is almost
a parody of the Biblical apocalyptic voice, but Frost knows
the difference between the two voices and would not deride
the first. This is the poem's saving grace.

Frost will appeal, then, only to those truths or half-truths
that we know by being human and extant. Hence there is
his trust in numinous anecdote, the story that begins as an
incident and flowers into a fable without losing the resilience
of contingency, illustrated in poems like "The Death of the
Hired Man," "The Ax-Helve," "Paul's Wife," "An Old
Man's Winter Night," and the terrible "Out, Out." These
poems find common ground between Jew, Gentile, American, European, Tory, Communist, Warren the Hired Man
and any tycoon you care to name, provided that each of these
imagined readers has retained his feeling for "the way things
are," his feeling for human axioms, in the press of rival commitments. Take a classic case in point:

            Some say the world will end in fire,
            Some say in ice.
            From what I've tasted of desire
            I hold with those who favor fire.
            But if it had to perish twice,

> I think I know enough of hate
> To say that for destruction ice
> Is also great
> And would suffice.

The problem of communication is clearly in abeyance for the life of this poem. What is rendered is a response to common experience, a psychological event brought to a degree of generalization without sacrificing its momentum. We can all share it, admiring in the syntax the speaker's control over the facts, his humility, knowing that the humility is nine-tenths of the control. There must be many readers who wonder why all poems can't communicate so easily. And they can point to many other poems—this one, for instance, in Yeats:

> Others because you did not keep
> That deep-sworn vow have been friends of mine;
> Yet always when I look death in the face,
> When I clamber to the heights of sleep,
> Or when I grow excited with wine,
> Suddenly I meet your face.

These poems are what they are, with finality. They move into central areas of experience, say what they have to say, and make no further demands. And there are hundreds of poems complete in this way—Wordsworth's "Complaint of a Forsaken Indian Woman," Synge's "Riders to the Sea," for example. I am reminded of Wallace Stevens, who said in an uncharacteristic moment in the *Adagia* that "Literature is the better part of life. To this it seems inevitably necessary to add, provided life is the better part of literature." Life is indeed the better part of these poems by Frost and Yeats, and this is why they enter the lives of their readers so unerringly. But they do not solve all our problems, and there are many areas of life that they do not touch and that we still retain, mostly to our distress.

When Yeats faced this problem he tried to undercut those contentious areas—mind, ideology, dogma, argument—and to effect human contact through those motives that are prior to all radical contention: the axioms of the body, our sense of the heroic, or even the Great Memory. Or again he would try to burn all contentions away with the great symbolic brand or flame that he invokes in several poems. Frost has his own strategy. He addresses us through our basic "drives" —nutritive, sexual, self-protective—through our sense of isolation, of idiosyncrasy. Thus he will present, as a parable of inner emptiness, a landscape at night and the snow obliterating the "quiddity" of things:

> And lonely as it is that loneliness
> Will be more lonely ere it will be less—
> A blanker whiteness of benighted snow
> With no expression, nothing to express.
>
> They cannot scare me with their empty spaces
> Between stars—on stars where no human race is.
> I have it in me so much nearer home
> To scare myself with my own desert places.

Responding to this poem, we warm to the speaker's tact, the high courtesy that leaves so much unspecified. The poet refrains from minute disclosures, because fine breeding and the circumstances of the case suggest that he should, not because he covets the murky splendors of ambiguity; he will be literal when the time comes. Meanwhile the poem reaches us because we have our own desert places. We share an incorrigible experience, contributing a little of the meaning from our own drought. This is how the poem works. But it would not work at all except for the speaker's tact. In Frost's poems a man has this "tact of words" if he can say:

> He fell at Gettysburg or Fredericksburg,
> I ought to know—it makes a difference which:
> Fredericksburg wasn't Gettysburg, of course . . .

Or if he can say this, he has it:

> They meet him in the general store at night,
> Preoccupied with formidable mail,
> Riffling a printed letter as he talks.
> They seem afraid. He wouldn't have it so:
> Though a great scholar, he's a democrat,
> If not at heart, at least on principle.

The tact goes with understatement and the preservation of decent limits, and it reveals itself most urbanely in the middle range of experience. Hence Frost's cultivation of the mean or tempered style, which affects ease of discourse:

> Spades take up leaves
> No better than spoons,
> And bags full of leaves
> Are light as balloons.
>
> I make a great noise
> Of rustling all day
> Like rabbit and deer
> Running away.
>
> But the mountains I raise
> Elude my embrace,
> Flowing over my arms,
> And into my face.
>
> I may load and unload
> Again and again
> Till I fill the whole shed,
> And what have I then?
>
> Next to nothing for weight
> And since they grew duller
> From contact with earth,
> Next to nothing for color.
>
> Next to nothing for use.
> But a crop is a crop,

> And who's to say where
> The harvest shall stop?

This poem is a liberal education, it justifies itself as easily as the crop. Wallace Stevens once agreed with someone who argued that in a poem the "something said" is important, but "only in so far as the saying of that particular something in a special way is a revelation of reality." And he added on his own behalf, "the reality so imposed need not be a great reality." ² I suppose he meant that it need not be a momentous reality, or that smaller realities will do for most poems; life and death need not hang on the word of every poem. The reality imposed in Frost's poem is large enough for the claims he makes. There is nothing glib, nothing portentous, in his assertion, for these notes are alien to the true Horatian "ease" that will not harden into the mold of formula. The decorum the poem serves is that of polite discourse, the statement—neither "low" nor "grand"—that knows its own range and is content. Frost's poems rarely make new meanings; mostly they remind us of ancient meanings and place them in settings that, perhaps for the first time, do them justice.

To propose Frost as a master of the "middle" style is at once to praise him, to point to his particular strength, and to mark his limitations. For it is useless to think of him as a poet in command of all the poetic resources. For one thing, he lacks the range of Eliot, from the remorseless acid of "The Fire Sermon"—a masterpiece of the "low" style—

> Unreal City
> Under the brown fog of a winter noon
> Mr. Eugenides, the Smyrna merchant
> Unshaven, with a pocket full of currants
> C.i.f. London: documents at sight,
> Asked me in demotic French
> To luncheon at the Cannon Street Hotel
> Followed by a weekend at the Metropole—

to the choruses from "The Rock," or "Burnt Norton"—a
poem that would have pleased Longinus—

> The Word in the desert
> Is most attacked by voices of temptation,
> The crying shadow in the funeral dance,
> The loud lament of the disconsolate chimera.

And Frost lacks that art of elevation by which a major poet
may sometimes, in a moment of grace, move into charged
meditation. There is Yeats:

> Some moralist or mythological poet
> Compares the solitary soul to a swan;
> I am satisfied with that,
> Satisfied if a troubled mirror show it,
> Before that brief gleam of its life be gone,
> An image of its state;
> The wings half spread for flight,
> The breast thrust out in pride
> Whether to play, or to ride
> Those winds that clamour of approaching night.

And there is Stevens:

> Was the sun concoct for angels or for men?
> Sad men made angels of the sun, and of
> The moon they made their own attendant ghosts,
> Which led them back to angels, after death.
>
> Let this be clear that we are men of sun
> And men of day and never of pointed night,
> Men that repeat antiquest sounds of air
> In an accord of repetitions. Yet,
> If we repeat, it is because the wind
> Encircling us, speaks always with our speech.

Frost never commands this kind of meditation. His own
kind is a slack affair, hardly more than whimsical patter,

especially in the longer poems. When he chooses to "raise" his style, it is usually to claim a "public" and representative emotion:

> The land was ours before we were the land's.
> She was our land more than a hundred years
> Before we were her people. She was ours
> In Massachusetts, in Virginia,
> But we were England's, still colonials.

This kind of thing would do well enough as a slogan, perhaps even as a pseudo-Emersonian essay, but not as a poem. I have no objection to the sentiments, and would vote for them if it were a question of voting and if I had a vote. But one of the functions of the imagination is to drive us harder than we are driven in the market place, to hold out against such simplicity, because the imagination is nothing if not critical. Indeed, sooner than let us sink into the loud clichés so dear to our hearts, the imagination will go to the very edge of subversion. In the present poem Frost has thrown aside his most engaging mask and picked up one that does him less than justice. The real Frost is like Antaeus, the giant whose strength depends upon contact with his mother, Earth; when Hercules lifts him off the ground, Antaeus is lost. The earth, which, as Frost tells us, is the right place for love, is also the right place for Frost's strength. When he abandons it and sings falsetto, he is betrayed by his familiars —slogan, pamphlet, evasion, whimsy.

Frost knows this, on the whole. He knows that his most reliable source of strength is the actual, the rock bottom, the bare human fact. Hence his piety toward everything elemental. We call it piety, he calls it love:

> I'd like to get away from earth awhile
> And then come back to it and begin over.
> May no fate wilfully misunderstand me

> And half grant what I wish and snatched me away
> Not to return. Earth's the right place for love:
> I don't know where it's likely to go better.

When Frost commits himself to the actual, his tone is nearly always beautifully poised, not with the poise of virtuosity—the trapeze artist's, William Empson's style—in-the-teeth-of-a-despair—but the steadier poise of humility and trust. This is the sign of his civility. But when this commitment breaks down or falls away in fear or weariness, he becomes strident, complacent, oracular. And sometimes, even in poems that otherwise are magnificent, he slips into self-pity:

> I have been one acquainted with the night.
> I have walked out in rain—and back in rain.
> I have outwalked the furthest city light.
>
> I have looked down the saddest city lane.
> I have passed by the watchman on his beat
> And dropt my eyes, unwilling to explain.
>
> I have stood still and stopped the sound of feet
> When far away an interrupted cry
> Came over houses from another street,
>
> But not to call me back or say goodbye;
> And further still at an unearthly height,
> One luminary clock against the sky
>
> Proclaimed the time was neither wrong nor right.
> I have been one acquainted with the night.

It is one of Frost's most impressive poems. Indeed, all that can be said against it is quickly said. The moral of the story is that the time is neither wrong nor right. We can't play Hamlet and curse the time for being out of joint, as Robinson did, for instance, in several poems that we have looked at. And yet Frost does, in a sense. He presents himself as the "man against the sky," the sensitive man keeping his own counsel in the black city. This is a song of experience, but unlike Blake's, it is a little ingrown. The city lane, the watchman, the rain, and the anonymous cry can hardly avoid becoming theatrical props to cosset the isolation and the tenacity of the silent hero. When Blake wanders through a blackened London, what he sees and hears is offered as evidence of misery—not, in the first instance at least, his. In fact, he detaches himself from the evidence so that it will stand there in its own right. Frost rarely manages to do this in his first-person poems; the events are invariably reflected back upon the nature of the man who was sensitive enough to notice them. This may help to explain why Frost's greatest poems are objective narratives—poems like "A Servant to Servants," "The Fear," and "Out, Out."

What is remarkable in the first of these poems is Frost's power to turn an anecdote of tiredness into a fable of radical dissociation, a dissociation felt by the speaker only locally, in literal terms, and resisted by her in the same terms:

> It seems to me
> I can't express my feelings any more
> Than I can raise my voice or want to lift
> My hand (oh, I can lift it when I have to).

And the deadpan speech goes on until suddenly the servant says:

> I have my fancies: it runs in the family.
> My father's brother wasn't right . . .

This is the flowering of what was darkly implicit from the beginning. And it is achieved without forcing the facts to deny themselves in the service of the tragic tone. Reading the poem makes one wonder if there are any facts from the dark side of life that it doesn't encompass or imply. And we think that it is closer to Hawthorne, Melville, and Faulkner than to anything else in modern American poetry.

"The Fear" is, of course, an early figuring of the drama

that is to be played again in "The Hill Wife." In the early poem the black presences that inhabit the world of man and wife are given spectral "body," as in a surrealist film. If these presences turn out, in the later poem, to be a tramp who walks away leaving behind him the image of a dank smile, and a dark pine scraping on the bedroom window, we are not therefore mistaken—even when the husband becomes himself a black presence, in "The Impulse" and "Home Burial." These presences are not specified in "Out, Out," but we have to assume their existence in order to make the fable endurable. They are discernible in the sweet scent of the sawdust, in the buzz saw that, snarling, leaped out at the boy's hand, and certainly in the stern, blameless practicality with which the onlookers, "since they/Were not the one dead," turned to their affairs:

> The buzz saw snarled and rattled in the yard
> And made dust and dropped stove-length sticks of wood,
> Sweet-scented stuff when the breeze drew across it.
> And from there those that lifted eyes could count
> Five mountain ranges one behind the other
> Under the sunset far into Vermont.
> And the saw snarled and rattled, snarled and rattled,
> As it ran light, or had to bear a load.
> And nothing happened: day was all but done.
> Call it a day, I wish they might have said
> To please the boy by giving him the half hour
> That a boy counts so much when saved from work.
> His sister stood beside them in her apron
> To tell them "Supper." At the word, the saw,
> As if to prove saws knew what supper meant,
> Leaped out at the boy's hand, or seemed to leap—
> He must have given the hand. However it was,
> Neither refused the meeting. But the hand!
> The boy's first outcry was a rueful laugh,
> As he swung toward them holding up the hand
> Half in appeal, but half as if to keep

The life from spilling. Then the boy saw all—
Since he was old enough to know, big boy
Doing a man's work, though a child at heart—
He saw all spoiled. "Don't let him cut my hand off—
The doctor, when he comes. Don't let him, sister!"
So. But the hand was gone already.
The doctor put him in the dark of ether.
He lay and puffed his lips out with his breath.
And then—the watcher at his pulse took fright.
No one believed. They listened at his heart.
Little—less—nothing—and that ended it.
No more to build on there. And they, since they
Were not the one dead, turned to their affairs.

Thinking of this poem, we recall what Frost said on several occasions, that poetry is what is lost in translation. But the present poem contradicts that aphorism, or at least modifies it so that it applies to some poems but not to others. I should prefer to argue, at the other extreme, that poetry is what survives translation. Goethe said that the important thing is what remains of a poet when he is translated into prose. This is a harsh test, and there is no present reason to enforce it, except to say that Frost's greatest poems could be separated from the rest by this means. And the present poem would survive the test. Charles Tomlinson says in one of his poems that "fact has its proper plenitude," and this is in line with our present argument. The plenitude of "Out, Out" is not, at least in the first instance, a verbal or linguistic plenitude; it is the plenitude of fact, of event, of plot, of what happened. And to this Frost adds the proper plenitude of modest words, which—when they have something to point at—point and take themselves off.

A question arises from Frost's poems in the present context: What are the possibilities for a poetry based upon little more than a shared sense of "the way things are"? Is this enough? Will it serve in place of those other "certainties" that are, for many readers, insecure?

Frost would seem to answer yes. Yeats relied on nervous improvisations, the record of exemplary lives, the pull of mind and body, or even religious patterns rented for the occasion of the poem. Eliot relied on Christian assumptions, some well in the light of day, others half-buried in the common language itself. Frost committed himself to the common ground he *knew* existed between himself and his putative reader. He knew, in several poems, that if he were to tell a moving story in a few common words, we would respond feelingly. And that, if not everything, was something. Hence he spent a lifetime finding out how much he could say on those terms. He is the poet most devoted to bare human gesture.

But this does not answer the question. Think of Frost and then of a poet like Traherne. Traherne "solves" the problems of his world, in many poems, by removing them to a higher ground on which only the pure can breathe. He annoys us when the removal arrangements are glib and automatic, especially when we feel that it cost him no real heartache to translate himself out of the human world. (Eliot often annoys us in this way too.) Frost is different. He doesn't solve the difficult problems, rather he evades them, mainly by living on the frontier, where a certain few problems arise so insistently that others may be ignored.

We will try again. The question before us is pretty close to Kenneth Burke's concerns in *Permanence and Change*, where he considers communication in its broadest sense as the sharing of sympathies and purposes. I. A. Richards would seem to answer our question, joylessly, by saying that once our attitudes and impulses are driven back upon their biological justification, those that are strong enough to survive are too crude to satisfy a finely developed sensibility. Such a sensibility, Richards warns us, cannot live by warmth, food, drink, and sex alone. But wait. Frost has shown in his poems that even if we are driven to rock bottom, to the biological imperative, enough remains to ensure the survival of human feeling, if not its constant operation. And that again is something. Warmth, food, fighting, drink, and sex are interim simplifications, local releases from the painful pursuit of "wholeness." Frost's poems acknowledge this, but without moving above rock bottom they also find interim peace in a bird twittering, "Let what will be, be," in flowers lodged but not dead, in women spinning their own cocoon of smoke. As to Burke, what he envisaged in *Permanence and Change* was not the preservation of a former homogeneity—he had Eliot's cultural program in his sights—but the establishment of a new one through the powers of fusion provided by a fresh unity of purpose.

Burke's writing at this point in *Permanence and Change* is unusually optative and hortatory. He speaks of cooperation to replace competition, yearning for a world devoted to ingratiation and persuasion. And he almost identifies style, piety, and decorum. It is a beautiful vision, almost a conceptual translation of *The Tempest,* and by its favored words it persuades toward its own end—words like *congregational, fusive, cooperative, participant, communicative, civic.* These are fine, resonant words, and the vision behind them glows with custom and good will. But—and here is our point—is the myth any more comprehensive than Frost's, the limitations of which we have seen? These myths differ in at least one crucial respect, which we will examine. But they are together in this, that they propose to build from the ground up, the ground being man as symbol-using animal. This is fine as far as it goes, but it doesn't go very far. And when is the fresh unity of purpose to emerge? And whose purpose will it be? And how will we prevent such a purpose from being a highly controversial linkage, just like the theological one?

Examining further the theological linkage, we find that Frost pretends to evade it, though in fact he rejects it out of hand. And although he was a gentleman, he would not have minded breaking other people's idols provided he could avoid being caught. Being caught, of course, would mean a fight on his hands that he could hardly hope to win by the famous charm, a matey wink, or a grin that said, "Take it easy, pal, I'm just a simple country boy." In Burke there is neither simple evasion nor simple rejection; there is, instead, translation. I have sometimes thought that what he offers in *Permanence and Change* is a method of "taking the harm out" of the Christian religion as an imperative by clinging to a secular version of it as an optative. In this respect his program is the reverse of Eliot's. Eliot, notably in his plays, uses the secular imprints of Christianity to push his audiences to the end of the line, into Christian worship itself. When he talks about the unconscious effect of poetry, this is really what he means and what he hopes for. Being a Christian, I should want the harm left in the Christian religion, and I should feel that Burke's program, however stylishly grounded upon the poetic metaphor, is feasible only if we all agree not to recall the divisive topics that he would translate out of dogmatic existence. And few of us could make or keep that promise. What life would be like in a Burkean condition of "pure" ingratiation I do not know. Most poems are the better for a good deal of impurity. And my own life seems to need a great deal of argumentative impurity to make it feel substantial. With that, we are back again in the gritty world of specific belief, specific commitment. Perhaps, then, Frost's poems provide at once the enactment of Burke's program and its critique. Reading Frost gives no scope for the trick-work of polemic. The best of his poems have a way of making the reader over in their own image, and this is their persuasive power. But they leave many of our stirrings unanswered.

There is one important element in Frost's poems that I have not discussed, but it is necessary to mention it at this stage, especially in the light of our speculations on *Permanence and Change*. I mentioned that Burke's vision of an ideal community would replace competition by cooperation. But of course there is no equivalent of this in Frost's poems. And this makes a difference. Burke would change the world by the sweetness of cooperation; Frost would leave the world pretty much as it is, only taking care to make himself strong enough to withstand it. And there are other differences. It often seems that everything in Frost's poems is to be explained as a nudging of temperament. Certainly the poems give an impression, through all their differences, of an identifiable temperament at work, answerable to no one. And this tends to make us conclude that there was no structure of conviction or idea in his society, in his background, from which the temperament emerged or to which it stands in any close relation. But this is wrong. If we look for such a structure in the America of Frost's youth, we find it—I shall argue—in the ideas of the Social Darwinists, especially in men like Herbert Spencer and William Graham Sumner and other voices that clamored in America from the 1870's up to the end of the century.

To support this it is necessary to bring the leading tenets of the Social Darwinists together, at least in rough paraphrase,[3] and to show their presence in a number of Frost's poems. The basic idea is that the natural world is a competitive situation in which the best competitors will win. Hence it follows that those who win are the best, and therefore the fittest to survive. Herbert Spencer believed that the pressure of subsistence upon population is bound to have a good effect on the human race. In any event, the whole effort of nature is to get rid of the weak, the unfit. "If they are sufficiently complete to live, they *do* live, and it is well they should live. If they are not sufficiently complete to live, they die, and it is best they should die." Hence the only feasible ethical standard is the right of every man to do as he pleases, subject only to the condition that he does not infringe upon the equal rights of others. (This is why good fences make good neighbors.) There is also the idea of the conservation of energy, or—as Spencer preferred to call it—the persistence of force. "Everywhere in the universe man observes the incessant re-distribution of matter and motion, rhythmically apportioned between evolution and dissolution. Evolution is the progressive integration of matter, accompanied by dissipation of motion; dissolution is the disorganization of matter accompanied by the absorption of motion." Hence Spencer inferred that anything that is homogeneous is inherently unstable, since the different effects of persistent force upon its various parts must cause differences to arise in their future development. Thus the homogeneous will inevitably develop into the heterogeneous. (Frost's version of this, in a poem of *In the Clearing,* is:

> A nation has to take its natural course
> Of Progress round and round in circles
> From King to Mob to King to Mob to King
> Until the eddy of it eddies out.[4]

And this belief also throws light upon his presentation of the family unit, in many poems, as a pretty desolate structure.) And, finally, the Darwinian view is that all changes in types of survival and kinds of fitness are considered without relation to ultimate values; there is no relevant value beyond survival itself. There is, of course, a milder version of this to which we would all subscribe: "the desire of the body is to continue, the deepest need of the mind is for order,"[5] and where there is a quarrel, the body claims priority. But the Social Darwinists went much further than this.

If we look at a few of Frost's poems in this setting, the

relation between his temperament and the ideas of Social Darwinism seems very close. There is the famous instance, "Two Tramps in Mud Time." The narrator is splitting wood when two tramps come by, and one of them drops behind, hoping to get the job for pay:

> Nothing on either side was said.
> They knew they had but to stay their stay
> And all their logic would fill my head:
> As that I had no right to play
> With what was another man's work for gain.
> My right might be love but theirs was need.
> And where the two exist in twain
> Theirs was the better right—agreed.

These arguments are strong, but the tramps don't get the job:

> But yield who will to their separation,
> My object in living is to unite
> My avocation and my vocation
> As my two eyes make one in sight.
> Only where love and need are one,
> And the work is play for mortal stakes,
> Is the deed ever really done
> For Heaven and the future's sakes.

So need is not reason enough. The narrator has need and love on his side, hence he survives and nature blesses him as the best man. The tramps are unfit to survive because they have only their need, and the Darwinist law is that they should not survive. And if people think that they should survive and should be helped to survive, there is another poem, "A Roadside Stand," that says of another kind of poor:

> It is in the news that all these pitiful kin
> Are to be bought out and mercifully gathered in
> To live in villages next to the theater and store

Where they won't have to think for themselves any more;
While greedy good-doers, beneficent beasts of prey,
Swarm over their lives enforcing benefits
That are calculated to soothe them out of their wits,
And by teaching them how to sleep the sleep all day,
Destroy their sleeping at night the ancient way.

This is the dogma of Herbert Spencer set to a tune characteristic of Robert Frost. And there are many poems that would document the case if it were necessary.

The shoddy part of all this, of course, is that one can only talk about the survival of the fittest if one has already survived. And the complacent acceptance of this fact induces a nasty tone in these poems that no amount of rural minstrelsy will evade. Complacency about war, for instance, proliferates through such poems as "The Flood," "On Looking Up by Chance at the Constellations," "A Serious Step Lightly Taken," "It Bids Pretty Fair," and this one, "Bursting Rapture":

> I went to the physician to complain,
> The time had been when anyone could turn
> To farming for a simple way to earn;
> But now 'twas there as elsewhere, any gain
> Was made by getting science on the brain;
> There was so much more every day to learn,
> The discipline of farming was so stern,
> It seemed as if I couldn't stand the strain.
> But the physician's answer was "There, there,
> What you complain of all the nations share.
> Their effort is a mounting ecstasy
> That when it gets too exquisite to bear
> Will find relief in one burst. You shall see.
> That's what a certain bomb was sent to be.

And then there is complacency about evil, as in the poem "Quandary," and complacency about waste, which is called "the good of waste," in "Pod of the Milkweed." In "New Hampshire" Frost says:

> We get what little misery we can
> Out of not having cause for misery.
> It makes the guild of novel writers sick
> To be expected to be Dostoievskis
> On nothing worse than too much luck and comfort.

As if this disposed of William Faulkner. In "Our Hold on the Planet" Frost argues from the fact that world population is increasing and therefore "surviving," that things can't be too bad:

> We may doubt the just proportion of good to ill.
> There is much in nature against us. But we forget:
> Take nature altogether since time began,
> Including human nature, in peace and war,
> And it must be a little more in favor of man,
> Say a fraction of one per cent at the very least,
> Or our number living wouldn't be steadily more,
> Our hold on the planet wouldn't have so increased.

In the little poem "Pertinax" he says:

> Let chaos storm!
> Let cloud shapes swarm!
> I wait for form.

He says it, of course, because he is a survivor, and he can afford to wait. And there is a poem with the fantastic title, "Evil Tendencies Cancel," to which the only response is "No, by God, they don't!":

> Will the blight end the chestnut?
> The farmers rather guess not.
> It keeps smoldering at the roots
> And sending up new shoots
> Till another parasite
> Shall come to end the blight.

We either gloss this over, or we accept the challenge it implies. If the chestnut is man, and the blight is evil, and the smoldering is pain and suffering, then what is this anticipated parasite that will end the evil blight? In what sense does one evil cancel out another? And even in such a transaction how can man gain? How can his suffering be reduced?

There is only one answer: Make sure that *you* are the one who survives; keep one step ahead of all the games. This is the moral of several poems—"A Drumlin Woodchuck," "In Time of Cloudburst," "A Leaf Treader," and many others. And the tone in which you do this is suggested by the poem "Bravado":

> Have I not walked without an upward look
> Of caution under stars that very well
> Might not have missed me when they shot and fell?
> It was a risk I had to take—and took.

This means, in effect, "*I* ignored God and *I* survived." And another version, which might well be the slogan of a reactionary politics today rather than an adornment of the New Frontier by its poet laureate, is "One Step Backward Taken":

> Not only sands and gravels
> Were once more on their travels,
> But gulping muddy gallons
> Great boulders off their balance
> Bumped heads together dully
> And started down the gully.
> Whole capes caked off in slices.
> I felt my standpoint shaken
> In the universal crisis.
> But with one step backward taken
> I saved myself from going.
> A world torn loose went by me.
> Then the rain stopped and the blowing
> And the sun came out to dry me.

If we bring most of this together, it seems to converge on those poems in which Frost defines his essential vision of man. And one poem seems particularly relevant, "The Figure in the Doorway." From a train traveling through mountains the narrator sees a man standing at his cabin door. He is utterly alone, no wife, no family, utterly self-reliant, far away from other people, societies, institutions:

> The miles and miles he lived from anywhere
> Were evidently something he could bear.
> He stood unshaken, and if grim and gaunt,
> It was not necessarily from want.
> He had the oaks for heating and for light.
> He had a hen, he had a pig in sight.
> He had a well, he had the rain to catch.
> He had a ten-by-twenty garden patch.
> Nor did he lack for common entertainment.
> That I assume was what our passing train meant.
> He could look at us in our diner eating,
> And if so moved uncurl a hand in greeting.

Social Darwinism petered out toward the end of the century; when the war came in 1914 its glibness and cruelty seemed repellent. (But it has emerged again in the 1960's.) In Frost it persisted through the wars, it persisted after Hiroshima, mainly because it was a matter of temperament rather than argument. And because it didn't have a label, it couldn't be inspected too closely. But it was there.

It follows that Frost's greatest poems are those in which he holds himself so firmly to the facts, devotes himself so lavishly to them, that they are, for the time being, everything there is. Even a meager list, which leaves out as many as it puts in, has to include these: the servant in "A Servant to Servants" saying "I shan't catch up in this world, anyway"; the pressure of the ladder in "After Apple-Picking"; the voice that says "Nothing" in "The Fear"; the sound like beating on a box in "An Old Man's Winter Night"; the

smile that "never came of being gay" in "The Hill Wife";
the great buck pushing through the water in "The Most of
It"; the horror on the girl's tongue in "The Subverted
Flower." And to acknowledge that the best poems are sometimes the famous poems, here is "After Apple-Picking"—or
rather, the end of it:

> For I have had too much
> Of apple-picking: I am overtired
> Of the great harvest I myself desired.
> There were ten thousand thousand fruit to touch,
> Cherish in hand, lift down, and not let fall.
> For all
> That struck the earth,
> No matter if not bruised or spiked with stubble,
> Went surely to the cider-apple heap
> As of no worth.
> One can see what will trouble
> This sleep of mine, whatever sleep it is.
> Were he not gone,
> The woodchuck could say whether it's like his
> Long sleep, as I describe its coming on,
> Or just some human sleep.

The noble, curial tone is supported by Frost's fidelity to the
facts of the case. Indeed, when he is at his best—as here—it is
characteristic of him to let the feeling ride upon the pre-
cision with which the facts are given. In this poem he is concerned with the quality of his tiredness, the nature of his
sleep, but these will come—in the poem—as they come in fact,
after he has done his job. First the job, the apples that are
gathered, then those that fell, and the cider-apple heap; and
only then the giving in, the tiredness, the sleep. There is as
much daring in the structure of this poem as there is in the
quirkiest details. (And, incidentally, what other poet would
start a poem with the line, "Back out of all this now too
much for us"?) This is where Frost really survives.

NOTES

1 Robert Frost, *Complete Poems* (New York: Henry Holt, 1949), p. 41.

2 Wallace Stevens, *The Necessary Angel* (New York: Knopf, 1951), p. 99.

3 What follows in these paragraphs is taken from Richard Hofstadter, *Social Darwinism in American Thought* (rev. ed.; Boston: Beacon Press, 1955), esp. pp. 36–37, 39, 41, 198.

4 Frost, *In the Clearing* (New York: Holt, Rinehart and Winston, 1962), p. 80.

5 John Peale Bishop, *Collected Essays* (New York: Scribners, 1948), p. 32.

CHAPTER 7

WALLACE STEVENS

IN "THE IDEA OF ORDER AT KEY WEST" Wallace Stevens sets up an imperious allegory to imply that in life we are sometimes victorious. The singer imposes upon reality her own imagination, until reality is taken up into her song and there is nothing but the song. And when the song is ended, the observers—Ramon Fernandez and the poet himself— find that even in their own eyes reality is mastered, more orderly; the sea and the night are fixed and disposed. And the poem ends:

> Oh! Blessed rage for order, pale Ramon,
> The maker's rage to order words of the sea,
> Words of the fragrant portals, dimly-starred,
> And of ourselves and of our origins,
> In ghostlier demarcations, keener sounds.[1]

By common agreement the sea is reality, things as they are that come to us without invitation or apology, often to be thought of as chaos. The fragrant portals are places of romance, realms of our desire; they are where we are when we rhyme "catarrhs" with "guitars." We may call them terraces of the irrational if we are prepared to think of the irrational as the unaccountable element in life as in poetry and to praise it, as Stevens did, in that sense.[2] And these fragrant portals, however splendidly irrational, are dimly starred, not sufficiently apportioned, not sufficiently understood, until the words for them are found and added. And the same applies to ourselves and our origins, whatever they are. We need for their safety "ghostlier demarcations, keener sounds." We need demarcations for a demonstrable order, ghostlier in the sense of more spiritual—which includes the sense of more spirited—and keener sounds for a more vivid ordering in the mind. For Stevens, the sea is not enough, reality is not enough. He needs the words of the sea, and if he cannot have them he will settle for words and let the sea look out for itself. But the greatest poem is words of the sea.

The question arises at once: What is the relation between the words (when we have found them) and the sea (when it has found us)? How do the words acquire authority—if they do? The ancient texts acquired authority from the structures of public belief that they endorsed and animated; the words were "in the script," [239] as Stevens says. Or they were parts of a tradition. But the situation, for Stevens, is changed. The past and its traditions are mere souvenirs, the structures of belief have dissolved in mid-air, and there is now (he says) no authority "except force, operative or imminent." [3] "There had been an age," he says in one of his poems, "when a pineapple on the table was enough." [4] It is not enough now. Hence there is no authority but the poet himself, no structures of belief but the structures he makes for his own appeasement. The poet's act of faith is: I believe in the inventions of my own productive imagination.

Stevens was driven to this assertion. At an early age he ceased to be a Christian, but he retained a deeply religious sensibility and spent a lifetime trying to console it for its loss. The loss and the attempted consolation are given in his most famous poem, "Sunday Morning." The loss, the heartbreak, come in phrases like "the holy hush of ancient sacrifice," and

> The tomb in Palestine
> Is not the porch of spirits lingering.
> It is the grave of Jesus, where he lay. [70]

The consolation is offered as "comforts of the sun," one's own imagination, liaisons, between the self and its environment, the continuity of "April's green," the splendor of life under death's shadow. There is no resolution, except in the sense that the poem ends when there is nothing more to be said; the loss remains. Stevens' entire work was an effort to find the consoling words, as if, in all his later poems, he were trying to find an answer for the questions raised, the losses registered, by the woman of "Sunday Morning." He would speak of reconciling us to ourselves "in those/True reconcilings, dark, pacific words." [*144*] In "The Man with the Blue Guitar" he invokes a poetry to "take the place/Of empty heaven and its hymns." [*167*] Like the general modern hero of William Empson's poems, Stevens will have to learn a style from a despair. If there is no truth, there is still fiction. Stevens says: ". . . in an age of disbelief, when the gods have come to an end, when we think of them as the aesthetic projections of a time that has passed, men turn to a fundamental glory of their own and from that create a style of bearing themselves in reality." [5] Or, as he puts it more succinctly: "We are conceived in our conceits." [*195*]

This is one way of saying what William Empson said in another, that "human nature can conceive divine states which it cannot attain," like the souls damned in hell who "knew the bliss with which they were not crowned." And Empson dramatizes the conceits, the consoling fictions:

All those large dreams by which men long live well
Are magic-lanterned on the smoke of hell;
This then is real, I have implied,
A painted, small, transparent slide.

These the inventive can hand-paint at leisure,
Or most emporia would stock our measure;
And feasting in their dappled shade
We should forget how they were made.

Feign then what's by a decent tact believed
And act that state is only so conceived,
And build an edifice of form
For house where phantoms may keep warm.[6]

This is as accurate a description of Stevens' *Collected Poems* as we are likely to devise: an edifice of form to replace the old structures. Many of the long poems are elaborately inventive hand paintings on slides; the projections return to assuage their inventor. And much of Stevens' energy is deployed to convince himself that he is not a phantom, that his life is not—as he called it on one occasion—a skeleton life.

But this is to anticipate. All we need say at this point is that Stevens gave up the search for truth, which he deemed a will-o'-the-wisp, and set about constructing his own fiction. The fiction would have several advantages: it would be in the image of its creator, it would be amenable to the whole range of his powers, it would always be under his control, like the art object that it would resemble to the point of identity. It would even change to suit its creator's desire for change. What more could one ask? The answer is: nothing more, except on those winter days on which the whole edifice of form would seem merely an arbitrary construction, a mere function of the will of its disconsolate creator On warmer days Stevens would say, "the imperfect is our paradise." [*194*] Things would be good for as long as they lasted, and when they died they would be superseded by other things. Thus the vacancy of life would be filled. Where there is nothing, you put yourself and your inventions, thereby raising desires and appeasing them. Life becomes a rhetorical situation in which you are your own audience. History becomes mythology; ideas that are or might be true are replaced by ideas that are undeniably beautiful.

There is one aspect of this that we should emphasize: history becomes mythology. There are some poets whose consciousness is historical. For these, tradition is a great drama of people and institutions, conflicts of values in their full temporal idiom. Allen Tate is a case in point. For him the meanings of history are resilient; they cannot be wished away by treating them as mere esthetic projections. And because Tate's consciousness is historical, even the timeless and the mythological are animated with the vitality of drama. In his poems—those like "The Mediterranean" and "To the Lacedemonians"—our forefathers are always alive. But in Stevens the past is not only dead but deadly. There is a remarkable passage of reminiscence in one of his essays in which he recalls a visit to the old Zeller house in the Tulpehocken, in Pennsylvania. He remembers a family of religious refugees, their Lutheran church, the graveyard, the cedar trees. Stevens describes these remnants only to emphasize the sense of abandonment and destitution, as he says, "the sense that, after all, the vast mausoleum of human memory is emptier than one had supposed." Later, when he went back to New York and visited the exhibition of books held by the American Institute of Graphic Arts, "the brilliant pages from Poland, France, Finland and so on," as he describes them, "books of tales, of poetry, of folk-lore, were as if the barren reality that I had just experienced had suddenly taken color, become alive and from a single thing become many things and people, vivid, active, intently trying out a thousand characters and illuminations." [7] This is Stevens in one of his most revealing aspects: he will entertain reality only when it has been refracted through the idiom of art, when the artist has certified it by giving it the seal of his own authority. This is the "mythology of self" that replaces history.

The loss of Christian belief and the loss of history are two parts of a unitary loss, just as, for Stevens, mythology of self and the supreme fiction are two parts of a unitary gain. Strategically, Stevens would deal with the loss by handing it over to people too destitute to have any other possessions, too low to deserve any. The people chosen for this indignity were the bourgeois-Christians, guardians of a middle-class culture. In "The Noble Rider and the Sound of Words" he speaks with some distaste of "the expansion of the middle

class with its common preference for realistic satisfactions."
And the distaste persists through the paragraph, so that even
when he speaks of modern communication as a method of
bringing us closer to one another and making us intimate
with people we have never seen, he goes on to say that these
people, unhappily, are intimate with us. And the next
sentence is a dismissal of the modern novel, the middle-
class consolation prize. Indeed, when Stevens thought of
such matters he invariably thought of the middle-class and
their crude force. In "Three Academic Pieces" he says that
"the resemblance of the profile of a mountain to the profile
of General Washington exists for that great class of people
who co-exist with the great ferns in public gardens, amplified music and minor education." [8] When we think of
modern writers and their contempt for the middle class we
often refer to Yeats, Eliot, and Valéry and reflect a little
upon the typist in "The Waste Land"; we seldom include
Stevens in the list. And yet we should. His distaste for the
middle class is as keen as Eliot's. And it shows itself only a
little more urbanely. Where Eliot sneers at girls who do
their own laundry, Stevens praises "the ignorant man." [9]
Where Eliot implies that there is a direct relation between
the health of the English language and the victory of the
Tory party, Stevens resuscitates certain images of nobility
and cultivates an imperial style.

We can put this another way, thinking a little further of
Stevens and Eliot. Common to both poets is a feeling that
the world of public affairs has been taken over by the middle
class. Hence, among other evils, there has been the replace-
ment of knowledge by power, the exclusion of contemplation, the degradation of mind. This partly explains one of
the crucial equations in modern literature, Eliot's equation
of virtue with consciousness. The clear implication of Eliot's
poetry is that the good life is the life of consciousness, that
the only really valid moments in life are the moments of

intense consciousness. In fact, much of Eliot's work can be considered as a translation of Walter Pater's exquisite moments into spiritual terms, so as to blur the distinction between the greatest sanctity and the greatest consciousness. Those who are incapable of such intense consciousness are beneath contempt and probably beneath the dignity of damnation. Much of Stevens' work, on the other hand, is an attempt to render to Pater the things that are Pater's.

And the first thing is consciousness itself. Stevens and Eliot are together in equating the good with the conscious, but Eliot goes on to press the correspondence toward an ethical and theological end, while Stevens' ends are incorrigibly esthetic. Hence where Eliot equates consciousness with sanctity, Stevens equates consciousness with vision, which is the imagination's sanctity. In "The Noble Rider and the Sound of Words" he speaks of the pressure of reality as "the pressure of an external event or events on the consciousness to the exclusion of any power of contemplation"; [10] and in "The Figure of the Youth as Virile Poet" he represents the poet as saying, "I am imagination, in a leaden time and in a world that does not move for the weight of its own heaviness." [11] Instead of the assembly line, the poet devotes himself to "incessant creation." [12] His leading terms are *imagination, metaphor, consciousness, creation, vision.* In the last chapter of *Marius the Epicurean* Marius, prostrate in fever, ponders the terms of his existence:

> Revelation, vision, the discovery of a vision, the seeing of a perfect humanity, in a perfect world—through all his alternations of mind, by some dominant instinct, determined by the original necessities of his own nature and character, he had always set that above the *having,* or even the *doing,* of anything. For such vision, if received with due attitude on his part was, in reality, the *being* something, and as such was surely a pleasant offering or sacrifice to whatever gods there might be, observant of him.[13]

To equate seeing with being, as Marius does, is entirely in
Stevens' spirit. I think of that passage in "Notes toward a
Supreme Fiction" in which Stevens invokes

> . . . a time
> In which majesty is a mirror of the self:
> I have not but I am and as I am, I am.   [*405*]

I also think of that later poem in which he says:

> And one trembles to be so understood and, at last,
> To understand, as if to know became
> The fatality of seeing things too well.   [*459*]

For theory I cite Stevens' gloss upon a line in "The River of
Rivers in Connecticut." The line reads, "And trees that lack
the intelligence of trees." [*533*] Explaining this to Renato
Poggioli, Stevens said: "This refers to the distortion of trees
not growing in conditions natural to them and not to houses
deprived of a setting of trees. The look of death is the look
of the deprivation of something vital." [14] It is entirely characteristic of Stevens to use the word "intelligence" when he
means a vital principle, the quality of being.

It is also characteristic of him, as it is of Marius, to put
seeing above *doing*. It is again as if the possibilities of action
were smeared by dirty bourgeois hands and Stevens were to
yield the entire realm of action and send it to the vulgar in
some distaste. After that he will console himself with the
reflection that "we live in the mind"; and if we do, "we
live with the imagination." [15] The poem is in that imperial
sense a rival world, set up in the service of contemplation,
an intransitive world. And within that world, of course, the
poet acts. Indeed, if the poet is Stevens, he carries all the unfulfilled acts that otherwise wander footloose and fretful in
an alien world and sets them astir in the nuances of the
poem. There, because their master is imperator, inquisitor
of structures, they will work or die. If you do not act in the

public world, and if you are not dead, you are likely to act in your private world with a vengeance.

Think of Vladimir Nabokov. If you draw a line from *Marius the Epicurean* to "Notes toward a Supreme Fiction" and produce it, after some years it will meet *Pale Fire,* the work of a man who brings "detachment" to an extremely fine art in the cause of his own delight. This is not to bring those three works into unseemly contact; it is merely to note a few of the possible modes of detachment. Nabokov goes through life in a space helmet so that he can construct objects eminently fit for his imagination to live in. Pater's Marius goes through life in search of "moments," exquisite conjunctions, flares of consciousness. Stevens went through life bisecting his life lines, to keep things clear or to get them straight. There is a time for being vice-president of the Hartford Accident and Indemnity Company, and there is a time for writing poems. In the first time a strong man moves competently through the world of public affairs; in the second, the same man builds a fortress of contemplation against the pressure of reality. In "Notes toward a Supreme Fiction" the major man comes, Stevens says,

> Compact in invincible foils, from reason,
> Lighted at midnight by the studious eye,
> Swaddled in revery, the object of
> The hum of thoughts evaded in the mind.   [388]

In "An Ordinary Evening in New Haven" Stevens says that "Plain men in plain towns/Are not precise about the appeasement they need." But a Platonist scholar, like Milton's, in his lonely tower in Hartford or elsewhere is more than precise about that appeasement; he is a scholar, almost a pedant, of appeasement. He is appeased when the imagination is fully occupied; and the imagination is fully occupied either with what it sees, or, seeing nothing, invents, constructs for the mental eye. A few phrases from

Stevens will mark this: "the hero of midnight," "not that which is but that which is apprehended," "fictive things," "let the lamp affix its beam," "words added to the senses," "the poem of the act of the mind," "the world as word," "the word is the making of the world," the scholar to whom his book is true."

We think of Stevens in this aspect of him, and then for contrast and sometimes for relief, we think of William Carlos Williams in any aspect of him. Williams had no interest in lonely towers of the imagination. He was never afraid that direct contact with the unimaginative would soil his own imagination. He lived a life of contact, not just because Whitman was its apostle but because he thought it the best life. Nothing human was alien to him. He was a great anthologist of human action, and he knew that the contribution of middle-class men to human life did not end with a taste for amplified music. There was more to be said, and he said some of it. He was never as eloquent as Stevens, he never had—in similar measure—Stevens' verbal resource, and he thought that a rough, human energy would answer all questions. He placed excessive trust in good intention, beginning with his own; he was always "one of us." And perhaps he was a little fey in singing as discoveries those things that any woman who has had a child knows by heart. He wrote too much, because there was too much to write and because he never mastered questions of scale and precedence. It is conceivable that his stories will wear better than his poems, because the stories keep him rooted in the particular incident, the human event before him, and many of the poems sound as if he were running for public office. Now that he has been dead for several years and we have only his poems, plays, stories, letters, essays, and memoirs, he lives for us as a way of life rather than as a corpus of finished work. He stands for all the possibilities implied in such words as *sympathy, action, suffering, person, love, place, time, America, fact, speech, truth.* Now that Stevens has been dead for several years, he lives for us as a body of work, and he stands for all the possibilities implied in such words as *contemplation, detachment, loneliness, impersonality, art, revery, vision.* We grow weary with Stevens when we cease to believe that "words alone are certain good," when we want more sea in the words. We become irritated with Williams when the poetic result seems less than the sum of its intentions. (But this again is to anticipate.)

It is necessary to effect these juxtapositions because Stevens invariably spoke of the imagination and reality as a grappling of opposites, using the idiom of action; but in fact we must understand his work in the idiom of knowledge and vision.[16] In "The Noble Rider and the Sound of Words" he speaks of the imagination "pressing back against the pressure of reality," "a violence from within that protects us from a violence without." In this sense the work of the imagination is "a vital self-assertion in a world in which nothing but the self remains, if that remains." [17] And again in this sense the imagination is the only force that defends us against the terror of reality. But Stevens pushed this to the strange conclusion that the mind's defense against the terror might well be successful—even in the case of war. Stevens could deal with war in his own special way by regarding it as one part of a warlike whole and setting up a rival "whole," a rival "world"—or several of them—which would engross the imagination and leave the spirit free. The way to cope with a terrible reality is to encompass it in the mind, and it matters not at all how this is done. As long as the imagination can grasp an object, the nature of the object does not matter, because its chief purpose, in Stevens' eyes, is to disclose the power of the imagination. Indeed, we should push this a little more. One way of putting it is that Stevens, who ceased to believe in the God of Christianity and found that there was nothing left to believe, filled the void with his own inventions. Another way of putting it is that when Stevens ceased to be a Christian he lost all the valid terminologies of action and knew that he could recover them—if at all—only by playing a part in a fictive drama of his own devising. Sometimes this was a comic part, as in "A High-Toned Old Christian Woman," sometimes it was the philosopher-king, sometimes Prospero—he had a large repertoire. The greatest role he would devise for himself would be God; the most splendid drama, a new creation; and he would play all the parts himself. His play would be called "The Supreme Fiction."

The poem to think of here is "Examination of the Hero in a Time of War." Stevens asks, "Unless we believe in the hero, what is there/To believe?" [275] But the hero cannot be located or named. Indeed, Stevens tries to coax him into existence by describing all the obsolete forms of him, the forms that no longer apply. He is not, for instance, the classic hero. He is not the bourgeois hero. He is not a person at all, not even an image. "There is no image of the hero."

> The hero is a feeling, a man seen
> As if the eye was an emotion,
> As if in seeing we saw our feeling
> In the object seen and saved that mystic
> Against the sight, the penetrating,
> Pure eye.

Perhaps it is better to say that we—our imaginations—are the man, the hero, since we are "capable of his brave quickenings." So Stevens is back where he started: the hero is the poet, type of the imaginative man. But the poem is not finished yet. Stevens keeps on trying:

> The hero
> Acts in reality, adds nothing
> To what he does. He is the heroic
> Actor and act but not divided.

This sounds somewhat like Aristotle's God in Book XII of the *Metaphysics,* the unmoved mover or pure act, and it may well be Stevens' humanist translation of it, in keeping with his earlier equation that says that God and the human imagination are one. Perhaps to emphasize that nothing supernatural is being mooted, Stevens in the next line makes the feeling humanistically "incarnate":

> Say that the hero is his nation,
> In him made one, and in that saying
> Destroy all references. This actor
> Is anonymous and cannot help it.

We need not go to the end of the poem. Once Stevens has devised his man-hero, he makes "the familiar man" extend his imagination to encompass the fiction, and the consoling transaction is complete.

How consoling it was to Stevens we have no way of knowing. It is difficult to believe that he was consoled by the conclusion reached in the poem, or indeed by any of his "conclusions." We can only assume that he was exhilarated by the actual procedure of writing the poem, by the manipulation of ideas, possibilities, connivances of language, by playing all the parts, by playing the most exhilarating of all roles, the Great Impresario, God. Instead of a God in whom he could not believe, Stevens set up a God in whom his belief was total.

This was one way of dealing with chaos, by playing the role of its Great Connoisseur, the God of Power who made the earth and heaven. Stevens goes beyond this: he first invents God and thereafter plays all His parts. And he comes close to saying this in "The Figure of the Youth as Virile Poet":

> . . . If we say that the idea of God is merely a poetic idea, even if the supreme poetic idea, and that our notions of heaven and hell are merely poetry not so called, even if poetry that involves

us vitally, the feeling of deliverance, of a release, of a perfection touched, of a vocation so that all men may know the truth and that the truth may set them free—if we say these things and if we are able to see the poet who achieved God and placed Him in His seat in heaven in all His glory, the poet himself, still in the ecstasy of the poem that completely accomplished his purpose, would have seemed, whether young or old, whether in rags or ceremonial robe, a man who needed what he had created, uttering the hymns of joy that followed his creation.[18]

This is what Stevens meant in that more famous statement of the poet's function: in an age of disbelief "it is for the poet to supply the satisfactions of belief, in his measure and in his style." [19] And it is also what he meant in "Variations on a Summer Day" when he said that "one looks at the sea" —at reality, shall we say—"As one improvises, on the piano." The only way to live is to improvise, in the absence of the great drama to devise little dramas, and, if nothing else, to arrange "happenings." And—finally, for this theme—it is what Stevens meant when he said that in the stress of modern life and modern art "reality changes from substance to subtlety." "Modern reality is a reality of decreation, in which our revelations are not the revelations of belief, but the precious portents of our own powers." [20]

This is one way, and for Stevens it includes all the other ways. The powers of the imagination appear differently in different settings. The imagination is sometimes the inventive will, sometimes the constructive will, very often the will-to-order, "the power that enables us to perceive the normal in the abnormal, the opposite of chaos in chaos." [21] In "Imagination as Value" Stevens quotes a long passage from Cassirer's *An Essay on Man* in which the climax of the theory of poetic imagination in romantic thought is given: the poetic imagination is now deemed to be the only clue to reality. Stevens quotes this and approves of it. And in his poems he pushes it to one of its available extremes. The reality disclosed by the poetic imagination is not Aladdin's cave; more often than not it is an acceptable fiction—call it "the world as word." [*268*]

I am arguing, then, that Stevens lost the terminology of action, put in its place a terminology of knowledge and vision, but tried to translate this second terminology into "active" terms, terms of drama and epic. If the effort succeeded, then knowledge would take on the hue of action, the connoisseur would be the hero, the connoisseur of chaos would be the tragic hero, and the exquisite moment of consciousness would be the moment of mastery. In line with this, Stevens speaks in "The Man with the Blue Guitar" of reducing "the monster to/Myself," the monster being nature, or reality, the reduction being a dramatic victory. In "Notes toward a Supreme Fiction" he elevates his tone and speaks of stopping the whirlwind, balking the elements. And there is "The Comedian as the Letter C," in which Stevens gives the search for knowledge as an epic pilgrimage, for which the appropriate tone is sometimes heroic, sometimes mock-heroic. This is his most elaborate essay in the translation of terminologies.

The comedian begins as a parody figure, Crispin, a European valet, a petit bourgeois. He is the imagination when it is less than itself, or a mere bourgeois shadow of itself, mere fancy, winner of easy victories, magister of ponds and shallow waters. In deep sea Crispin is "a skinny sailor peering in the sea-glass." Hence, Stevens says, "the valet in the tempest was annulled," and he became "an introspective voyager," a modern Candide, or a Passe Partout going round the world of himself in eighty days. But he is already changing; the sea is changing him, has changed him. He found that "his vicissitudes had much enlarged/His apprehension." But his most important discovery is that he is consoled only by his own imagination:

                                He perceived
        That coolness for his heat came suddenly,
        And only, in the fables that he scrawled
        With his own quill . . .

But he is still vulnerable, and when he is struck by the
storm in Yucatan he takes refuge, like the other victims, in
the cathedral of ancient ways. Nevertheless he is growing in
imagination, will, desire, and scruple. He plans a colony of
the spirit to protect his new intelligence. He takes stock
and finds himself still bland. And he plunges more deeply
than ever into the natural, the contingent. Time passes.
Reality encompasses him, silences him, blots out his words.
This seems to be the end of his story. Will he make it his
tragedy? Or will he treat his failure as an instance of all
failure, and by becoming its connoisseur, at once master it
and change it? Stevens asks:

        Was he to company vastest things defunct
        Arointing his dreams with fugal requiems?
        Was he to company vastest things defunct
        With a blubber of tom-toms harrowing the sky?
        Scrawl a tragedian's testament? Prolong
        His active force in an inactive dirge.

Or "Should he lay by the personal and make/Of his own
fate an instance of all fate? [*41*] This is very largely what
he does in the "Esthétique du Mal," the poem in which
Crispin's epic pilgrimage is extended into new territory.
Meanwhile Crispin persists. He marries, settles down, has
four daughters. His new life is good and comfortable even
if there is less of it than he once thought necessary and its
quality is more condign than he ever thought desirable. He
wants to live, in thought, more recklessly, tracking the
"knaves of thought," but he lives as he can, lives the life in
front of him, and concludes "fadedly" with a tolerable stock
of losses and gains.

When Stevens continues Crispin's story in the "Esthét-ique," he drops the mock-heroic tone and the whimsical wit. Instead of the earlier intuitions of reality in terms of sea and storm, the new confrontation sets the hero in a world of evil and death. The hero's scruple has deepened, so the occasion for parody is over. At one point he says:

> It may be that one life is a punishment
> For another, as the son's life for the father's.
> But that concerns the secondary characters.
> It is a fragmentary tragedy
> Within the universal whole. The son
> And the father alike and equally are spent,
> Each one, by the necessity of being
> Himself, the unalterable necessity
> Of being this unalterable animal.
> This force of nature in action is the major
> Tragedy. This is destiny unperplexed,
> The happiest enemy. And it may be
> That in his Mediterranean cloister a man,
> Reclining, eased of desire, establishes
> The visible, a zone of blue and orange
> Versicolorings, establishes a time
> To watch the fire-feinting sea and calls it good,
> The ultimate good, sure of a reality
> Of the longest meditation, the maximum,
> The assassin's scene. Evil in evil is
> Comparative.   [*323–324*]

The major tragedy is the force of nature in action, because man can deal with this force only deviously, by knowledge. And the only way he can deal with one evil is to say that it is comparative, only part of a greater evil, which we must evade as best we can. This part of the poem ends:

>   The assassin discloses himself,
>   The force that destroys us is disclosed, within
>   This maximum, an adventure to be endured

With the politest helplessness. Ay-mi!
One feels its action moving in the blood.

In "Extracts from Addresses to the Academy of Fine Ideas" the philosophic assassins shot it out and the best man won. His prize was the right to sing a liaison between himself and the night, a song in chaos that consoled him. In the "Esthétique" the assassin is nature's henchman, the heavy gangster, and gangland's methods are evil and death, "an adventure to be endured/With the politest helplessness." It sounds like Hamlet in Act V, expressing his politest helplessness to Horatio with illustrations of falling sparrows. But the difference is that Hamlet with all his veerings and ambiguities has something still to do. He has to be God's henchman, the unpaid assassin, he has to kill Claudius and hand on a purified kingdom through Horatio to Fortinbras. Stevens' hero has nothing to do. The "Esthétique," a humanist's progress, has nothing to say about evil except that it is comparative. So the poem drifts away in yet another hymn to the credences of summer.

The problem persists: in chaos, what can a man do? Can he do anything? Is there any use in committing oneself to "the destructive element," Conrad's sea of things? Or can one man differ from another only in the degree of his knowledge, the brilliance of his vision?

Stevens was not Conrad. He was not Kierkegaard. He made no leaps of faith. Of his heroes this must be said: by their words ye shall know them. Even when he sets the scene for a great drama, as in "Prologues to What is Possible," with the boat at sea and the hero standing at the prow, the object is never an India to be reached or a giant to be slain; it is always a word, a humanist Logos:

As he traveled alone, like a man lured on by a syllable without
    any meaning,
A syllable of which he felt, with an appointed sureness,

That it contained the meaning into which he wanted to enter
. . .   [*516*]

Williams called it "a redeeming language." Stevens' answer would run somewhat on these lines: The only way to deal with chaos is to become its connoisseur; the only answer to a world of chaos is a new world verified by the imagination or an old world redeemed by the imagination. These worlds —if we drive Stevens hard to admit it—are worlds of knowledge; no more, no less.

If the ideal solution is to make over the whole world as word—and this takes more than anyone can give at any moment—Stevens' heroes practice their art by trial runs of language. In the "Esthétique" he says:

> Natives of poverty, children of malheur,
> The gaiety of language is our seigneur.   [*322*]

And if we say that this is mere escapism, Stevens will agree and compose several pages to defend this recourse as being eminently natural. In "The Well Dressed Man with a Beard" the one thing remaining is "a speech/Of the self that must sustain itself on speech." [*247*] In "Asides on the Oboe" he describes the impossible possible philosophers' man:

> He is the transparence of the place in which
> He is and in his poems we find peace.   [*251*]

In "Of Modern Poetry" the great poet is a great actor, but more than that he is a great rhetorician, "saying the right thing," finding the satisfactions we need.

But do we need more than consoling sounds? Sometimes we do. And Stevens acknowledged the need at least once. In the "Esthétique" he says:

> He disposes the world in categories, thus:
> The peopled and the unpeopled. In both, he is
> Alone. But in the peopled world, there is,

Besides the people, his knowledge of them. In
The unpeopled, there is his knowledge of himself.
Which is more desperate in the moments when
The will demands that what he thinks be true?   [323]

Usually the will is not so demanding. It is satisfied to conceive only such things as are in its own image, in keeping
with that Proposition (LIV) in Spinoza's *Ethics* which says
that "The mind endeavors to conceive only such things as
assert its power of activity." These conceptions form the
"third world" that Stevens invokes, distinct from the
peopled world and the unpeopled world. In the "third
world" the will is much easier to please; it accepts whatever
is as true, including the consoling structures that have no
other ground but the nature of the will itself:

It accepts whatever is as true,
Including pain, which, otherwise, is false.
In the third world, then, there is no pain.

So far, so good; but it is a dry world, when all is said.
The world as word has many consolations, but as Stevens
asks,

What lover has one in such rocks, what woman,
However known, at the center of the heart?   [323]

This is the saving pressure and the saving grace of
Stevens' later poems. It would have been quite possible for
him at that stage to write a purely Platonic poetry, to move
about in the vacuum of principles, Ideas, essences, forms,
numbers, and theorems. He could have done this, because
the nature of language would have allowed him to do it
and he had verbal gifts that would have enabled him to do
virtually anything he chose. He was gifted in that lavish
way. If an effect were linguistically attainable, Stevens would
attain it. And he was always tempted to live in such a
vacuum. We tend to say that he was bound to the world by

the gaiety of the world, by the *vif* of things. Not so. He said farewell to Florida when he chose to do so, and the decision did not stifle his poetry. At one extreme he was quite capable of writing poems to take the place of mountains. And it is unwise to chart directions in Stevens' poetry or to say that he did this in the early poems and that different thing in the later poems. At any moment he was liable to write a poem that would confound the cartographer. The most we can say about the later poems, in this line of comment, is that "Notes toward a Supreme Fiction" virtually exhausted the poet's love of structures, fictions, and hypotheses. In *The Rock,* for instance, Stevens is just as loyal as ever to the imaginative powers, but he deploys them far less on hypothetical structures, enclosures of fiction, and far more on what is "there," such as it is. He will never be content to play the "flat historic scale," but when he looks at the world now he sees—for one thing— more people around the place, human acts and sufferings that compel his attention, rather than object lessons in epistemology. More and more the poet's will demands that what he thinks be true.

We can make the point by thinking of two poems. In "The Idea of Order at Key West" the imagination is embodied in the singer, and reality is the sea. And as the song proceeds we are told, "the sea,/Whatever self it had, became the self/That was her song, for she was the maker." And in fact, "there never was a world for her/Except the one she sang and, singing, made." We must say, then, that the situation is entirely favorable to the imagination; the figure is all imagination, and the reality—such as it is—is merely a function of the imagination. When I say that the figure is all imagination, I take this phrase from a passage in "The Noble Rider and the Sound of Words," where Stevens explains why Plato could yield himself to the figure of the charioteer and the winged horses but we can't. (I give several sentences because they are crucial.) The reason is this:

> The imagination loses vitality as it ceases to adhere to what is real. When it adheres to the unreal and intensifies what is unreal, while its first effect may be extraordinary, that effect is the maximum effect that it will ever have. In Plato's figure, his imagination does not adhere to what is real. On the contrary, having created something unreal, it adheres to it and intensifies its unreality. . . . The reason why this particular figure has lost its vitality is that, in it, the imagination adheres to what is unreal. What happened, as we were traversing the whole heaven, is that the imagination lost its power to sustain us. It has the strength of reality or none at all.[22]

Can we not say of Stevens' poem that the imagination adheres to the unreal and intensifies what is unreal, and that while its effect on first reading is extraordinary, that effect is the maximum effect it will ever have?

We say this with some insistence because it is endorsed by many of Stevens' later poems, particularly by those poems in which the poet's will demands that what he thinks be true. And of these I choose one of Stevens' greatest poems, "The River of Rivers in Connecticut." It is short enough to quote in full:

> There is a great river this side of Stygia,
> Before one comes to the first black cataracts
> And trees that lack the intelligence of trees.
>
> In that river, far this side of Stygia,
> The mere flowing of the water is a gayety,
> Flashing and flashing in the sun. On its banks,
>
> No shadow walks. The river is fateful,
> Like the last one. But there is no ferryman.
> He could not bend against its propelling force.
>
> It is not to be seen beneath the appearances
> That tell of it. The steeple at Farmington
> Stands glistening and Haddam shines and sways.

It is the third commonness with light and air,
A curriculum, a vigor, a local abstraction . . .
Call it, once more, a river, an unnamed flowing,

Space-filled, reflecting the seasons, the folk-lore
Of each of the senses; call it, again and again,
The river that flows nowhere, like a sea.　[*533*]

The river is a condition of being, short of its dissolution. Its dissolution, the loss of its vital principle, is ahead, but the river is still in time and place. The flowing of the water is the gaiety of reality, the *vif* of things. No shadow walks; the river is real, not a function of our selves, our wills. And this river in Connecticut is just as momentous, as fateful, as the Styx. Just as much depends upon it. If we take an oath upon it, the consequences of breaking it are just as grave. "But there is no ferryman." In Stevens' early poems, wherever there is a sea, a river, a force of nature or reality, there is a man or woman of imagination to master it, like the singer in "The Idea of Order at Key West." In the later poems Stevens is prepared to concede to the river a propelling force stronger than us—we have not invented it—or at least stronger than us in action. In knowledge, a man can still acknowledge the river, thereby ensuring the interpenetration of reality and the imagination. On this occasion—not in Key West—the imagination adheres to what is real: the river is the Connecticut River, verified by Haddam and Farmington. The mind acknowledges the reality attested by appearances, flashing and flashing. It then conceives a force beneath the flowing river, a force of which the flashing waters are verifiable manifestations. This invisible force is the "third commonness with light and air." It is the mythology of its region, reflecting the seasons, "the folk-lore/Of each of the senses." And in that mode it flows nowhere, like the flecked river of "This Solitude of Cataracts," "Which kept flowing and never the same way twice, flowing/Through many places, as if it stood still in one . . . ," [*424*] like reality itself, like the sea.

Glossing this a little, I would say that the imagination, which in many of Stevens' poems adds a "puissant flick" to what is real, and thus conveys the feeling of the thing (which is what it had lacked), gives the region of Connecticut its mythology. The real Connecticut is made "more acute by an unreal," as he says in "The Bouquet." Indeed, there is a little poem in which Stevens says:

> A mythology reflects its region. Here
> In Connecticut, we never lived in a time
> When mythology was possible—But if we had—
> That raises the question of the image's truth.
> The image must be of the nature of its creator.
> It is the nature of its creator increased,
> Heightened. It is he, anew, in a freshened youth
> And it is he in the substance of his region,
> Wood of his forests and stone out of his fields
> Or from under his mountains.[23]

And there is an essay called "Connecticut," one of Stevens' last pieces, in which he gives his feeling of the place in prose and says: "Now, when all the primitive difficulties of getting started have been overcome, we live in the tradition which is the true mythology of the region and we breathe in with every breath the joy of having ourselves been created by what has been endured and mastered in the past." [24]

This is a new note in Stevens. The historic scale has lost its flatness; the past is alive, long live the past. The mythology is to its region as tradition is to time, as the "unreal" is to the real, as feeling is to fact. The image in these last great poems is of the nature of its creator, but it is also true, as Haddam and Farmington are true. Hence when the will demands that what the poet thinks be true, the will is satisfied. This is the composure of these last poems. The imagination is less imperious, more humane. It knows that to impose is not to discover. In "The Course of a Particular," when the leaves cry, Stevens says:

> It is not a cry of divine attention,
> Nor the smoke-drift of puffed-out heroes, nor human cry.
> It is the cry of leaves that do not transcend themselves,
> In the absence of fantasia, without meaning more
> Than they are in the final finding of the air, in the thing
> Itself, until, at last, the cry concerns no one at all.[25]

It is still knowledge. Stevens is loyal to his vision. But even here the later poems exhibit a marvelous scruple. In "The Sail of Ulysses" Stevens equates knowledge with life, but then he says:

> Yet always there is another life,
> A life beyond this present knowing,
> A life lighter than this present splendor,
> Brighter, perfected and distant away,
> Not to be reached but to be known,
> Not an attainment of the will
> But something illogically received,
> A divination, a letting down
> From loftiness, misgivings dazzlingly
> Resolved in dazzling discovery.[26]

This is, to quote a phrase from the same poem, "the joy of meaning in design/Wrenched out of chaos." The squirming facts still exceed the squamous mind, but "relation appears." In "The River of Rivers in Connecticut" relation appears as a propriety of diction, a justice of cadence, "most happily contrived."

NOTES

[1] Wallace Stevens, *Collected Poems* (London: Faber and Faber, 1955), p. 130. Hereafter page references to this book are given, italicized, in brackets.
[2] Stevens, "The Irrational Element in Poetry," *Opus Posthumous* (New York: Knopf, 1957), pp. 216 ff.
[3] Stevens, *The Necessary Angel* (New York: Knopf, 1951), p. 17.

4 *Ibid.*, p. 85.

5 *Opus Posthumous*, p. 209.

6 William Empson, *Collected Poems* (London: Chatto and Windus, 1955), pp. 102, 32–33.

7 *The Necessary Angel*, pp. 101–102.

8 *Ibid.*, pp. 17–18, 76.

9 *Opus Posthumous*, pp. 160, 173, 178.

10 *The Necessary Angel*, p. 20.

11 *Ibid.*, p. 63.

12 *Ibid.*, p. 73.

13 Walter Pater, *Marius the Epicurean* (London: Macmillan, 1898), II, 162.

14 Stevens, *Mattino Domenicale, ed altre poesie* (Turin, 1954), p. 185.

15 *The Necessary Angel*, p. 140. See also *Opus Posthumous*, p. 164.

16 See Kenneth Burke, *The Rhetoric of Religion: Studies in Logology* (Boston: Beacon Press, 1961), pp. 38–39: "First, I would set 'Dramatism' against 'Scientism.' In so doing, I do not necessarily imply a distrust of science as such. I mean simply that language in particular and human relations in general can be most directly approached in terms of *action* rather than in terms of *knowledge* (or in terms of 'form' rather than in terms of 'perception'). The 'Scientistic' approach is via some such essentially epistemological question as 'What do I see when I look at this object?' or 'How do I see it?' But typical 'Dramatistic' questions would be: 'From what, through what, to what, does this particular form proceed?' or 'What goes with what in this structure of terms?' or 'How am I "cleansed" by a tragedy (if I am cleansed)?' Either approach ends by encroaching upon the territories claimed by the other. But the *way in* is different, Dramatism beginning with problems of act, or form, and Scientism beginning with problems of knowledge, or perception."

17 *The Necessary Angel*, p. 171.

18 *Ibid.*, p. 51.

19 *Opus Posthumous*, p. 206.

20 *The Necessary Angel*, pp. 174, 175.

21 *Ibid.*, p. 153.

22 *Ibid.*, pp. 6–7.

23 *Opus Posthumous*, p. 118.

24 *Ibid.*, p. 295.

25 *Ibid.*, pp. 96–97.

26 *Ibid.*, pp. 101–102.

CHAPTER 8

THEODORE ROETHKE

THERE IS A POEM called "Snake" in which Theodore Roethke describes a young snake turning and drawing away and then says:

> I felt my slow blood warm.
> I longed to be that thing,
> The pure, sensuous form.
>
> And I may be, some time.[1]

To aspire to a condition of purity higher than any available in the human world is a common urge. Poets often give this condition as a pure, sensuous form, nothing if not itself and nothing beyond itself. But it is strange, at first sight, that Roethke gives his parable in the image of a snake, because snakes tend to figure in his poems as emblems of the sinister. In "Where Knock is Open Wide" one of the prayerful moments reads: "I'll be a bite. You be a wink./Sing the snake to sleep." In "I Need, I Need" the term "snake-eyes" is enough to send its owner packing. And there is this, in "The Shape of the Fire":

Up over a viaduct I came, to the snakes and sticks of another
    winter,
A two-legged dog hunting a new horizon of howls.

But this is at first sight, or at first thought, because Roethke, more than most poets, sought a sustaining order in the images of his chaos, and only those images would serve. If you offer a dove as answer to a snake, your answer is incomplete, an order not violent enough. Hence when the right time came, in "I'm Here," Roethke would find that a snake lifting its head is a fine sight, and a snail's music is a fine sound, and both are joys, credences of summer. As Roethke says in "The Longing," "The rose exceeds, the rose exceeds us all."

But he did not sentimentalize his chaos. He lived with it, and would gladly have rid himself of it if he could have done so without an even greater loss, the loss of verifiable life. When he thought of his own rage, for instance, he often saw it as mere destructiveness. In one of his early poems he said: "Rage warps my clearest cry/To witless agony." And he often resorted to invective, satire, pseudonymous tirades, to cleanse himself of rage and hatred. In one of those tirades he said, "Behold, I'm a heart set free, for I have taken my hatred and eaten it." But "Death Piece" shows that to be released from rage is to be—quite simply—dead. And the price is too high. This is one of the reasons why Roethke found the last years of W. B. Yeats so rewarding, because Yeats made so much of his rage, in the *Last Poems, The Death of Cuchulain,* and *Purgatory.* In one of his own apocalyptic poems, "The Lost Son," Roethke says, "I want the old rage, the lash of primordial milk," as if to recall Yeats' cry, "Grant me an old man's frenzy." And in "Old Lady's Winter Words" he says: "If I were a young man,/I could roll in the dust of a fine rage . . ."; and in "The Sententious Man": "Some rages save us. Did I rage too long? /The spirit knows the flesh it must consume." Hence Roethke's quest for the saving rage. Call it—for it is this— a rage for order. He was sometimes tempted to seal himself against the rush of experience, and he reminds himself in "The Adamant" that the big things, such as truth, are sealed against thought; the true substance, the core, holds itself inviolate. And yet man is exposed, exposes himself. And, in a sense, rightly so. As Yeats says in the great "Dialogue of Self and Soul":

I am content to live it all again
And yet again, if it be life to pitch
Into the frog-spawn of a blind man's ditch.

In "The Pure Fury" Roethke says, "I live near the abyss."
What he means is the substance of his poetry. The abyss is
partly the frog-spawn of a blind man's ditch, partly a ditch
of his own contriving, partly the fate of being human in a
hard time, partly the poet's weather. As discreetly as possible
we can take it for granted, rehearsing it only to the extent of
linking it with the abyss in other people. Better to think of
it as the heart of each man's darkness. In "Her Becoming"
Roethke speaks of it in one aspect:

> I know the cold fleshless kiss of contraries,
> The nerveless constriction of surfaces—
> Machines, machines, loveless, temporal;
> Mutilated souls in cold morgues of obligation.

And this becomes, in the "Fourth Meditation," "the dreary
dance of opposites." (But so far it is common enough.)

It is still common enough when Roethke presents it
through the ambiguities of body and soul. In "Epidermal
Macabre" Roethke, like Yeats in *The Tower*, wishes the
body away in favor of a spirit remorselessly sensual:

> And willingly would I dispense
> With false accouterments of sense,
> To sleep immodestly, a most
> Incarnadine and carnal ghost.

Or again, when the dance of opposites is less dreary, Roethke
accepts with good grace the unwinding of body from soul:

> When opposites come suddenly in place,
> I teach my eyes to hear, my ears to see
> How body from spirit slowly does unwind
> Until we are pure spirit at the end.

Sometimes the body is "gristle." In "Praise to the End" Roethke says, "Skin's the least of me," and in the "First Meditation" it is the rind that "hates the life within." (Yeats' "dying animal" is clearly visible.) But there were other moments, as there were in Yeats. In "The Wraith" the body casts a spell, the flesh makes the spirit "visible," and in the "Fourth Meditation" "the husk lives on, ardent as a seed."

Mostly in Roethke the body seems good in itself, a primal energy. And when it is this it features the most distinctive connotations of the modern element: it is a good, but ill at ease with other goods. Above all, it does not guarantee an equable life in the natural world. More often than not in these poems man lives with a hostile nature, and lives as well as he can. In "I Need, I Need" intimations of waste, privation, and insecurity lead to this:

> The ground cried my name:
> Good-bye for being wrong.
> Love helps the sun.
> But not enough.

"I can't marry the dirt" is an even stronger version, in "Bring the Day," echoing Wallace Stevens' benign "marriage of flesh and air" while attaching to it now, as courageously as possible, the bare note, "A swan needs a pond"; or, more elaborately in another poem, "A wretch needs his wretchedness." The aboriginal middle poems have similar cries on every page: "These wings are from the wrong nest"; "My sleep deceives me"; "Soothe me, great groans of underneath"; "Rock me to sleep, the weather's wrong"; "Few objects praise the Lord."

These are some of Roethke's intimations of chaos. They reach us as cries, laments, protests, intimations of loss. Most of Roethke's later poems are attempts to cope with these

intimations by becoming—in Stevens' sense—their connoisseur. In "The Dance" Roethke speaks of a promise he has
made to "sing and whistle romping with the bears"; and
whether we take these as animals or constellations, the
promise is the same and hard to keep. To bring it off at all,
Roethke often plays in a child's garden, especially in poems
like "O Lull Me, Lull Me," where he can have everything
he wants by having it only in fancy. "Light fattens the rock,"
he sings, to prove that good children get treats. "When I say
things fond, I hear singing," he reports, and we take his word
for it; as we do again when we acknowledge, in a later poem,
that "the right thing happens to the happy man." Perhaps
it does. But when Roethke says, "I breathe into a dream,/
And the ground cries . . . ," and again, "I could say hello
to things;/I could talk to a snail," we think that he protests
too much, and we know that his need is great. Roethke is
never quite convincing in this note, or in the hey-nonny
note of his neo-Elizabethan pastiche. Even when he dramatizes the situation in the "Meditations of an Old Woman"
the answers come too easily. In two stanzas he has "the earth
itself a tune," and this sounds like a poet's wishful dreaming.
Roethke may have wanted the kind of tone that Stevens
reached in his last poems, an autumnal calm that retains the
rigor and the feeling but banishes the fretful note, the whine,
the cry of pain. But Stevens earned this. And Yeats earned
it too, in poems like "Beautiful Lofty Things." Roethke
claimed it without really earning it. Here is a stanza from
"Her Becoming":

> Ask all the mice who caper in the straw—
> I am benign in my own company.
> A shape without a shade, or almost none,
> I hum in pure vibration, like a saw.
> The grandeur of a crazy one alone!—
> By swoops of bird, by leaps of fish, I live.
> My shadow steadies in a shifting stream;

I live in air; the long light is my home;
I dare caress the stones, the field my friend;
A light wind rises: I become the wind.

And here is Stevens, in a passage from "The Course of a Particular":

The leaves cry. It is not a cry of divine attention,
Nor the smoke-drift of puffed-out heroes, nor human cry.
It is the cry of leaves that do not transcend themselves,
In the absence of fantasia, without meaning more
Than they are in the final finding of the air, in the thing
Itself, until, at last, the cry concerns no one at all.

How can we compare these two passages except to say that Stevens speaks with the knowledge that there have been other days, other feelings, and the hope that there will be more of each, as various as before? Roethke speaks as if the old woman were now released from time and history and the obligations of each, released even from the memories that she has already invoked. There is too much fantasia in Roethke's lines, and this accounts for a certain slackness that fell upon him whenever he tried too hard to be serene. Stevens' poem is, in the full meaning of the word, mature; Roethke's is a little childish, second-childish. Stevens would affirm, when affirmation seemed just, but not before. Roethke longed to affirm, and when the affirmation would not come he sometimes—now and again—dressed himself in affirmative robes.

But only now and again. At his best he is one of the most scrupulous of poets. In "Four for Sir John Davies," for instance, the harmony between nature and man that Davies figured—the orchestra, the dance, the music of the spheres— is brought to bear upon the poem, critically and never naïvely or sentimentally. The divinely orchestrated universe of Davies' poem is more than a point of reference but far less than an escape route. For one thing, as Roethke says, "I need a place to sing, and dancing-room," and for another, there is no dancing master, and for a third, there isn't even at this stage a dancing partner. So he must do the best he can in his poverty. And if his blood leaps "with a wordless song," at least it leaps:

> But what I learned there, dancing all alone,
> Was not the joyless motion of a stone.

But even when the partner comes and they dance their joy, Roethke does not claim that this makes everything sweet or that nature and man will thereafter smile at each other. In the farthest reach of joy he says:

> We danced to shining; mocked before the black
> And shapeless night that made no answer back.

The sensual cry is what it is, and there are moments when it is or seems to be final, but man still lives in the element of antagonisms. In "Four Quartets" the "daunsynge" scene from Sir Thomas Elyot testifies to modes of being, handsome but archaic; it answers no present problem. Nor does Sir John Davies, who plays a similar role in Roethke's sequence. And even before that, in "The Return," man in the element of antagonisms feels and behaves like an animal in his self-infected lair, "With a stump of scraggy fang/Bared for a hunter's boot." And sometimes he turns upon himself in rage.

When Roethke thinks of man in this way, he often presents him in images of useless flurry. Like Saul Bellow's Dangling Man, he is clumsy, ungainly, an elephant in a pond. Roethke often thinks of him as a bat—by day, quiet, cousin to the mouse; at night, crazy, absurd, looping "in crazy figures." And when the human situation is extreme, Roethke thinks of man as a bat flying deep into a narrowing tunnel. Far from being a big, wide space, the world seems a darkening corridor. In "Bring the Day!" Roethke says,

"Everything's closer. Is this a cage?" And if a shape cries
from a cloud as it does in "The Exorcism," and calls to
man's flesh, man is always somewhere else, "down long corridors." (Corridors, cages, tunnels, lairs—if these poems
needed illustration, the painter is easily named: Francis
Bacon, keeper of caged souls.)

In "Four for Sir John Davies" the lovers, Roethke says,
"undid chaos to a curious sound," "curious" meaning careful as well as strange and exploratory. In this world to undo
chaos is always a curious struggle, sometimes thought of as
a release from constriction, a stretching in all directions, an
escape from the cage. In "What Can I Tell My Bones?"
Roethke says, "I recover my tenderness by long looking,"
and if tenderness is the proof of escape, long looking is one
of the means. In *King Lear* it is to see feelingly. In some of
Roethke's poems it is given as, quite simply, attention. In
"Her Becoming" Roethke speaks of a "jauntier principle of
order," but this is to dream. What he wants, in a world
of cages and corridors, is to escape to an order, an order of
which change and growth and decay are natural mutations
and therefore acceptable. In many of the later poems it will
be an order of religious feeling, for which the punning motto
is, "God, give me a near."

The first step, the first note toward a possible order, is to
relish what can be relished. Listening to "the sigh of what
is," one attends, knowing, or at least believing, that "all
finite things reveal infinitude." If things "flame into being,"
so much the better. "Dare I blaze like a tree?" Roethke asks
at one point, like the flaming tree of Yeats' "Vacillation."
And again Roethke says, "What I love is near at hand,/
Always, in earth and air." This is fine, as far as it goes, but
it is strange that Roethke is more responsive to intimations
of being when they offer themselves in plants than in people; and here, of course, he differs radically from Yeats. In
the first version of "Cuttings" he is exhilarated when "the

small cells bulge," when cuttings sprout into a new life, when bulbs hunt for light, when the vines in the forcing house pulse with the knocking pipes, when orchids draw in the warm air, when beetles, newts, and lice creep and wriggle. In "Slug" he rejoices in his kinship with bats, weasels, and worms. In "A Walk in Late Summer" being "delights in being, and in time." In the same poem Roethke delights in the "midnight eyes" of small things, and in several poems he relishes what Christopher Smart in *Jubilate Agno* calls "the language of flowers." Everywhere in Roethke there is consolation in the rudimentary when it is what it is, without fantasia. It is a good day when the spiders sail into summer. But Roethke is slow to give the same credences to man. Plants may be transplanted, and this is good, but what is exhilarating reproduction in insects and flowers is mere duplication in people. Girls in college are "duplicate gray standard faces"; in the same poem there is talk of "endless duplication of lives and objects." Man as a social being is assimilated to the machine; the good life is lived by plants. In the bacterial poems, weeds are featured as circumstance, the rush of things, often alien but often sustaining. "Weeds, weeds, how I love you," Roethke says in "The Shape of the Fire." In the "First Meditation," "On love's worst ugly day,/ The weeds hiss at the edge of the field . . ." In "What Can I Tell My Bones?" "Weeds turn toward the wind weed-skeletons," presumably because "the dead love the unborn." But in "Praise to the End!" when the water's low and romping days are over, "the weeds exceed me."

There are two ways of taking this, and Roethke gives us both. Normally we invoke the rudimentary to criticize the complex: the lower organism rebukes the higher for falling short of itself, as body rebukes the arrogance of vaunting mind or spirit. This works on the assumption that what is simple is more "natural" than what is complex, and that lower organisms have the merit of such simplicity. Or, alternatively, one can imply that the most exalted objects of our human desire are already possessed, in silence and grace, by the lower organisms. Roethke often does this. In "The Advice," for instance, he says:

> A learned heathen told me this:
> Dwell in pure mind and Mind alone;
> What you brought back from the Abyss,
> The Slug was taught beneath his Stone.

This is so presumably because the slug had a teacher, perhaps the dancing master who has retired from the human romp. Roethke doesn't commit the sentimentality of implying, however, that all is sweetness and light in the bacterial world, and generally he avoids pushing his vegetal analogies too far. In his strongest poems the bacterial is featured as a return to fundamentals, a syntax of short phrases to represent the radical breaking-up that may lead to a new synthesis. In grammatical terms, we have broken the spine of our syntax by loading it with our own fetishes. So we must begin again as if we were learning a new language, speaking in short rudimentary phrases. Or, alternatively, we learn in simple words and phrases, hoping that eventually we may reach the light of valid sentences. In this spirit Roethke says, in a late poem, "God bless the roots!—Body and soul are one!" The roots, the sensory facts, are beneath or beyond doubt; in "The Longing" Roethke says, "I would believe my pain: and the eye quiet on the growing rose." Learning a new language in this way, we must divest ourselves at this first stage of all claims to coherence, synthesis, or unity. This is the secular equivalent of the "way of purgation" in "Four Quartets," and it serves a corresponding purpose, because here too humility is endless. If our humility is sufficient, if we attend to the roots, to beginnings, we may even be rewarded with a vision in which beginning and end are one, as in the poem "In Evening Air":

Ye littles, lie more close!
Make me, O Lord, a last, a simple thing
Time cannot overwhelm.
Once I transcended time:
A bud broke to a rose,
  And I rose from a last diminishing.

We can see how this goes in the first stanzas of "Where Knock is Open Wide":

A kitten can
Bite with his feet;
Papa and Mama
Have more teeth.

We can take this as pure notation, the primitive vision linking things that to the complex adult eye seem incommensurate. But the adult eye is "wrong," and it must go to school again if it is ever to say, "I recover my tenderness by long looking." Roethke's lines are "intuitions of sensibility," the ground of our beseeching, acts of the mind at the very first stage, long before idea, generalization, or concept. And this is the only way to innocence—or so the poem suggests. Then he says in the second stanza:

Sit and play
Under the rocker
Until the cows
All have puppies.

Here the aimlessness of the kitten stands for the innocence of game and apprehension. The play is nonchalant, and it conquers time by the ease of its reception. Time is measured by the laws of growth and fruition, not by the clock. In this sense it is proper to say, as Roethke does in the next stanza:

His ears haven't time.
Sing me a sleep-song, please.
A real hurt is soft.

In Christopher Smart's "A Song to David" (the source of the title of the present poem [2]) stanza 77 includes the lines:

> And in the seat to faith assigned
> Where ask is have, where seek is find,
> Where knock is open wide.

The cat's ears haven't time because they don't ask for it. If time is for men the destructive element, that is their funeral, and mostly their suicide. "Sing me a sleep-song, please" is a prayer to be released from time. "A real hurt is soft" is an attempt to render human pain as pure description, to eliminate self-pity. And the appropriate gloss is the second stanza of "The Lost Sun"—"Fished in an old wound,/ The soft pond of repose"—to remind us that the primitive vision is at once harsh and antiseptic. (Roethke himself sometimes forgot this.) Hence these intuitions of rudimentary sensibility are exercises, akin to spiritual exercises, all the better if they are caustic, purgative, penitential. The exercises are never finished, because this is the way things are, but once they are well begun the soul can proceed; the energy released is the rage for a sustaining order.

The search for order begins easily enough in Roethke. Sometimes, as we have seen, it begins in celebration, relishing what there is to relish. Or again it may begin by sounding a warning note. The early poem "To My Sister" is a rush of admonition designed for survival and prudence. "Defer the vice of flesh," he tells her, but on the other hand, "Keep faith with present joys." Later, Roethke would seek and find value in intimations of change and growth, and then in love, normally sexual love. Many of the love poems are beautiful in an Elizabethan way, which is one of the best ways, and whether their delicacy is entirely Roethke's own or partly his way of acknowledging the delicacy of Sir Thomas Wyatt is neither here nor there. Some of the love poems are among Roethke's finest achievements. I would choose "The Renewal," "I Knew a Woman," "The Sensualists," "The Swan," "She," and "The Voice"— or this one, "Memory":

> In the slow world of dream,
> We breathe in unison.
> The outside dies within,
> And she knows all I am.
>
> She turns, as if to go,
> Half-bird, half-animal.
> The wind dies on the hill.
> Love's all. Love's all I know.
>
> A doe drinks by a stream,
> A doe and its fawn.
> When I follow after them,
> The grass changes to stone.

Love was clearly a principle of order in Roethke's poems, but it never established itself as a relation beyond the bedroom. It never became dialogue or *caritas*. Outside the bedroom Roethke became his own theme, the center of a universe deemed to exist largely because it had such a center. This does not mean that the entire universe was mere grist to his mill; he is not one of the predatory poets. But on the other hand, he does not revel in the sheer humanity of the world. Indeed, his universe is distinctly underpopulated. Even Aunt Tilly entered it only when she died, thereby inciting an elegy. This is not to question Roethke's "sincerity"; poems are written for many reasons, one of which is the presence of poetic forms inviting attention. But to indicate the nature of Roethke's achievement it is necessary to mark the areas of his deepest response and to point to those areas that he acknowledged more sluggishly, if at all. I have already implied that he responded to the human modes of being only when a specific human relation touched him and he grasped it. He did not have that utter assent to other people, other lives, that marks the best poetry of William Carlos Williams or Richard Eberhart, the feeling that human life is just as miraculous as the growth of an orchid or the "excess" of a rose. Indeed, one might speculate along these lines: that Roethke's response to his father and mother and, in the love poems, to his wife was so vivid that it engrossed all other responses in the human world. It set up a monopoly. And therefore flowers and plants were closer to him than people.

Even when he acknowledged a natural order of things, Roethke invariably spoke of it as if it did not necessarily include the human order or as if its inclusion of that order were beside the point. The natural order of things included moss growing on rock, the transplanting of flowers, the cycle of mist, cloud, and rain, the tension of nest and grave, and it might even include what he calls, rather generally, "the wild disordered language of the natural heart." But the question of the distinctively human modes of life was always problematic. In Roethke's poems human life is endorsed when it manages to survive a storm, as in "Big Wind," where the greenhouse—Roethke's symbol for "the whole of life"—rides the storm and sails into the calm morning. There is also the old florist, standing all night watering the roses, and the single surviving tulip with its head swaggering over the dead blooms—and then Otto.

To survive, to live through the weeds—in Roethke's world you do this by taking appropriate security measures. Property is a good bet. In "Where Knock is Open Wide" there is a passage that reads:

> That was before. I fell! I fell!
> The worm has moved away.
> My tears are tired.
>
> Nowhere is out. I saw the cold.
> Went to visit the wind. Where the birds die.
> How high is have?

The part we need is the last line, "How high is have?" This virtually identifies security with property. In several poems Roethke will pray for a close relation to God, and this will rate as security, but in the meantime even property in a material sense will help. And because he lived in our own society and sought order from the images of his chaos, security and property normally meant money. In "The Lost Son," for instance, there is this:

> Good-bye, good-bye, old stones, the time-order is going,
> I have married my hands to perpetual agitation,
> I run, I run to the whistle of money.
>
>   Money money money
>   Water water water

And even if he wrote two or three poems to make fun of this, the fact remains: property and the fear of dispossession, money and the lack of it, were vivid terms in his human image. Property was money in one's purse, more reliable than most things—more reliable than reason, for instance.

In his search for a viable and live order Roethke used his mind for all it was worth, but he would not vote for reason. He did not believe that you could pit the rational powers against the weeds of circumstance and hope to win. When he spoke of reason it was invariably Stevens' "Reason's click-clack," a mechanical affair. In one poem Roethke says, "Reason? That dreary shed, that hutch for grubby schoolboys!" Indeed, reason normally appears in his poems, at least officially, as a constriction. Commenting on his poem "In a Dark Time," Roethke said that it was an attempt "to break through the barriers of rational experience." [3] The self, the daily world, reason, meant bondage; to come close to God you had to break through. These things were never the medium of one's encounter with God, always obstacles in its way. For such encounters you had to transcend reason; if you managed it, you touched that greater thing that is the "reason in madness" of *King Lear*. The good man takes the risk of darkness. If reason's click-clack is useless, there remains in man a primitive striving toward the light. Nature, seldom a friend to man, at least offers him a few saving analogies, one being that of darkness and light. Much of this is given in the last stanzas of "Unfold! Unfold!":

> Sing, sing, you symbols! All simple creatures,
> All small shapes, willow-shy,
> In the obscure haze, sing!

> A light song comes from the leaves.
> A slow sigh says yes. And light sighs;
> A low voice, summer-sad.
> Is it you, cold father? Father,
> For whom the minnows sang?

> > A house for wisdom; a field for revelation.
> > Speak to the stones, and the stars answer.
> > At first the visible obscures:
> > Go where light is.

To go where light is: the object is self-possession, sometimes featured as a relation to the world:

> > I lose and find myself in the long water;
> > I am gathered together once more;
> > I embrace the world.

To be one's own man, to come upon "the true ease of myself," to possess oneself so fluently as to say, "Being, not doing, is my first joy"—these are definitive joys when "the light cries out, and I am there to hear." If it requires "the blast of dynamite" to effect such movements, well and good. At any cost Roethke must reach the finality in which, as he says in "Meditation at Oyster River," "the flesh takes on the pure poise of the spirit." (This is his version of Yeats' "Unity of Being.") Hence he admires the tendrils that do not need eyes to seek, the furred caterpillar that crawls down a string, anything that causes movement, gives release, breaks up constriction. In the natural world there is growth, the flow of water, the straining of buds toward the light. And in the poet's craft these move in harmony with the vivid cadence, fluency, Yeats' "tact of words," the leaping rhythm.

For the rest, Roethke's symbolism is common enough. The life-enhancing images are rain, rivers, flowers, seed, grain, birds, fish, veins. The danger signals are wind, storm, darkness, drought, shadow. And the great event is growth, in full light. "The Shape of the Fire" ends:

To have the whole air!
The light, the full sun
Coming down on the flowerheads,
The tendrils turning slowly,
A slow snail-lifting, liquescent;
To be by the rose
Rising slowly out of its bed,
Still as a child in its first loneliness;
To see cyclamen veins become clearer in early sunlight,
And mist lifting out of the brown cattails;
To stare into the after-light, the glitter left on the lake's surface,
When the sun has fallen behind a wooded island;
To follow the drops sliding from a lifted oar,
Held up, while the rower breathes, and the small boat drifts
    quietly shoreward;
To know that light falls and fills, often without our knowing,
As an opaque vase fills to the brim from a quick pouring,
Fills and trembles at the edge yet does not flow over,
Still holding and feeding the stem of the contained flower.

The flower, contained, securely held in a vase filled with water and light—with this image we are close to the core of Roethke's poetry, where all the analogies run together. The only missing element is what he often called "song," the ultimate in communication, and for that we need another poem, another occasion. One of his last poems, a love poem, ends:

> We met to leave again
> The time we broke from time;
> A cold air brought its rain,
> The singing of a stem.
> She sang a final song;
> Light listened when she sang.

If light listens, if light attends upon a human event, then the event is final. Kenneth Burke has pointed out that Roethke tends to link things, whenever there is a choice, by means of a word in the general vocabulary of communication. We need only add this, that when the relation is as close as a relation can be, the participants "sing," and there is singing everywhere, singing and listening. "The light cries out, and I am there to hear."

Pushed to their conclusion, or followed to their source, these analogies would run straight to the idea of God, or rather to the image of God. And taking such stock in the symbolism of creation and light, Roethke could hardly have avoided this dimension. Nor did he. One of his last and greatest poems is called "The Marrow":

> The wind from off the sea says nothing new.
> The mist above me sings with its small flies.
> From a burnt pine the sharp speech of a crow
> Tells me my drinking breeds a will to die.
> What's the worst portion in this mortal life?
> A pensive mistress, and a yelping wife.
>
> One white face shimmers brighter than the sun
> When contemplation dazzles all I see;
> One look too close can make my soul away.
> Brooding on God, I may become a man.
> Pain wanders through my bones like a lost fire;
> What burns me now? Desire, desire, desire.

Godhead above my God, are you there still?
To sleep is all my life. In sleep's half-death,
My body alters, altering the soul
That once could melt the dark with its small breath.
Lord, hear me out, and hear me out this day:
From me to Thee's a long and terrible way.

I was flung back from suffering and love
When light divided on a storm-tossed tree;
Yea, I have slain my will, and still I live;
I would be near; I shut my eyes to see;
I bleed my bones, their marrow to bestow
Upon that God who knows what I would know.[4]

The first stanza is all alienation—from nature and man and the self. The second is preparation for prayer, a relation with God as the light of light, source of the sun. The third is the prayer itself to the ground of all beseeching. In the fourth and last stanza the loss of selfhood is associated with the breakup of light on a storm-tossed tree, the emaciation of the human will; and then the last gesture—the voiding of the self, restitution, atonement (a characteristic sequence in late Roethke).

From the poems I have quoted, it might seem that Roethke was concerned with only one thing—himself. And this is true. But in his case it does not mean what it usually does. It does not mean that he is thrilled by his own emotions or that he spends much time in front of his mirror. The saving grace in Roethke, as in Whitman, is the assumption that he is a representative instance, no more if no less. When Roethke searches for value and meaning he assumes that this is interesting insofar as it is representative and not at all interesting when it ceases to be so. This is the source of Roethke's delicacy, as of Whitman's. When he says, in "I Need, I Need," "The Trouble is with No and Yes," or when he says, in "The Pure Fury," "Great Boehme rooted all in Yes and No," he advances this choice as a universal predicament rather than a proof of his own tender conscience. Again, in "The Waking" and other poems of similar intent, when he says, "I learn by going where I have to go," he is not claiming this as a uniquely sensitive perception; the line points to areas of feeling important because universal. And when he says, "Light takes the Tree; but who can tell us how?" the question is given with notable modesty, although indeed Roethke could have staked a higher claim for it, since it is the basis of several of his own religious poems. The motto for this delicacy in Roethke is a line from "The Sententious Man": "Each one's himself, yet each one's everyone." And there is the "Fourth Meditation" to prove that Roethke was never really in danger of solipsism.

With these qualifications, then, it is permissible to say that he was his own theme and to consider what this means in the poems—with this point in mind, however, that Whitman's equations were not available to Roethke. Roethke was not content to think of the self as the sum of its contents, even if he had Yeats to tell him that a mind is as rich as the images it contains. He would try to accumulate property, but only because he thought of property as a protective dike; behind the dike, one could live. But he never thought of this as having anything to do with the "nature" of the self. The self was problematic, but not a problem in addition. In one of his last and most beautiful poems, "In a Dark Time," he said:

> A man goes far to find out what he is—
> Death of the self in a long, tearless night,
> All natural shapes blazing unnatural light.
>
> Dark, dark my light, and darker my desire.
> My soul, like some heat-maddened summer fly,
> Keeps buzzing at the sill. Which I is *I*? [5]

That is still the question. In the early poems Roethke held to the common romantic idea of "the opposing self," the self defined by its grappling with the weeds of circumstance; hence, as Hopkins said, "Long Live the Weeds." Much later, Roethke was to consider this more strictly, notably in a poem like "The Exorcism," where he asks in a beguiling parenthesis, "(Father of flowers, who/Dares face the thing he is?)" And this question is joined to several bacterial images of man partaking uneasily of several worlds, beasts, serpents, the heron and the wren. In "Weed Puller" man is down in a fetor of weeds, "Crawling on all fours,/Alive, in a slippery grave."

Many of the middle poems feature a declared loss of self, often given as division, absence. In "Where Knock is Open Wide" Roethke says:

> I'm somebody else now.
> Don't tell my hands.
> Have I come to always? Not yet.
> One father is enough.
>
> Maybe God has a house.
> But not here.

There is a similar feeling in "Sensibility! O La!" and in "The Shimmer of Evil" perhaps the most explicit of all versions is, quite simply, "And I was only I"—which leads almost predictably but nonetheless beautifully to "There was no light; there was no light at all." The later poems tend to reflect upon the nature of the self by listing its demands; behind the love poems there is the assertion that "we live beyond/Our outer skin" even when the body sways to music. And much of this feeling culminates in the lovely "Fourth Meditation," which begins with many intuitions of sensibility and goes on to this:

But a time comes when the vague life of the mouth no longer suffices;
The dead make more impossible demands from their silence;
The soul stands, lonely in its choice,

Waiting, itself a slow thing,
In the changing body.

> The river moves, wrinkled by midges,
> A light wind stirs in the pine needles.
> The shape of a lark rises from a stone;
> But there is no song.

This is a later version of the predicament, loss of self, which cries through the middle poems. In "The Lost Son" he says:

> Snail, snail, glister me forward,
> Bird, soft-sigh me home.
> Worm, be with me.
> This is my hard time.

And a few lines later we read: "Voice, come out of the silence./Say something." But there is no song in that "kingdom of bang and blab." In Roethke's poems song is proof that infinity clings to the finite. In "Old Lady's Winter Words" he says, "My dust longs for the invisible." What he wants is given in phrase, image, and rhythm: "the gradual embrace/of lichen around stones"; "Deep roots"; and, quite directly:

> Where is the knowledge that
> Could bring me to my God?

The only knowledge is reason in madness.

Theodore Roethke was a slow starter in poetry. He survived and grew and developed without attaching himself to schools or groups. He was never a boy wonder; he was never fashionable as the Beat poets were fashionable; most of the currents of easy feeling left him untouched, unmoved. He never set up shop as a left-wing poet or a right-wing poet or a Catholic poet or a New England poet or a Southern poet or a California poet. He never claimed privilege in any region of feeling. This was probably as good for his poetry as it was bad for his fame. He made his way by slow movements, nudgings of growth, like his own plants and flowers. But he grew, and his poems got better all the time —so much so, that his last poems were his greatest achievements, marvelously rich and humane.

Along the way he was helped by friends, often poets like Louise Bogan and Marianne Moore, but this is another story, not mine to tell. He was, however, helped also by other writers, earlier poets, and some of this story may be told, and the telling should disclose something of the poetry. Clearly, he was a careful, scrupulous poet. There are lines and phrases here and there that show that he was prone to infection, picking up things from lesser poets, like Dylan Thomas, and keeping them beyond the call of prudence. But the poets who really engaged him were those who offered him a challenge, a mode of feeling, perhaps, that he himself might not possess, or possessed without knowing that he did. The Elizabethan song-poets, and especially John Donne, challenged him in this way, and his own love poems reflect not only their own feeling but the strenuous competition of the Elizabethan masters. And then there were poets like Davies and Smart who disclosed certain modes of feeling and belief that were not so deeply a personal challenge but a measure of the time in which we live. And there were the great modern masters whom he could hardly have avoided hearing. He learned a lot from T. S. Eliot—mainly, I think, how to be expressive while holding most of his ammunition in reserve. And this often comes through the verse as a cadence, as in this passage from "I'm Here":

> At the stream's edge, trailing a vague finger;
> Flesh-awkward, half-alive,
> Fearful of high places, in love with horses;
> In love with stuffs, silks,
> Rubbing my nose in the wool of blankets;
> Bemused; pleased to be;

> Mindful of cries,
> The meaningful whisper,
> The wren, the catbird.

Consider the rhetoric of the short phrase, at once giving and taking; Eliot is a great master in these discriminations. Think of this passage in "East Coker":

> In the middle, not only in the middle of the way
> But all the way, in a dark wood, in a bramble,
> On the edge of a grimpen, where is no secure foothold,
> And menaced by monsters, fancy lights,
> Risking enchantment.

Other cadences Roethke got from other poets—from Hopkins, notably, especially from "The Wreck of the Deutschland," which Roethke uses in the poem about the greenhouse in a storm, "Big Wind":

> But she rode it out,
> That old rose-house,
> She hove into the teeth of it,
> The core and pith of that ugly storm . . .

From Joyce Roethke learned one kind of language for the primitive, the rudimentary, the aboriginal, especially the Joyce of the *Portrait of the Artist as a Young Man,* bearing hard on the first chapter; and *Finnegans Wake* showed him one way of dealing with the unconscious. And there is Wallace Stevens. Roethke disapproved of Stevens' procedures in argumentative theory, but in fact he learned some fundamental lessons from Stevens. When he says, "I prefer the still joy," he is Stevens' pupil, conning a lesson he could well have done without. And I think he found in Stevens a justification of, if not an incitement to, his own propensity for the "pure moment." In one of his later poems he says, "O to be delivered from the rational into the realm of pure song." And if pure song is pure expression or pure communication, it is also close to Stevens' "hum of thoughts evaded in the mind." Stevens seems to me to be behind those poems in which Roethke longs for essence, for an essential "purity," or finds it in a still moment. He records it in a passage like this, for instance, from the "First Meditation":

> There are still times, morning and evening:
> The cerulean, high in the elm,
> Thin and insistent as a cicada,
> And the far phoebe, singing,
> The long plaintive notes floating down,
> Drifting through leaves, oak and maple,
> Or the whippoorwill, along the smoky ridges,
> A single bird calling and calling;
> A fume reminds me, drifting across wet gravel;
> A cold wind comes over stones;
> A flame, intense, visible,
> Plays over the dry pods,
> Runs fitfully along the stubble,
> Moves over the field,
> Without burning.
>> In such times, lacking a god,
>> I am still happy.

And Stevens is behind those poems in which Roethke presents the "single man" who contains everything:

> His spirit moves like monumental wind
> That gentles on a sunny blue plateau.
> He is the end of things, the final man.

When Whitman comes into the later poems, such as "Journey to the Interior," he shows Roethke how to deal with natural forms without hurting them, so that "the spirit of wrath becomes the spirit of blessing"; or how to give one thing after another without lining them up in symbolist rivalry, so that he can say "Beautiful my desire, and the place of my desire"; or how to preserve one's own integrity even

when beset by "the terrible hunger for objects." But Whitman was a late consultant to Roethke. Much earlier, and
toward the end of his poetic life, he attended upon Yeats'
poems and contracted debts handsomely acknowledged in
the "In Memoriam" and again in "The Dance." To Roethke
—or so it seems from the poems—Yeats stood for the imperious note, concentration, magnificent rhetoric clashing against
the bare notation, the dramatic play of self and soul.

> What's madness but nobility of soul
> At odds with circumstance? The day's on fire!
> I know the purity of pure despair,
> My shadow pinned against a sweating wall.
> That place among the rocks—is it a cave,
> Or winding path? The edge is what I have.

It peters out somewhat. Yeats would not have praised the
last line. But the rest is very much in Yeats's shadow, particularly the Yeats of "Coole Park and Ballylee, 1931." The
dramatic occasion; the landscape, moralized with a large
showing; the poet, finding correspondences and emblems in
herons, wrens, swans; nature with her tragic buskin on—
these are the Yeatsian gestures. And, to take them a little
further, Roethke knows that if he proposes to learn a high
rhetoric he must do it in earnest. So he begins with the
magisterially rhetorical question, then the short declaration,
not yet intimate, "The day's on fire!" and only then the
despair. And even now it is given as knowledge rather than
romantic exposure, so that even the shadow, the other self,
is presented as an object of contemplation before the poet
acknowledges the feeling as his own in "a sweating wall."

One of the odd things in this list of relationships, however, is that it is quite possible to think of Roethke as one
of the best modern poets without troubling about the fact
that he was, after all, an American poet. When reading
Stevens or Frost or Williams or Robert Lowell we are con-

stantly aware that we are reading American poets; but this is not an insistent element in Roethke. Indeed, it is quite clear that he bears no special relation to either of the dominant traditions in American poetry—New England and the South. Temperamentally he is not too far away from such writers as Hawthorne, Melville, or James. Like them, in his quite different way, he was concerned with the wounded conscience, the private hazard. But while it is obviously proper in some sense to relate the poems of Robert Lowell to this tradition, it has little bearing on Roethke's work. And the tradition of the South can be ruled out. This suggests that the discussion of American literature in terms of these two traditions may by now have lost much of its force. To think of the New England tradition as scholastic, autocratic, and logical, and the Southern tradition as humanistic, Ciceronian, grammatical, and rhetorical is fine as far as it goes,[6] but its relevance clearly fades in regard to poets like Roethke. This may well be the point to emphasize, that Roethke and many of the poets of his generation took their food wherever they could find it. Yeats could well be more useful to them than, say, Hawthorne, because they saw their problems as being human, universal, in the first instance, and American problems only by application and inference. Roethke committed himself to his own life. He thought of it as a human event of some representative interest. And he set himself to work toward lucidity and order without turning himself into a case study entitled "The Still Complex Fate of Being an American." This is one aspect of Roethke's delicacy. Contemporary American poets, for the most part, are not going his way; they insist upon their complex fate and would not live without it. But Roethke's way of being an American is an eminently respectable way, and part of his achievement is that he makes it available to others.

"The Far Field"[7] is a distinguished example of this delicacy. It has four unequal sections. The first is a dream

of journeys, journeys without maps, featuring imprisonment, attenuation of being, the self "flying like a bat deep
into a narrowing tunnel" until there is nothing but darkness. It is life in a minor key, diminished thirds of being.
The second stanza translates these into major terms, images
of force, aggression, suffering, death, dead rats eaten by rain
and ground beetles. But the poet, meditating upon these
images, thinks of other images, of life, movement, freedom,
everything he means by "song." And these natural configurations lead to thoughts of life as cycle, evolution and return,
proliferations of being, the whole process of life, which the
poet calls "infinity"; what Wallace Stevens in "The
Bouquet" calls "the infinite of the actual perceived,/A freedom revealed, a realization touched,/The real made more
acute by an unreal." In the third section the poet feels a
corresponding change in himself, a moving forward, a quick-
ening, and as he commits himself to earth and air he says,
"I have come to a still, but not a deep center." Naturally it
feels like a loss, another diminution of being, even if the
sense of life-ordained process is strong. And this feeling leads
straight into the fourth and last section:

> The lost self changes,
> Turning toward the sea,
> A sea-shape turning around,—
> An old man with his feet before the fire,
> In robes of green, in garments of adieu.
>
> A man faced with his own immensity
> Wakes all the waves, all their loose wandering fire.
> The murmur of the absolute, the why
> Of being born fails on his naked ears.
> His spirit moves like monumental wind
> That gentles on a sunny blue plateau.
> He is the end of things, the final man.
>
> All finite things reveal infinitude:
> The mountain with its singular bright shade

Like the blue shine on freshly frozen snow,
The after-light upon ice-burdened pines;
Odor of basswood on a mountain-slope,
A scent beloved of bees;
Silence of water above a sunken tree:
The pure serene of memory in one man,—
A ripple widening from a single stone
Winding around the waters of the world.

Roethke says: "The end of things, the final man"; Stevens asserts in "The Auroras of Autumn":

There is nothing until in a single man contained,
Nothing until this named thing nameless is
And is destroyed. He opens the door of his house
On flames. The scholar of one candle sees
An Arctic effulgence flaring on the frame
Of everything he is. And he feels afraid.

The difference is that Stevens identifies the man with his imagination, and his imagination with his vision—and insists upon doing so. And the imagination feeds upon as much reality as it can "see" and values only that; what it can't see won't hurt or help it. The scholar has only this one candle. Roethke's man is not a scholar at all, or if he is, he is an amateur, perhaps a mere teacher. His imagination is partly his memory, which offers hospitality to sights, sounds, and smells, and partly his conscience, and partly his feeling for modes of being that he cannot command, directions that he cannot chart. Hence his poems are the cries of their occasions, but rarely cries of triumph. This is what makes his later poems the noble things they are, stretchings of the spirit without fantasia or panache. "Which is the way?" they ask, and if they include God in their reply they do so with due deference, knowing that one can be "too glib about eternal things," too much "an intimate of air and all its songs."

Another way of putting it is that the poems, especially

the middle poems, are cries of their occasions, sudden, isolated cries. The later poems turn cries into prayers, praying for a world order, a possible world harmony of which the cries are part, like voices in polyphony. The self in exposure is monotone; a sustaining society is polyphony; God is the Great Composer. The poet's ideal is the part song, music for several instruments, what the Elizabethans called "broken music." In "In Evening Air" Roethke says, "I'll make a broken music, or I'll die." In such poems as "The Marrow" and "In a Dark Time" he made a broken music at once personal and—in Stevens' sense—noble. And then, alas, he died.

NOTES

1 Theodore Roethke, *Words for the Wind* (Bloomington: Indiana Univ. Press, 1961), p. 181.

2 I owe this to James S. Southworth.

3 Roethke, "The Poet and the Poem," *New World Writing, No. 9* (Philadelphia: J. B. Lippincott, 1961), pp. 214–219.

4 Roethke, *The Far Field* (New York: Doubleday, 1964), pp. 89–90.

5 *Ibid.*, p. 79.

6 See H. M. McLuhan, "Poe's Tradition," *Sewanee Review,* LII (1944), pp. 31ff.

7 *The Far Field,* pp. 25–28.

CHAPTER 9

ELIZABETH BISHOP

IN MARCH 1938 *Partisan Review* published a story by Elizabeth Bishop called "In Prison," one of those stories which, like John Berryman's "The Imaginary Jew," James Merrill's "Driver," and Yvor Winters's "The Brink of Darkness," are particularly salient in their bearing upon their authors, upon each writer's work as a whole. Bishop wrote two such stories: the second is "In the Village," a companion piece to "In the Waiting Room" and other poems. It is never clear why a poet with no special inclination to fiction writes a story: it is hardly enough to assume that the poet wants a change of pace or the different conditions of form and composition which arise in fiction. Elizabeth Bishop wrote several pieces of prose, including "Rainy Season" and "The Hanging of the Mouse," short pieces which suggest that her imagination sometimes ran to marginal conceits, bizarreries of experience for which her customarily neat stanzas were unsuitable. Her few poems of Paris in her first book, *North and South* (1946), emerge from Surrealist interests which, in any official sense, didn't last long: she continued to keep herself alert to the surrealism of everyday life rather than to that of Aragon, Bréton, de Chirico, and Ernst; she did not cultivate Surrealism as a procedure. Nevertheless, the stirrings it appeased continued in her work, however subdued. I mention the matter at this early point because the received sense of Bishop's work, so far as I can judge it, makes her poetry sound far more domestic than it is. Her poems seem to me elusive; they rarely coincide with the evidence to which they testify. When we try to specify their tone, or the afterimage they leave in our mind, we find nothing entirely producible, the aura of the poetry is extraordinarily hard to account for. When we hear Bishop reading her poems, we find the reading not flat but flattened, as if she chose to discard as pretentious or indecent several more striking manners well within her range. Constance Rourke once remarked upon the indefinite identity of American art; as if the feelings in each case settled upon the expressive form available to them only with misgiving and restlessness. Bishop's poems seem always at one with themselves, and we are inclined to assume that their forms took possession of their substance easily and without remainder, form and feeling coming together as if by mutual vocation. It may be true; but it would be a mistake to act, from the start, upon such an assumption, taking every appearance of security at its form and word.

A sentence from "In Prison" will point us toward the poems: "One must be *in;* that is the primary condition." (1) In prison, but not only there; in one place rather than another; living in the interior rather than upon the coast, or the other way round; in one family, one generation, rather than another; in one space, alone or with other people; in one's poem, in the rarefied but crucial sense in which a poet is in her poem and, taking a longer view, in her poetry. The dictionaries say that "in" is "the preposition expressing the relation of inclusion, situation, position, existence, or action, within limits of space, time, conditions, circumstances, etc." Bishop's poetry is such a preposition; its major relations are those of presence and absence, if we think of presence as presence of mind as much as coming into the scene of an action; and if we think of absence as featuring loss, loss of loves and houses, shelters, security.

It is common to describe Bishop's poetry as a poetry of place, and to report that particular poems resort to Nova Scotia, New England, New York, Paris, Florida—"the state with the prettiest name"—Mexico, Brazil. A poet who calls her books *North and South, A Cold Spring* (1955), *Questions of Travel* (1965), and *Geography III* (1976) is drawing attention to them as earthwork, and inviting the reader to read the poems with that emphasis in view.

The poems may turn out to require other categories: they would
be odd indeed if the category of time could be sequestered while
reading them. But an emphasis is clearly marked. (2)

II

Elizabeth Bishop was born in Worcester, Massachusetts, on
February 8, 1911. Her father died when she was eight months
old. Her mother, mentally ill, spent long periods in hospital; she
was taken, when Elizabeth was five, to a mental hospital in
Dartmouth, Nova Scotia. Elizabeth never saw her again. The
child was brought up partly by her grandparents in Nova Scotia, partly by her mother's older sister in Boston. When she was
sixteen, she went to a boarding school near Boston, and from
there to Vassar College. When she graduated, she moved to New
York, and travelled in France and Italy. From 1938 she spent
ten years in Key West, Florida. In 1942 she met, in New York,
a Brazilian, Lota Costellat de Macedo Soares, and, beginning in
1951, they shared a house near Petrópolis in Brazil, and an
apartment in Rio de Janeiro. Bishop wrote a book about Brazil,
and stayed there for fifteen years, writing her poems and translating some poetry by modern Brazilian poets. In 1966 she returned to the United States, teaching poetry at various univer-
sities and especially at Harvard; in 1974 she took an apartment
in Boston. She died in the winter of 1979. So far as appearances go, her life was not dramatic. But one never knows about
drama.

III

One never knows about travel, either. For some poets, it means
freedom, mobility, new thresholds, new images. Some poets, like
Stevens, don't need to go far; they can imagine what it would
be like to go further. Some, like William Carlos Williams, stay
at home and make a virtue of that choice. It is safe to assume
that Bishop lived in far places so that she could mind her own
business. Besides, living abroad, she came naturally upon im-

ages congenial to her poetry: abroad, you need a map, some ease in the language, access to the lore, and the various artifacts which take possession of your space; conventions, newspapers, photographs, pictures, back numbers of the *National Geographic.*

If you start in Massachusetts or Nova Scotia and go south to Florida and further south to Brazil, you are likely to bring with you a question you would do well to hold in abeyance: is it different in kind, or is it—Brazil, for instance, starting at Santos—more of the same? Not that Bishop's poems are, in any limited sense, descriptive. If you want to know what São Paulo is like, or at least what it was like in 1935, Lévi-Strauss's *Tristes Tropiques* will tell you as much as you want to know. Bishop's poems don't compete: her book on Brazil is more informative. But exotic travel alerted her to correspondences between natural life and human life; she was alive to them before she went south, but Brazilian images sharpened this sense in her by offering it more extreme provocation.

I concede: even in her first poems, she was alert. In "The Map" "these peninsulas take the water between thumb and finger / like women feeling for the smoothness of yard-goods." In "The Imaginary Iceberg" one wave doesn't merely follow another; "waves give in to one another's waves," repetition, for Bishop, here betokening concessiveness. In "The Bight," white boats, piled up, stove in, lying against one another, are "like torn-open, unanswered letters." In "A Summer's Dream," a boarding house, painted blue, is streaked "as though it had been crying." A taxi-meter, in "Letter to N.Y." "glares like a moral owl." A very odd comparison is made in "Questions of Travel," where having to listen to rain is like having to listen to politicians' speeches; but, when you think of it, it is exactly judged. In "Going to the Bakery"—a Rio bakery—"the gooey tarts are red and sore." Sore? Yes, if you see the sheen on them as too much, an inflammation. In "The Moose" fog settles down upon the vegetables and flowers.

in gray glazed cabbages,
on the cabbage roses
and lupins like apostles.

Apostles; because they are so upright, and they are usually seen together in lines, maybe eleven or twelve of them, standing like witnesses waiting to be called or messengers to be sent; and because they are never the chief flower of the garden. Is Bishop, then, a latter-day Metaphysical poet? No; because she glances at these conceits, but leaves them, too, at a glance; she never drives them as far as they might conceivably go. In "Chemin de Fer" the little pond where the dirty hermit lives lies "like an old tear / holding onto its injuries / lucidly year after year." Imagine what Marvell would do with that conceit, if he chose to do anything with it. Lucidly: because there is no reason why the lucidity which maintains the injury should dim, or lapse; maintained as it is not by determination, which would have to be renewed, but by absolute conviction, unquestioned and unquestionable. In "The Man-Moth" the moth climbs up the facades, "his shadow dragging like a photographer's cloth behind him"; because, this time, concentration of will depends upon the exclusion of darkening possibilities. And in "Wading at Wellfleet" the glinting waves are compared to knife-blades attached to the wheels of Assyrian chariots in some old battle:

The war rests wholly with the waves:
they try revolving, but the wheels
give way; they will not bear the weight.

Nearly a Metaphysical figure, this one, but it stops just short of the stage of development at which the question of pretentiousness would arise; and then the further question, of feeling, in the particular case, strong enough to ride over such a question and set it beside the point.

In all these instances, Bishop is patiently engaging with the otherness of the natural world, drawing it, by the force of provisional comparison, toward the world she already knows. For

the moment, something there is like something here; that is all
she insists on reflecting. The likeness is valid, perhaps, only at
one point or in one respect. Lupins are like apostles, but mostly
unlike them: the comparison, to be just, must retain likeness and
unlikeness for the tension between them. The risk such a poetry runs is that of dissolving the otherness, so that the correspondences are facile; the natural world, opaque in much of its
character, is forced to give up its otherness and to give in to the
subjective imagination. Bishop wants to discover that the opacity of the natural world is not absolute; that the mind can deal
with such a world and remain patient before it; patient, not dis-
traught beyond endurance. But she doesn't want the foolish
victory of showing that the mind is—what it isn't—omnipotent.

Analogies and correspondences enliven the poet's sense that
while we live, as Stevens once felt, in a place that is not our own
and, much more, not ourselves, we may still live there with dignity. The conditions set for our living are not intolerable. We
don't need to suffuse the world with our mystery to make it
habitable. There is, indeed, no classic method, unless it is, as
Eliot said, to be very intelligent. But that virtue is not enough.
There are several kinds of intelligence, and the only one that
counts is the one that consists with thoughtfulness, the larger
considerations, care for the feelings provoked or violated on the
particular occasion. In "Roosters," one of Bishop's heartbreak-
ing and yet heartmending poems, the crowing cocks are like us
in some respects; they strut and terrorize, shout senseless orders all over the town, fight and destroy one another. But there
are holy sculptures in which the crowing cock is figured between an amazed Christ and bewildered Peter; and the moral
of the story is forgiveness. "Deny, deny" is not all the roosters
cry. Bishop's poem leaves the roosters as alien to us as they ever
were; all the more so because of their similarities to us. But the
poet's mind, recalling what others have felt, opens a space between the murderous cocks and the range of meaning they have
for us: her poem recalls that range, and gathers strength from
one of the traditions which have proposed to understand it. The

poem ends with the morning and its other interests; the sun, "the day's preamble / like wandering lines in marble." Preamble: a word very much of our human world, like "lines," a word for preliminary efforts to write, to understand; and a word, too, which goes back into the world we haven't made, the marble. Goes back into life considered as process:

> The sun climbs in,
> following 'to see the end',
> faithful as enemy, or friend.

The sun resolves the matter, but only by brightening the day; the roosters stop their crowing. The poem ascribes to the sun nothing more than, in our terms, curiosity, or whatever quality it is which prompts us to see an event to its end. "Faithful"? Faithful to what? To the event itself, as something to be seen, or even seen through. It is a question of unity. We live in a place that is not ourselves. How then do we live, given such a world? The easy way is to pretend that the world is ourselves, and to conspire with every appearance that makes the pretense at all feasible. Bishop's way is harder and more respectable: to see how far one's sense of analogy and correspondence will go, consistent with intelligence, and to cope with whatever remains. Sometimes, when the analogies come to an apparent end, Bishop feels only division, self-division, and in one poem, "The Weed," she deals with it by recourse to one of the better traditions for this exigency.

"The Weed," Bishop told Ashley Brown, "is modelled somewhat on George Herbert's 'Love unknown'," a poem she thought "almost surrealistic." (3) It seems clear that she came to Herbert's poem by way of Coleridge, who praised it in the *Biographia Literaria* as an example of the neutral style common to poetry and prose, but shook his head over it, nonetheless, as exhibiting "the characteristic fault of our elder poets," by which it conveyed "the most fantastic thoughts in the most correct and natural language." Bishop liked the poem, I think, for precisely the quality in it which troubled Coleridge: she had her own sense

of decorum, but it accommodated notably vigorous tension between fantastic thoughts and a convincingly easy or natural idiom. "Love unknown" is a dialogue between a Christian voice—
victim of God's attention—and a detached voice in a position to
review the attention. The two speakers may indeed be one, the
same speaker in two roles or moods, expansive and explicative,
a good talker and a good listener. Or we might give them Yeatsian names, self and soul. The self reports that one day he offered his master a gift of fruit, "and in the middle plac'd my
heart." But the master threw the heart into a font, and washed
it in a stream of blood which issued from a rock. Then the master threw the soul into a cauldron marked Affliction, to make
it supple. Released from the cauldron, the self resorted to its
bed for rest and sleep; but found that someone "had stuff'd the
bed with thoughts. / I would say *thorns*"; a linguist, whatever else.
The soul then tells the self that only good was intended:

> The Font did onely, what was old, renew:
> The Caldron suppled, what was grown too hard:
> The Thorns did quicken, what was grown too dull.

In "The Weed" the speaker dreams of her death, and of her
final thought standing frozen there in her heart. A weed grows
up, pushing through the heart, sending out a leaf on each side.
The heart begins to change, and splits apart into two streams
which flow through the black grains of earth and threaten to
sweep the weed away. But it survives, heavy with drops of water:

> The weed stood in the severed heart.
> 'What are you doing there?', I asked.
> It lifted its head all dripping wet
> (with my own thoughts?)
> and answered then: 'I grow', it said,
> "but to divide your heart again".

The severed heart is one of Bishop's motifs, but she presents it
as the price, high but not outrageous, which has to be paid for
the boon of being alive. Unity would be better, if it could be
had without loss and without, as in Herbert's allegory, hard-

heartedness and dullness. In "The Weed" the weed-deflected
stream is made of racing images

> (As if a river should carry all
> the scenes that it had once reflected
> shut in its waters, and not floating
> on momentary surfaces.)

—which I take as denoting Bishop's ambivalence about experience itself, and the memory of it. The good that nothing should
be lost is balanced against the evil that everything we have ever
done and suffered must be remembered: "shut in its waters" is
a threat as much as a possession. The alternative, figured as
"floating / on momentary surfaces," means a high price, too, that
no experience is allowed to "take," or to make, at last, a difference.

Bishop returned to the motif of severance in one of her last
poems, "Sonnet," where the primary condition of being *in* is
evaded or transcended, but at a price:

> Caught—the bubble
> in the spirit-level,
> a creature divided;
> and the compass needle
> wobbling and wavering,
> undecided.
> Freed—the broken
> thermometer's mercury
> running away;
> and the rainbow-bird from the narrow bevel
> of the empty mirror,
> flying wherever
> it feels like, gay!

More like one of Emily Dickinson's exclamations than like Herbert's parable, this poem moves from "caught" to "freed" in a
way which qualifies each of those chapter-headings. Caught, yes,
but in a condition which makes possible the responsiveness of

compass-needle and spirit-level. Both of these instruments are undecided, in the sense that every decision has to be made anew and afresh, and no prior decision helps. Each decision is delicate and arduous, but from it comes whatever ardor enlivens such a life. Freed; but in terms so deeply qualified as to make the freedom hardly better than nominal. A thermometer tells of fever, fire in the blood; a mirror tells of division; a mirror records no heart but some appearances. An empty mirror says nothing about division by saying nothing about anything: a broken thermometer doesn't allay fever merely by withholding report of it. Bishop's imagination, Romantic in this poem rather than Metaphysical, turns a shape into a rainbow-bird, a humming-bird of South America, and releases it along with the desire for release in whatever form. But there is a gap between the desire, figured most richly in the rhythm of the last lines— the rhetorical endlessness of "wherever" and the last gesture, after the comma, "gay"—and the analogies called upon to release it. Spirit-level, compass, thermometer, and rainbow-bird do their poetic duty, but they speak more clearly of division accepted than of division resented; such resentment as there is, in this case, is carried by the music of the words rather than by their syntax.

But the figure which seems to represent the human mind most clearly in Bishop's poems is the sandpiper, in the poem of that name. Sandpiper is the common name of any limicoline or shore-wading bird other than plover or snipe. That it lives between water and land is much of its poetic significance. The geographer Carl Sauer has argued, in an essay on "Seashore—Primitive Home of Man?", that "a riparian location is indicated for man's earliest living." Habitat by the waterside, he maintains, "is the most general term proposed for the primitive ecology of mankind, be it along stream, lake, or seashore." (4) One thinks of William Empson's "Arachne": "Twixt devil and deep sea, man hacks his caves." Bishop's poem represents the sandpiper as running along the wet sand:

> He runs, he runs to the south, finical, awkward,
> in a state of controlled panic, a student of Blake.

Presumably the panic comes with the world, sand, waves; the control comes as a possibility with Blake. But the bird is not in control; he is preoccupied, "looking for something, something, something." If it were sufficient to be a student of Blake, one would see a world in a grain of sand and a heaven in a wild flower; hold infinity in the palm of one's hand and eternity in an hour. But the sandpiper's studies are incomplete, or they don't really solve the hard questions:—

> Poor bird, he is obsessed:
> The millions of grains are black, white, tan, and gray,
> mixed with quartz grains, rose and amethyst.

The sandpiper, presumably, can't make head or tail of these grains of sand; but can't take his eyes off them. The poet, conspiring with the documentary character of language, gives them a few rudimentary names, hoping the corresponding distinctions will, in practice, be enough. But it is primitive dealing, under whatever name.

Panic is never far away from Bishop's feeling. The mind does what it can, and it is not negligible, but there is always something beyond what can be known and possessed, a margin of opacity beyond anyone's endeavors. Obsession is the mind's state when it can't take for granted or leave well alone; subject is fixed upon object without any real hope of understanding it; fixed, nonetheless. What is left? Nothing much, unless it is the human will to endure, to survive.

"The Man-Moth" is Bishop's supreme poem on this predicament. Based on a misprint—manmoth for mammoth—the poem construes man's life in a city—New York, presumably, where Bishop lived in 1935, when she wrote the poem—as a moth's emergence from beneath the streets, his climb up the sidewall of the buildings toward the moon, which he thinks is a hole in the tent of the sky. He must climb to see for himself, and he must fail. Each night, like man, he dreams his recurrent dreams; he rides the subways, because there is nothing else to do. The poem ends:—

> If you catch him,
> hold up a flashlight to his eye. It's all dark pupil,
> an entire night itself, whose haired horizon tightens
> as he stares back, and closes up the eye. Then from the lids
> one tear, his only possession, like the bee's sting, slips.
> Slyly he palms it, and if you're not paying attention
> he'll swallow it. However, if you watch, he'll hand it over,
> cool as from underground springs and pure enough to drink.

This extraordinary stanza goes, to use a few phrases from Stevens's "Notes Toward a Supreme Fiction," "from the poet's gibberish to / The gibberish of the vulgate and back again." The words are as ordinary as Herbert's, and their arrangement is just as "natural" as his. The trope is fantastic not in its origin but in its end. A poet gifted in fancies and conceits might have thought of man as a moth and given him much the same nightly routine which he gets in Bishop's poem; but no mere conceitist would find the terrible logic fulfilled in turning the moth into a man again, shifty and desperate, trying to hide his sole possession. The tear protects the eye, fends off the flashlight's glare: in other poems it contains its own light, but here it seems to signify man's will, which he sometimes does well to conceal. Gibberish: one gibbers, as R. P. Blackmur said by way of gloss on Stevens's phrases, "before a reality too great, when one is appalled with perception, when words fail though meaning persists." Or when, as in Bishop's poem, the words fail in every respect except to stand and speak for the human will, where there is nothing else to vouch for.

There is another poem to read in the same spirit, where the analogies invoked have to do not with the mind but with the will. I think of both as Bishop's Kafka-poems, without implying an obligation. "The Armadillo" is famous, partly because it set Robert Lowell writing in a way which issued in "Skunk Hour."

Both poems, as Lowell remarked, "use short line stanzas, start with drifting description and end with a single animal." (5) It is not much to say, except for the reference to drifting description. Lowell means, I take it, descriptive writing which goes on its way as if it were just passing the time, not claiming anything much for the events and objects described: these rather than nothing, the description seems to say.

A poem in ten stanzas of four lines each, mostly short, three or four feet, rhyming, half-rhyming, or off-rhyming, "The Armadillo" starts off as if it meant to describe the fire balloons which are released, illegally because dangerously, at night in Rio. Five stanzas describe this in a fairly neutral style, but there is an occasional grace-note to hint that more than description is planned. The paper chambers flush and fill with light "that comes and goes, like hearts." Some of the balloons are carried off by the wind, and the poet watches them

> receding, dwindling, solemnly
> and steadily forsaking us

as if she were still thinking of hearts, affections, passions, and their withdrawal. The first half of the poem is description as drifting as the balloons, with only those two touches of analogy to show that at any moment an ostensibly casual sentence can go an unintended way or strike a nerve. Sometimes the balloons turn dangerous, as passion does. Bishop describes the danger; how a balloon fell, splattering "like an egg of fire" against the cliff behind the house, and the flame ran down and burned two nesting owls and a baby rabbit; and an armadillo left the scene,

> rose-flecked, head down, tail down.

The poem ends, in italics:—

> Too pretty, dreamlike mimicry!
> O falling fire and piercing cry
> and panic, and a weak mailed fist
> clenched ignorant against the sky!

Up to this point, the poem has been first descriptive, then narrative: now, in the vocative mood, verbs recede from action to gesture. Bishop rarely aspires to the grand style, but these four lines justify the surge. Four lines, three of them with end-rhymes, making the fourth stand out like a fist: each line a perfect iambic tetrameter. The first line sets the pattern, modified by the break, with "pretty," in the middle of the second foot. The second line reasserts the pattern, and the break in the phrasing coincides with the second foot, but the sense runs over into the third line—"and panic," the only noun without its adjective. The third line ends with iambics, the pattern quite regular, but the last words of it, monosyllables, are spoken as if they made a spondee—"mailed fist," so that the line seems to enact the gesture it describes—"and a weak mailed fist / clenched ignorant against the sky." The syntax directs the challenge across the metres to the end. "Weak" and "ignorant" are near enough to one another to mime the rift between knowledge and will; nothing we know avails, there remains only the force of will, a mimicry of power, helpless but, in its way, beautiful. Armadillo, the dictionary says, is the name of several species of burrowing animals peculiar to South America; specially distinguished by the bony armor in which their whole body is encased, and by the habit of rolling themselves, when captured, into an impregnable ball, sheltered by this armor.

When the force of will—or mimicry of that force—is in question, the poem to read, besides "The Armadillo," is "The Unbeliever," another allegory in a seventeenth-century mode but, this time, taking its bearing and motto from Bunyan: "He sleeps on the top of a mast." In the First Part of *The Pilgrim's Progress* Christian dreams that he came upon three men fast asleep, "with fetters upon their heels." Their names were Simple, Sloth, and Presumption. Trying to arouse them, he shouted: "You are like them that sleep on the top of a mast." The reference is to Proverbs, xxiii, 34: "Yea, thou shalt be as he that lieth down in the midst of the sea, or as he that lieth upon the top of a mast." "The Dead Sea is under you," Christian cries,—"a gulf that hath no bottom." To which Simple answers: "I see no danger"; and Sloth, "Yet a little more sleep!"; and Presumption, "Every vat must stand upon its own bottom." So they lay down to sleep again, and Christian continued on his way. Bishop's poem retains the three speakers, but distances their characters: they are the unbeliever, a cloud, and a gull. The cloud would correspond to Bunyan's Simple if Bishop's poem were at all religious or doctrinal, but it is entirely secular. What she ascribes to the cloud is modern subjectivity; this character is "secure in introspection." The gull would correspond to Bunyan's Presumption: a visionary, imperious in his certainty. Up here, he says, "I tower through the sky / for the marble wings on my towertop fly." The unbeliever sleeps on the top of his mast "with his eyes closed tight." He is not, apparently, a master of knowledge: nor does he claim anything for consciousness. He dreams, but not of reason. Evidently he is concentrated upon a purpose not prescribed by consciousness but by instinct, self-defense, self-preservation:—

> The gull inquired into his dream,
> which was, "I must not fall.
> The spangled sea below wants me to fall.
> It is hard as diamonds; it wants to destroy us all".

"The spangled sea" is an allusion rather than an invention: it is well established, as in Tennyson's "The spangle dances in bight and bay." It has often been used of the sky, spangled with stars. In every use I have seen, it has the force of distance, gaudy carelessness, indifference to the human feelings dazzled by its glitter. The metallic quality is strident: hard as diamonds. The sea, in Bishop as in Stevens, is the reality which has to be mastered or appeased. In "The Unbeliever" the moral of the story is that the sea is omnivorous, indifferent to nice distinctions between one aesthetic attitude and another: "it wants to destroy us all," and can be prevented, presumably, only by force of will. "I must not fall."

Vigilance, despite every appearance of sleep, is Bishop's counsel. In Bunyan, as in Proverbs, sleep is the time of spiritual danger, when evil is seeking whom he may devour and finds no resistance. What corresponds to vigilance, in Bishop's poetry generally, is mobility of responsiveness, an intelligence not restless but ready. The rhetoric of her poems arises from attentiveness; she pays attention, listening to "the music of what happens," living with no armor except vigilance. She does not resort to an ideology, or to any other device which would deal with experience chiefly by forestalling it. She does not suppose that paying attention will ward off every ghost. Her tone of voice—and it seems entirely appropriate to use such a phrase in her case—is always admitting that beyond an uncertainly placed point there is no certainty: our acts of appropriation are bound to fail. It is absurd to be effusive in such a world. But there is every reason for vigilance, for keeping the mind on the alert. As in the last lines of Bishop's "Florida":—

> Cold white, not bright, the moonlight is coarse-meshed,
> and the careless, corrupt state is all black specks
> too far apart, and ugly whites; the poorest
> post-card of itself.
> After dark, the pools seem to have slipped away.
> The alligator, who has five distinct calls:
> friendliness, love, mating, war, and a warning—
> whimpers and speaks in the throat
> of the Indian Princess.

Vigilance here appears as a quality of the mind that makes distinctions; between cold white and bright—a distinction Bishop was ready to make on ordinary occasions, saying of Marianne Moore that "her eyes were bright, not 'bright' as we often say about eyes when we really mean alert; they were that too, but also shiny bright and, like those of a small animal, often looked at one sidewise . . . ." Or between moonlights fine-meshed and coarse-meshed. Or, another distinction, between different acts of mind, as here between description and discrimination—"the careless, corrupt state," corrupt because careless of the issues the state should care for. Or a distinction between tones, as in the last lines about the alligator, where the reader is not allowed to have the noun completed by the verb—"whimpers"— till a suitable context has been readied for it, a discrimination of five alligator-noises none of which necessarily coincides with the whimper audible on this occasion. It is not precisely Stevens's Florida, "venereal soil," but compatible with it.

Vigilance is one of Bishop's ways of controlling panic, keeping the mind on guard. Another is to control the rate at which intimations of danger and nothingness are acted upon. She once praised Hopkins for his power of timing, "the releasing, checking, timing, and repeating of the movement of the mind according to ordered systems." The ordered systems, in any particular poem, are not official; they seem to have to do with the relation between the sense-value of the words and, like a net in tennis, a metrical scheme in some degree regular. The sense plays across the official metrical pattern, and the art of the play is timing. Bishop early recognized in Hopkins what she soon came to master for herself. As for her ordered systems: her favorite plan, in such poems as "The Armadillo" and "At the Fishhouses," is to start with a common scene—it may be nearly anything—and set description going, as if the scene were describing itself, casually; and then to let the appearance of casualness darken, as it will, by coming upon unintended nuances, coincidences of language which turn the poem into a minefield. Gradually, the poetry seems to decide not to ignore what the meddling words have turned up. The poet's timing accommodates these turns, and responds to them. Otherwise put: her system begins with what she calls—without referring to any system—"self-forgetful, perfectly useless concentration," and it goes on by taking the risk of anything the concentration turns up.

"At the Fishhouses" begins in this way: an evening down by the fishhouses where an old man is working on his nets, waiting for the herring boats to come in. Seemingly aimless description: the five fishhouses, the wheelbarrows and tubs, an old capstan, a chat with the man about the declining population in the village. Then the sea, "cold dark deep and absolutely clear": but as if "absolutely" reminded the poet of othernesses terrible rather than enhancing, the tone of the poem changes to meet the exigency:—

> Cold dark deep and absolutely clear,
> element bearable to no mortal,
> to fish and to seals . . .

One seal in particular; and the ominous note is suppressed as the poet recalls seeing the seal, years ago. But the note reasserts itself, having waited for the reminiscence to end, and it comes in the same words:—

> Cold dark deep and absolutely clear,
> the clear gray icy water . . .

Note to the reader: watch out, when Bishop repeats a word, it never means what it has already said. The second "clear" is turned toward "gray" and "icy." But again, the darkening is fended off, as the poet turns her eyes away from the sea, back, toward the hills and the trees:—

>   . . . Back, behind us,
> the dignified tall firs begin.
> Bluish, associating with their shadows,
> a million Christmas trees stand
> waiting for Christmas.

A detail, a detour of mind, which justifies our own: the lines, as Charles Tomlinson has pointed out, (6) are an allusion to Marianne Moore's "An Octopus," which in turn alludes to a passage in Ruskin. Near the end of *Modern Painters,* there is a curious passage in which Ruskin tries to explain why Turner couldn't paint pine-trees with any success, Other trees "yield to the form and sway of the ground, clothe it with soft compli-

ance, are partly its subjects, partly its flatterers, partly its com-
forters." But the pine

> "rises in serene resistence, self-contained":—Nor can I ever without
> awe stay long under a great Alpine cliff, far from all house or work
> of men, looking up to its companies of pines, as they stand on the
> inaccessible juts and perilous ledges of the enormous wall, in quiet
> multitudes, each like the shadow of the one beside it—upright, fixed,
> spectral, as troops of ghosts standing on the walls of Hades, not
> knowing each other—dumb for ever. You cannot reach them, can-
> not cry to them;—those trees never heard human voice; they are
> far above all sound but of the winds. No foot ever stirred fallen leaf
> of theirs. All comfortless they stand, between the two eternities of
> the Vacancy and the Rock; yet with such iron will that the rock it-
> self looks bent and shattered beside them—fragile, weak, inconsis-
> tent, compared to their dark energy of delicate life, and monotony
> of enchanted pride:—unnumbered, unconquerable. (7)

If we find ourselves inclined to mock the passage, the reason is
that we are embarrassed by the evidence of feelings we regard
as silly or archaic. If we agree with Tomlinson that "unnum-
bered, unconquerable" is a misplaced organ-note, it is because
we think everything is both numbered and conquered. Sublimity is difficult, now that travel and color photographs of Alpine
scenery have removed the sentiment of "awe." But mountain
gloom and mountain glory were still available to Ruskin: he had
no cause to be ashamed of expressing these sentiments.

Marianne Moore recalled the passage when she was writing
"An Octopus," a poem in some sense—however tenuous—about
the glacial Big Snow Mountain, Mount Rainier, though it is not
a poem in Ruskin's spirit. Moore was impressed by Ruskin's insistence that the ability to see is rarer than the ability to think,
but on this occasion the mountain is neither to be seen nor
thought of. The poem consists of darting phrases which make
leaps of mind across themes—the flora, fauna, and animalia of
a glacial mountain—which could not be deemed responsible for
any of them. Moore eschews dealing with the sublime, and re-

places it with a choreography of relations intelligible so long as the question of their plausibility is not raised. At one point she alludes to Ruskin, chiefly to subdue what she regards as his shamelessness. His pines become firs:—

> The fir-trees, in 'the magnitude of their root systems',
> rise aloof from these maneuvers 'creepy to behold',
> austere specimens of our American royal families,
> 'each like the shadow of the one beside it.
> The rock seems frail compared with their dark energy of life',
> its vermilion and onyx and manganese-blue interior expensive-
>   ness
> left at the mercy of the weather; (8)

The passage retains more of Ruskin than the lines in quotation marks: the aloofness and austerity of the trees, their superiority to the rock. But Moore's sensibility, civic in its refusal to be sublime, involves trees and rock at once in social considerations. The passage is dominated not by intensities of landscape but by social idioms—"our American royal families" and the rock's "expensiveness"—which speak more of Veblen than of Ruskin.

Bishop's lines—

> . . . Back, behind us,
> the dignified tall firs begin.
> Bluish, associating with their shadows,
> a million Christmas trees stand
> waiting for Christmas. The water seems suspended
> above the rounded gray and blue-gray stones.
> I have seen it over and over, the same sea, the same,
> slightly, indifferently swinging above the stones,
> icily free above the stones,
> above the stones and then the world.

—conflate Ruskin and Moore without being awed by the one or dazzled by the other. She, too, disowns sublimity, but brings further the subduing process and subdues the subduer. Moore removes the mystery from Ruskin by forcing the reader, instead of letting himself be awed into vertigo, to pause upon each phrase long enough to work out what it is doing there, the delay giving time for the awe to evaporate. Bishop curbs both Ruskin and Moore; Ruskin, by leaving only a trace of the willpower he ascribes to the trees ("Bluish, associating with their shadows"); Moore, she curbs by letting the reader move forward more quickly, the impediment of Moore's forcepped phrases removed. The reader's eyes, like her own, turn back to stones and water, without further cognitive ado. Bishop has lifted her eyes to the trees, but not to derive from them a domestic parable. The notion that the firs stand waiting for Christmas doesn't drive the passage beyond the neutral style for which, after Ruskin and Moore, she has settled. When she turns back to the water and the stones, what the syntax mimes, in its dragging repetitions, is the mind's fixation on the sea and its indifference; its freedom unlimitedly greater than ours. And as the indifference of one element means the indifference of all—

> If you should dip your hand in,
> your wrist would ache immediately,
> your bones would begin to ache and your hand would burn
> as if the water were a transmutation of fire
> that feeds on stones and burns with a dark gray flame.
> If you tasted it, it would first taste bitter,
> then briny, then surely burn your tongue.

According to Heraclitus, water is indeed a transmutation of fire: the relevant fragment reads, in Philip Wheelwright's translation: "The transformations of fire are: first, sea; and of sea, half becomes earth, and half the lightning-flash." That Nature is a Heraclitean fire is a notion more congenial to Bishop than to Hopkins, who couldn't bear a Heraclitean cosmology until it was transformed into the Christian doctrine of resurrection. Bishop doesn't look for anything more than what may be divined by putting your hand in cold Northern water, and letting the ache continue till it seems like burning. The poem ends:—

If you tasted it, it would first taste bitter,
then briny, then surely burn your tongue.
It is like what we imagine knowledge to be:
dark, salt, clear, moving, utterly free,
drawn from the cold hard mouth
of the world, derived from the rocky breasts
forever, flowing and drawn, and since
our knowledge is historical, flowing, and flown.

More difficult than they seem, these lines treat knowledge, too, as otherness; for the moment, it is just as foreign as the sea or any other element that is "not ourselves." Bishop is refusing the consolation of philosophy; regarding knowledge not as mine, yours, or hers, but as defined more by its origin in otherness than its end in us: "drawn from . . . derived from the rocky breasts" distances knowledge from us who claim to possess it, and gives it back to the elements, its first company. "And since / our knowledge is historical"; as distinct, presumably, from real or elemental knowledge. Historicism can mean nearly anything, but Bishop's phrase seems to take it strictly, and refers to what the O. E. D. calls "the attempt to view all social and cultural phenomena, all categories, truths, and values, as relative and historically determined, and in consequence to be understood only by examining their historical context, in complete detachment from present-day attitudes." Historicism, in that sense, would be congenial to a Northerner who found herself living in a South where different axioms prevailed; living there, too, with sympathies and enchantments she could not have anticipated in Worcester, Mass.

IV

"Our knowledge is historical," in a particular and perhaps limiting sense. Bishop's poems act upon knowledge geographical rather than historical. It is true that memory is vivid in her poems, but she does not relish it as a property. Her sense of loss and lapse is acute, but she seems to need to establish herself in space rather than in time; especially since her sense of home is gravely qualified. The notion of home and residence is rarely more than provisional in her poetry, even though her conviction of being real seems to depend more upon houses and places and her presence in them than upon historical epiphanies, golden spots of time. In "Five Flights Up" she envies bird and dog who find their questions—if they are questions—answered simply by having day succeed night:—

> He and the bird know everything is answered,
> all taken care of,
> no need to ask again.
> —Yesterday brought to today so lightly!
> (A yesterday I find almost impossible to lift.)

To lift: to lift its burden, enforced remembrance; or to retain it, lifting it out of the slough of everything gone and forgotten. The first is more probable, given the tone in which bird and dog are envied.

An American option, this. One of the motives of American poetry since Emerson has been to remove the privilege of history; to refuse the European afflatus with its claim upon privileged acts and monuments. It is American rhetorical practice to treat every detail as if it were equal to everything else; in Marianne Moore's poems, as Hugh Kenner has observed, the act of seeing makes every object of attention equal in at least that democratic respect. Moore's quotations are more likely to come from newspapers or magazines, the *Illustrated London News* or such, than from accredited masterpieces; implying that a mind ready to pay attention will find its readiness repaid in unlikely ways.

But the American rhetoric of space has taken some extreme forms. "I take SPACE to be the central fact to man born in America, from Folsom cave to now," Olson asserted in the first sentence of *Call Me Ishmael* (1947). The assertion isn't in Bishop's spirit. Space and geography are her terms, but understood rather as Sauer understood them when he proposed "historical geography" as a study of "the series of changes which the cultural landscapes have undergone," the development, as he put it, "of the present cultural landscape out of earlier cultures and the natural landscape." And he quoted von Humboldt, who pointed out that "in classical antiquity the earliest historians made little attempt to separate the description of lands from the narration of events the scene of which was in the areas described." Herodotus and Polybius were geographers as much as historians. Historical geography resumes history, even while it finds its material in a particular area or region.

Space, then, is the element of Bishop's poems, but not in any sense of propaganda or rejection. She has a need to feel at home in the world; secure in her bearing. Panic besets such a person through an appalling sense of displacement. Her best poems are preoccupied with her being in a world most of which she can't believe we know, since our knowledge is merely a bundle of sentiments, fears, anxieties, misgivings, which nothing dragged or rescued from the past can alleviate. Her best poems: my list includes, in no special order, "Poem," "Love Lies Bleeding," "The Unbeliever," "Roosters," "Cootchie," "Anaphora," "Over 2000 Illustrations and a Complete Concordance," "Five Flights Up," "The Bight," "At the Fishhouses," "Cape Breton," "Insomnia," "One Art," "The Prodigal," "The Monument," "Brazil, January 1, 1502," "Questions of Travel," "The Armadillo," "Sandpiper," "Going to the Bakery," "In the Waiting Room," "Crusoe in England," "The Moose," and "The End of March."

I haven't included one of Bishop's best-known poems, "The Fish." I still find its ending coy, and too much a matter of self-congratulation. But in any case I associate "The Fish" with the one occasion on which I had any communication with Bishop, and the occasion does me little credit. I had published, in *Poetry*, an essay called "After Reading Hannah Arendt," the gist of which was to say that after reading Arendt's books I found most of the current poetry I was reading small beer. Unfortunately, I chose "The Fish" to illustrate the point; the poem was in high repute, but I was troubled by the preening note at the end of it, when the speaker throws the fish back into the water. Soon after the essay appeared, I had a letter from Bishop, not indeed remonstrating but saying that her poem wasn't intended as a major statement and that comparison with a political philosopher's work of a lifetime was hardly appropriate. There the matter ended. Presumably I had already regretted the essay, having got some irritation off my chest. I didn't take up the correspondence with Bishop.

I want now to look at two poems which seem to me remarkable even by Bishop's achieved standards.

"Over 2000 Illustrations and a Complete Concordance" is a poem about seeing, and the good of seeing; which means that it is about imagining and remembering. The poet, say, is looking through a gazetteer; not the text, only the pictures. The first pictures, of the Seven Wonders of the World, are too stale to be imagined. There is no merit in it. Other scenes, of the Holy Land, are sufficiently foreign to be construed: an Arab, pointing, could be plotting against "our Christian Empire." In another picture the human figure could be imagined as "far gone in history or theology"; ardent, perhaps, in espousing the first or defining the second. The poem is printed continuously, in *The Complete Poems 1927–1979*, except for two line-breaks, the first at the end of the gazetteer-section, the second at the end of the personal recollections. In earlier printings, only the second line-break occurred. But in any case it goes naturally enough in three sections.

The second section drifts out of the gazetteer into personal recollections of travel: Newfoundland, Rome, Mexico, Volubilis, Dingle, Marrakesh, and an unnamed Arab graveyard. These are recalled fairly casually, but there are signs of dissatisfaction, as if the poet were asking herself, "What, in the end, do these episodes mean; or do they, in any conceiveable way, matter?" It is common for poets to worry about memory. In the "Epilogue" to his *Day by Day* Robert Lowell writes:—

I want to make
something imagined, not recalled.

Wordsworth thought memory and imagination compatible forms of energy, but Blake thought memory a nuisance, alien to the original and originating power of imagination. We don't know what Bishop thought about it. She gives each little episode, in this second section, what she thinks it's worth, and the last episode, the Arabian one, is given some weight. But the section breaks off. After the pause, indicated in all printings by the line-break, the poem ends:—

> Everything only connected by 'and' and 'and'.
> Open the book. (The gilt rubs off the edges
> of the pages and pollinates the fingertips.)
> Open the heavy book. Why couldn't we have seen
> this old Nativity while we were at it?
> —the dark ajar, the rocks breaking with light,
> an undisturbed, unbreathing flame,
> colorless, sparkless, freely fed on straw,
> and, lulled within, a family with pets,
> —and looked and looked our infant sight away.

Difficult, again, and it looks easy. It seems generally assumed that "everything only connected by 'and' and 'and' " is Bishop's rueful expression of the random or pointless character of her experiences. David Kalstone's interpretation of the poem goes along this line; Childhood memories of etchings of the Holy Land in an old Bible, he says, "make her yearn for something beyond the *and* and *and* of pointlessly accumulated travel." (9) Anyone who travels a good deal is likely to have such a mood. But I'm not convinced. Bishop could have such a mood and still feel that a syntax of ands is good enough. How much order or syntax a life needs, is a personal matter: some lives get along quite well on the least degree of order compatible with its being order at all. Other lives have to have a pattern in place before-hand, so that every new experience fulfills a prior requirement. It would be possible to read Bishop's line in a tone of elation, if you felt that you wanted your life to have a lot of risk or randomness. The line may be a punning allusion to Margaret Schlegel's "Only connect the prose and the passion," in *Howards End*. The point about "and" is that it joins things which are roughly equivalent, or things strikingly different: that is why the conjunction is needed, and it's far more patient than "but" or "therefore."

There's another problem with the last line of the poem: "and looked and looked our infant sight away." John Ashbery has said that after twenty years—the poem first appeared in *Partisan Review* in 1948—"I am unable to exhaust the meaning and mysteries of its concluding line . . . and I suspect that its secret has very much to do with the nature of Miss Bishop's poetry: looking, or attention, will absorb the object with its meaning." (10) Kalstone gives several possible interpretations, without committing himself to any. "Where or when is *away*? Is it a measureless absorption in the scene? Or, on the contrary, a loss of powers, as in 'to waste away'? Or a welcome relinquishment, to be gathered back into the world of childhood, to return to 'infant' sight—it keeps its Latin root, 'speechless'." If the line is restored to its sentence, "Why couldn't we have seen . . . ," it seems to long for a kind of seeing in which, absorption in the object being so complete, the child would not be aware of herself as seeing: she would not be aware of the gap across which the act of seeing would throw its energy. Adults can't see in that way or with that degree of absorption; they are always aware of themselves as seeing. Memory is always aware of itself as memory, and is grateful, in Proust's way, for involuntary occasions and chance encounters. The act of imagining could be such a seeing, especially if it were the kind of imagining that Keats, Coleridge, and Hazlitt attributed to Shakespeare; dramatic rather than egotistical. Shakespeare gives imagined things a life of their own, he does not lend them his own life or force them to receive it.

The other poem I want to look at is "Crusoe in England." Bishop went back to *Robinson Crusoe* and thought the book "aw-

ful," pious, "all that Christianity." She remembered a visit to
Aruba, long before it became a resort: the island was full of small
volcanoes. So she got the notion of seeing Crusoe again with all
the Christianity left out.

Crusoe is back in England, remembering, musing with himself, talking to himself, having nothing better to do. It is good
talk, even if no one is there to listen: communication, we are
free to infer, is not the only motive of speech. Words alone may
not be, as Yeats once thought, certain good, but they are good
for certain things, one of which is to adorn or caress an experience long gone:—

> When all the gulls flew up at once, they sounded
> like a big tree in a strong wind, its leaves.
> I'd shut my eyes and think about a tree,
> an oak, say, with real shade, somewhere.

Not only a gorgeous sound but a wonderful stroke, that phrase,
"its leaves," Crusoe's mind going back to the detail when the
sentence was already complete but the sound of sense needed
a little more. What the lines mime is not the gulls flying but
Crusoe's feeling, flying with them. The revisions and additions
in the other lines—"a tree, / an oak, say, with real shade, somewhere"—mark Crusoe's desire not merely to commit himself to
his thinking but to make the most of it; as one does by shutting
one's eyes to begin with.

Crusoe's comparisons are always—what else could they be
expected to be?—domestic and personal. His volcanoes looked
as if they had "their heads blown off," the waterspouts have "their
heads in cloud, their feet in moving patches / of scuffed-up
white," the spouts are—in a flourish of making the most of
them—"sacerdotal beings of glass":—

> . . . All the hemisphere's
> left-over clouds arrived and hung
> above the craters—their parched throats
> were hot to touch

—an odd passage, incidentally, because the grammar seems to say that "parched throats" refers to the clouds, but the sense of the whole makes the phrase refer to the craters and has the clouds hanging above them because the craters are hot to touch.

Crusoe's nightmares, too, turn a baby goat into a baby's throat—by a slip of the rhyme which becomes a slitting of flesh. But they are mostly nightmares of imprisonment, of "islands spawning islands" and of Crusoe having to live "on each and every one"

> . . . eventually,
> for ages, registering their flora,
> their fauna, their geography

—as if perception, too, were a form of imprisonment; which it is, given that any faculty imposes the compulsion to practice it, with a purpose or not:—

> Just when I thought I couldn't stand it
> another minute longer, Friday came.
> (Accounts of that have everything all wrong.)
> Friday was nice.
> Friday was nice, and we were friends.
> If only he had been a woman!

I hear an allusion to Eliot's "Whispers of Immortality": "Grishkin is nice"; but the repetition—Friday was nice—is more to the point, Crusoe's words hovering upon the image, caressing it. "Pretty to watch; he had a pretty body": we think of Bishop as a decorous poet, but her erotic sense was keen. No wonder she loved Billy Holiday's music and wrote "Songs for a Colored Singer" with its superb

> I'm going to go and take the bus
> and find someone monogamous.

In "Crusoe in England" Bishop's repetitions, as in Lady's blues, mime the sense that our losses and woes are in language, just as poignantly as Crusoe's body is on the island and, in dream, on all the other islands.

Back in England—

> Now I live here, another island,
> that doesn't seem like one, but who decides?

Crusoe is even more isolated than he was in his un-renamable one. Friday is long dead. Crusoe's will is idle. The things which had meant most to him—his knife, which had "reeked of meaning, like a crucifix"—are inert. His eyes rest on these things, but there is no life in them, or indeed in him. Hopkins has a note in his Journal: "What you look hard at seems to look hard at you." Crusoe says of his knife: "Now it won't look at me at all." Meaning, Crusoe's musing seems to say, arises from need and the power of will as provoked by need. I take the poem to be about the loss of radiance, of aura—to use Walter Benjamin's word—as objects lose the life we have given them, and we too lose much of ourselves. Arthur Symons once wrote of the dance: "The picture lasts only long enough to have been there."

V

Bishop's poetry, on all the available evidence, is justly admired. Her reputation is very high, deservedly so. But the poetry is associated with other poetries, and inaccurately for the most part. She was herself responsible for its association with Marianne Moore. Her weakest poem is "Invitation to Marianne Moore," a girlish exercise. She has published, in *Vanity Fair,* a beautiful account of her friendship with Marianne Moore over many years, and of her admiration, mentioned but not elucidated, of Moore's poetry. (11) So it has become standard critical practice to speak of Moore when speaking of Bishop. Charles Tomlinson has described the relation as "clearly decisive." But it is neither clear nor decisive. My account of Bishop's allusion to Moore and to Ruskin suggests, what should be clear enough without it, that Bishop's poetry is not at all like Moore's. John

Ashbery is the only critic of Bishop who has made the point with adequate emphasis: "the two poets couldn't be more different," he said; "Miss Moore's synthesizing, collector's approach is far from Miss Bishop's linear, exploring one." There, indeed, we have the right emphasis. Bishop's way in poetry is to set something going—a line, in the fisherman's sense, too—and see where it goes when she gives it the freedom, as well as the probable limitations, of a mind speaking. Moore's way is that of a curator of a museum, assembling items to make a collection which will enhance the viewer's life by setting up tense relations, one item to another, making the exhibition a field of force. In "Objects and Apparitions," Bishop praises Joseph Cornell's boxes in which "things hurry away from their names." Nothing like this could be said of Bishop's poems, in which things couldn't hurry away from their names because the naming, the sound of naming, and the mind and the language conspiring to name, constitute the poetry. Bishop was fascinated by things-inside-things; Cornell's boxes, Moore's poems. (12) But her own practice, in poetry, was altogether different: expansive, letting out plenty of line, the play of mind, hand, and eye.

Some particular affiliations, too, seem to me off the mark. It is standard practice to compare "The Moose" with Frost's "The Most Of It." I see no resemblance; their parables recite quite opposite lessons. In "The Moose" the animal is a source of wonder and joy to the bus-driver and the passengers who see it; it is folded within assumptions as sweet as they are comforting. There is no danger. Frost's poem speaks in a far harsher voice, and of experience not at all comforting: the great buck that crashes through the undergrowth is unappeasably other, and the poem repudiates Wordsworthian kinship.

But the associations which have been attached most misleadingly to Bishop's poems are those of her contemporaries and friends: Randall Jarrell, John Berryman, and—most emphatically—Lowell. Stonington: Rio: a well-known photograph, Lowell's four poems to Bishop, Bishop's obituary poem "North

Haven": evidence enough of friendship, tributes going both ways. But Lowell and Bishop were very different poets.

VI

On December 19, 1953, *The New Yorker* published Bishop's extraordinarily touching story "In the Village": it was clearly enough autobiographical, a recollection of having heard, as a child, her mother screaming before she went away for the last time into madness. The story sets the mother's scream against another sound, that of the blacksmith's hammer and anvil: "the pure note: pure and angelic." Between the two sounds, there are other recollections: the mother having a new dress made for her; the child, every morning, taking the cow Nelly to the pasture; the mother's possessions, bits and pieces, broken in the mail from Boston; Mr. McLean's dog Jock; the village; the child, sent to buy humbugs at Mealy's shop; someone's haybarn going on fire.

The story has much to do with sounds, and even more with echoes. Echoing is like remembering: the vibrations flow and waver and seem to disappear, but it is easy to fancy that they don't, that they merely drift into a purer state. The story begins: "A scream, the echo of a scream, hangs over that Nova Scotian village." It is as if an experience could go from existence into essence, becoming the essence of itself, like Keats's unheard melodies. The poet John Hollander has written a book about echoing, recurrence and repetition in poetry. In Bishop's poetry, a scream, becoming the echo of itself, changes its element and stays in the poet's mind as a stain on the blue sky; the same, and different, a slight darkening at the edge of primary colors. When something becomes the essence of itself, it becomes permanent, with such permanence as time and memory have.

In the story, the diverse recollections of the village, of the child's being in the village, are called up as if to displace the mother's terrible scream. But there is a sense, throughout, of the child holding her breath, waiting for one sound and saved by the bell of another:—

> "Now there is no scream. Once there was one and it settled slowly down to earth one hot summer afternoon; or did it float up, into that dark, too dark, blue sky? But surely it has gone away, forever."

The child hears the sound of hammer and anvil again, and it seems to issue from the elements: "It is the elements speaking: earth, air, fire, water." Beautiful sound, it displaces, or gives the sense of displacing, the terrible human contingencies, the things that can only be lost, time being what it appears to be:—

"All those other things—clothes, crumbling postcards, broken china; things damaged and lost, sickened or destroyed: even the frail almost-lost scream—are they too frail for us to hear their voices long, too mortal?"

Even if the art of losing isn't hard to master, it's never completely mastered. The feeling at the end of "In the Village" is extraordinarily compacted: in one sense, the child has to rid her life of the scream, even if its echo becomes, like a stain, indelible: in another, the scream, too, comes to seem human, all-too-human, as passing as anything else; "the frail, almost-lost scream." The only comparison I can offer, for its tone of voice, is Emily Dickinson's poem that begins "It might be lonelier without the loneliness"; where the loneliness, long lived with, has becomes a presence, making a place for itself and for her. What Bishop's story speaks of, in letting the mind play over the two sounds, is the desire to be released from the whole human state—from Yeats's "the fury and the mire of human veins"—and at the same time and with no less force, the desire not to be released but to be held within it. The first part of the desire is pastoral; to be released from time, to sink to rest in elements that have no knowledge of themselves and therefore no history: the second part is to live, with all its pain, in time and the knowledge of ourselves in time.

In 1962, *The Kenyon Review* published "The Scream," a poem

by Robert Lowell "derived from Elizabeth Bishop's story 'In the Village'." The poem, eight stanzas of five lines, makes Bishop's story more explicitly subjective: not "the child" but "I." The first six stanzas use Bishop's words to tell of the scream, the cow Nelly, the blacksmith's shop, the mother coming and going away, the dressmaker fitting the purple dress, the dress looking like the garb worn by figures in the illustrated Bible. The last two stanzas use Lowell's own words, except for a reversion to Bishop's in the last two lines:—

> Later, she gave the scream,
> not even loud at first . . .
> when she went away I thought
> "But you don't have to love everyone,
> your heart won't let you!"

> A scream! But they are all gone,
> those aunts and aunts, a grandfather,
> a grandmother, my mother—
> even her scream—too frail
> for us to hear their voices long.

The break into explicitness, the child's thought in the first of these stanzas, can be accommodated in Lowell's poetry from *Life Studies* to *Day by Day:* it is the achievement of that poetry—allowing for an indisputable waning near the end—to maintain a flexed if risky decorum in which virtually anything in an imperfect life can be put on show by deeming the life itself to be simultaneously put on trial. Lowell's later poetry makes a show of itself, and calls upon the sense of drama which is fulfilled by public occasions, protest-marches, symbolic gestures, and riots in the street. As if to say: may I now become the hero of my time, having long been its victim? But to gloss the matter in these terms is to see how different Lowell's and Bishop's poetries are. No detail of "In the Village" warrants Lowell's extension of it, if strict loyalty to the nature of Bishop's art is the criterion. The child's outburst is compatible with Lowell's art—which is not dismayed by lurid testimony—but not with Bishop's. Bishop's sensibility is shy of disclosure, and likes to keep its meaning a little aside from whatever spectacle it produces to account for it.

Lowell's way of being a poet in his time was by taking every manifestation it provided as being a challenge and a provocation addressed specifically to him; not to him "personally," one was to understand, but to him "as poet." The frantic character of his time, as he saw and suffered it, was answered by an imagination more Jacobean than patrician. Bishop's way of being a poet in her time was by containing herself, as far as possible, in patience. Panic was as close to her as violence and rage and the show of violence were to Lowell, but she confided more of herself to silence and patience; she survived her time not by abstaining from its occasions but by waiting them out. Not complacently; but with composure equal and opposite to the stress that made it necessary.

NOTES

1. "In Prison," *Partisan Review*, IV, 4: March 1938, p. 4.

2. All quotations from Bishop's poetry are taken from *The Complete Poems 1927–1979* (New York: Farrar, Straus, Giroux, 1983).

3. Ashley Brown, "An Interview with Elizabeth Bishop," in Lloyd Schwartz and Sybil P. Estess (eds.), *Elizabeth Bishop and Her Art* (Ann Arbor: University of Michigan Press, 1983), p. 295.

4. Carl Sauer, *Land and Life*, edited by John Leighly (Berkeley and Los Angeles: University of California Press, 1963), pp. 300–312.

5. Robert Lowell, "On 'Skunk Hour,'" reprinted in *Elizabeth Bishop and Her Art*, p. 199.

6. Charles Tomlinson, "Looking Out for Wholeness," *Times Literary Supplement*, June 3, 1983, p. 575.

7. John Ruskin, *Modern Painters*, Part VI, Ch. ix, par. 8, "The Leaf Shadows."

8. Marianne Moore, *Selected Poems* (London: Faber and Faber, 1935), p. 96.

9. David Kalstone, *Five Temperaments* (New York: Oxford University Press, 1977), p. 27.

10. John Ashbery, review of *The Complete Poems: New York Times Book Review*, June 1, 1969. Reprinted in *Elizabeth Bishop and Her Art*, p. 204.

11. "Efforts of Affection: A Memoir of Marianne Moore," *Vanity Fair*. June 1983, pp. 44–60.

12. In 1963 Bishop sent Flannery O'Connor a gift, an altar in a bottle, as

O'Connor described it: ". . . an altar with Bible, chalice, and two fat candles on it, a cross above this with a ladder and the instruments of the crucifixion hung on it, and on top of the cross a rooster. It's all wood except the altar cloth and the rooster and these are paper, painstakingly cut out and a trifle dirty from the hands that did it. Anyway, it's very much to my taste." (The hands that did it were Brazilian and local.) Flannery O'Connor, *The Habit of Being*, edited by Sally Fitzgerald (New York: Farrar, Straus, Giroux, 1979), p. 519.

13. *The Kenyon Review*, XXIV, 4 (1962).